Broadcast Ne

MW01283187

Broadcast News and Writing Stylebook is the go-to resource for writing broadcast news, offering readers the know-how to write excellent stories for television, radio, podcasts and online media.

Through clear and concise chapters, this text provides the fundamental rules of broadcast news writing, teaching readers how to craft stories on government, crime, weather, education, health, sports and more. It covers the necessary mechanics news writers need to know, including the nuances of reporting, grammar, style and usage. This new seventh edition is updated with the latest on how stations incorporate online and social media strategies, as well as insights into the directions local news is headed. Author Robert A. Papper has over a quarter century of broadcast news and industry research experience and once again updates this vital text with the information necessary for being a successful news writer today. Also available for this edition is an Instructor's Guide, found on the book's webpage.

Whether you're a student seeking to learn the mechanics of successful broadcast news writing or a working professional looking for a definitive reference for your desk, *Broadcast News and Writing Stylebook* offers a comprehensive guide to writing for television, audio and beyond.

Robert A. Papper is Adjunct Professor at the Newhouse School at Syracuse University. A graduate of Columbia College and the Columbia Graduate School of Journalism, he has worked as a producer, writer and manager at television stations in Minneapolis, Washington, DC, San Francisco, Columbus, Ohio and radio stations in Maine and Indiana. He has won both the top award in broadcast journalism (duPont-Columbia) and the top award in broadcast journalism education (Ed Bliss Award).

Praise for Previous Editions

"This book will teach you how to tell a visual story well, using all the tools. The new edition of Bob Papper's classic shines a light for the digital age and will show you the way."

Bob Dotson, former NBC News National Correspondent and *New York Times* best selling author

"Papper's text has long earned accolades as a comprehensive and engaging guide to broadcast reporting, covering everything from interviewing to ethics, from writing for the ear to writing for the eye, from effective narrative techniques to the basics of proper usage and grammar. For those of us teaching Broadcast Journalism during these rapidly changing times in news, this new edition is a terrific addition to our teaching toolkit."

Judy Muller, Professor, USC Annenberg School, USA

"This edition has excellent tips for writing sound broadcast news copy and has now been updated with information from Papper's outstanding surveys of the news industry, advice from professional journalists, as well as ideas on the best practices for using new technology such as drones."

G. Stuart Smith, Professor, Hofstra University, USA

"This latest edition of Papper's well-respected style manual for broadcast news comes only two years after the previous release. Papper restructured the manual to forefront fundamentals of broadcast journalism, beginning with a chapter on ethics. Modest revisions follow. . . . The manual is strongest when it remains focused on the details of style and usage elaborated by real-world examples. . . . While the title suggests an audience limited to students of broadcast news, the style and usage sections of the manual have value for writers of any discipline composing podcasts or other new media work."

G. Wilsbacher, University of South Carolina

Broadcast News and Writing Stylebook

SEVENTH EDITION

Robert A. Papper

Routledge
Taylor & Francis Group

NEW YORK AND LONDON

Seventh edition published 2021
by Routledge
52 Vanderbilt Avenue, New York, NY 10017

and by Routledge
2 Park Square, Milton Park, Abingdon, Oxon, OX14 4RN

Routledge is an imprint of the Taylor & Francis Group, an informa business

First edition published by Pearson Education, Inc 1995
Sixth edition published by Routledge 2017

Library of Congress Cataloging-in-Publication Data
Names: Papper, Robert a, 1947– author.
Title: Broadcast news and writing stylebook / Robert A. Papper.
Other titles: Broadcast news writing stylebook | Broadcast news and
    writing stylebook
Description: 7th edition. | New York : Routledge, 2021. | Includes
    bibliographical references and index.
Identifiers: LCCN 2020010397 (print) | LCCN 2020010398 (ebook) |
    ISBN 9780367405564 (hardback) | ISBN 9780367422677 (paperback) |
    ISBN 9780367823030 (ebook)
Subjects: LCSH: Broadcast journalism—Authorship. | Journalism—Style
    manuals. | Report writing.
Classification: LCC PN4784.B75 P36 2020 (print) | LCC PN4784.B75 (ebook) |
    DDC 808.06/607—dc23
LC record available at https://lccn.loc.gov/2020010397
LC ebook record available at https://lccn.loc.gov/2020010398

ISBN: 978-0-367-40556-4 (hbk)
ISBN: 978-0-367-42267-7 (pbk)
ISBN: 978-0-367-82303-0 (ebk)

Typeset in Utopia
by Apex CoVantage, LLC

Visit the eResources: www.routledge.com/9780367422677

For Sol, Renee, Dana, Cristian, Daisy,
Matt, Bria, Zack, Jen, Xavier, Sloan,
Kate and especially Carole

Contents   •••••

Acknowledgments   • • • • •

Broadcast News and Writing Stylebook was first published in 1986 – more than 30 years ago. The first book of its kind, it was initially designed for professionals, and the Ethics and Excellence in Journalism Foundation in Oklahoma enabled the book to be distributed to every TV station and radio newsroom in the country. I am forever grateful to the Foundation for its support.

I am also indebted to so many friends and colleagues who have read (and re-read) this book and offered so many valuable suggestions. My thanks to active and past practitioners, faculty members, former students and friends: Laird Anderson, Dave Arnold, Mary Baer, Ken Barcus, Andy Barth, Alex Batres, Steve Bell, Jackie Benson, Amanda Billings, Ed Bliss, Merv Block, Justin Burton, Tim Calahan, Mark Christian, Kurt Christopher, Dane Claussen, Liz Claman, Ron Comings, Bob Conley, Evan Cornog, Carol Costello, Christine Davidson, Sue Drucker, Camilla Gant, John Doolittle, Bob Dotson, Emily Edwards, Irving Fang, Mike Ferring, Kelly Fincham, Brad Fitch, Carol Fletcher, Kymberly Fox, Wayne Freedman, Eric Galvan, Jeff Gillan, Peter Goodman, Tom Grimes, Jessica Harrington, Steve Hartman, Craig Helfant, Dave Hickcox, Chris James, Kelli Johnson, Steve Johnson, Phil Jurey, Laura Kaufmann, Mike Kiernan, Eric Knecht, Bill Knowles, Nick Kotz, John Larson, Rebecca Lewis, Bill Louthan, Carol Luper, Jim Mancari, Mark Masse, Christine Caswell McCarron, Jack McWethy, Mel Mencher, Cody Miller, Nick Mills, Joe Misiewicz, Beth Montagno, John Morris, Mackie Morris, Phillip Moyer, Mike Murrie, Chad Myers, Mark Neerman, Jacki Ochoa, Nathan O'Neal, Stacie Osadchaya, Charles Osgood, Jenn Palilonis, Bill Payer (who developed much of the guide to super usage), Ian Pearson, Jeff Porche, Deborah Potter, Lou Prato, Andy Rooney, Matthew Seeman, Colleen Seitz, Robert Siegel, Marc Silverstein, Gregg Smith, Mary Spillman, Susan Stamberg, Leeza Starks, Alan Thompson, Carl Twentier, Peter Valencia, Dan Van Benthuysen, Sara Vesser, Deb Wenger, Stephanie Wheatley, Lafe Williams, Maria Williams-Hawkins, Amy Wood and others that I'm undoubtedly forgetting. WSYX-TV, KPIX-TV, KRNV-TV, KSNV-TV, KERO-TV, WTOV-TV, WWJ and other stations across the country.

Most of all, I want to thank my wife Carole. Along with putting up with me and this book generally, she read and critiqued so much of this material . . . through so many drafts and so many editions. The English teacher in her did its best not to let me get away with abusing our language too much. She tried.

Bob Papper
Adjunct Professor, Broadcast and Digital Journalism
S.I. Newhouse School of Public Communication
Syracuse University

1

● ● ● ● ●

Ethics, Legality and the RTDNA and SPJ Codes of Ethics

● ● ● ● ●

Ethics

Proper ethical decision-making shouldn't be tough. After all, it's just doing what's right, isn't it? Yes, but apparently that's harder to do – or perhaps harder to stick to – than it sounds.

Inventing quotes and interviews, stealing (plagiarizing) columns, inadequate fact-checking, running PR-supplied video or stories as if they're news . . . the list of print and broadcast news failures has been widely reported.

The toll on the public's perception of journalism is incalculable. The notion that it might be necessary to tell people not to cheat or invent or plagiarize seems absurd. Surely some things should go without saying. Apparently not.

Broadcast appears to have less of a problem with invented quotes and stories, but it's probably just the nature of the beast. Television must have pictures, and it's hard to fake that, although one network did use its "green screen" to make it look like their reporters were outside on location rather than inside a studio. Broadcast also relies heavily on bites which it either has or it doesn't. Since broadcast journalists seldom ever quote (other than running bites), making them up would most often be a meaningless exercise.

There are still plenty of potential failings available. Getting the bites right doesn't prevent them from being taken out of context. And editing one part of a bite to another could well change the meaning of what someone said.

Where broadcasters can and too often do go wrong:

■ Stations periodically run video that they get from public relations or government sources without identifying the source of the video. A few stations were embarrassingly burned when it turned out that they ran PR-supplied video complete with a PR-supplied "reporter" – again, without identifying the source of the video.

■ A number of stations have run what looked like news interview programs without identifying that the people interviewed had paid to be on the program. The stations justified the practice by arguing that active news people didn't produce or host the show. But a more relevant question is what the audience thought.

■ Electronic altering of images is now so easy that it's not hard for the unscrupulous or thoughtless to change backgrounds, signs or other visual elements. Of course, this is also a danger in print.

There are probably two bigger threats to journalistic credibility and integrity. Not unique to broadcast, to be sure, but problematic.

1. Advertiser influence. Is a station willing to take on an advertiser if that advertiser has done something wrong? Think about how often you've seen news reports – print or broadcast – critical of a local car dealer. Hardly ever.
2. Sensationalizing and the consequent cheapening of the news. It's probably worse in promos and teases than the news stories themselves, but that's not a distinction the audience is going to make or care about. Every time journalists say a word, every time a picture airs, media credibility is on the line. It's infinitely easier to damage a reputation than regain one.

A useful guideline: If you wouldn't tell the audience everything you did to gather and report the story, then don't do it.

Advocacy journalism (like that practiced by Michael Moore in *Sicko* and *Capitalism: A Love Story*) has its place and a long history in this country. But it's not what we do day in and day out. The news audience shouldn't be able to determine where a reporter stands politically based on what's supposed to be an impartial report. At the same time, allowing a politician to make a blatantly false claim – without challenging that assertion – misleads and disserves the audience. It's all in how you handle the material.

Years ago, when I was news director at a public radio station, I called in one of our reporters to ask whether she was aware that a bite she used from a state legislator was factually incorrect? Yes, she was aware of that, she said. So why did she run it? Because he said it, and he's a state legislator. Not the right answer. Our primary – really, our only – obligation is to our audience. You cannot run factually inaccurate information without ensuring that the audience is told what is true. Running a factually inaccurate bite and explaining what the facts really are may make sense if you're dealing with someone who frequently invents information, and you're trying to demonstrate that. But if that's not what you're doing, then you're just using up precious air time for no particular reason or working at belittling someone. We are in the business of telling people the truth about events. Everyone is entitled to his or her opinion, but they are not entitled to their own facts. Don't censor opinions . . . but don't mislead your audience on facts.

While charges of bias get more attention, journalism is probably more at risk from the sheer volume of mistakes made every day. Talk to anyone who has been touched by the news, and they'll complain about how a reporter confused dates, misspelled the name of the street or town or people, misstated the number of something. The list goes on and on. Death by a thousand cuts. There will always be issues of interpretation or emphasis. Someone may feel that a journalist didn't emphasize a particular point enough or left a subtle misimpression. That's a different and debatable issue. Not open to interpretation or debate is getting the facts right.

Journalism is neither rocket science nor brain surgery, but everyone needs to remember that people's lives, livelihoods and reputations are at stake in virtually every story.

Consider this a plea for more care and attention to detail to help preserve your reputation, the reputation of the news outlet you work for and, most importantly, the reputation of the people whose lives you touch.

Ethics isn't simply a topic handled in one chapter of a book. You'll find issues involving ethical decision-making and ethical behavior in almost every chapter.

● ● ● ● ●

Fake News and the Question of Whether Facts Are Facts

Journalists and news organizations have been under attack to an extent not seen since the early days of the republic. Constant railing against the media and stirring up anti-journalist fervor in a large crowd and among extremist groups have made journalism an increasingly dangerous profession. Four journalists were shot dead in Maryland in 2018.

Fake news exists – primarily in material invented by political operatives in this country and in other countries – aimed at disrupting the American political system or specific candidates or simply to sow distrust in the media.

Every news organization is likely to make a mistake now and then. But there's a difference between error and fake news. Fake news operations don't apologize for their mistakes; they were intentional, after all. Real news organizations make corrections and apologize for errors and omissions.

We also need to draw critical distinctions between facts and opinions. Facts are facts. They may be subject to differing interpretations, but the facts themselves are immutable. Again, different people may interpret those facts in different ways and draw differing meanings or conclusions from them. But the facts, themselves do not change.

The president of the United States may say that he didn't say something. But, in the final analysis, he either did or did not, and there's likely a record of that fact. He may wish he hadn't said it; he may feel that he has misspoken; he may have changed his mind. But none of that alters the fact of whether he said it.

Supporters and detractors may all have opinions on whether the president's comments were appropriate or not . . . whether they were well thought out or reckless . . . whether they were cogent or irrational. And all those people have a right to their opinions, and a journalist should seek out differing opinions and perspectives. But none of those opinions change the facts. So when a presidential aide said – as she did – that there were "alternative facts" . . . that's simply not true. There may be additional facts that come to bear on a topic. There are undoubtedly plenty of differing opinions about those facts. But there's really only one set of facts.

●●●●●

Trust in the Media

A lack of trust in the news media is clearly a significant problem today, but whether that's getting better or worse seems to depend on the interpretations of the same data.

Gallup has been surveying trust in the news media since 1972. That year, 68% said they trusted the news media a great deal or a fair amount. The number actually rose to a peak of 72% in 1976 (think shades of Watergate).

The next time Gallup surveyed news media trust was in 1997, and the level of trust was down to 53%. It remained in the 50s until 2004, then it dipped to 44% . . . rising to 50% in 2005 . . . then back in the 40s until 2016, when it fell to an all-time low of 32%. Trust in news media went up to 41% in 2017 and to 45% in 2018.

That 2018 number led Gallup to issue a release in October of 2018 entitled, "US Media Trust Continues to Recover from 2016 Low."

But just a month before that, *Columbia Journalism Review* published an article entitled, "Most Americans say they have lost trust in the media." The article was based on a new Knight Foundation and Gallup poll. Yes, that's the same Gallup.

But the results are based on two different surveys conducted in June 2018 (in conjunction with Knight) and September (for Gallup's own survey). And the methodology was different. Gallup's simple trust in media survey was conducted via phone; the Knight-sponsored survey was far more detailed and done online by a Gallup-recruited panel. Online surveys are relatively inexpensive and easy to do, but a lengthy online survey means you're dealing with a subset of the country because you're excluding those without internet at home and almost certainly those without high-speed internet at home (because the survey would take too long without a high-speed connection).

The two surveys present their own caution to journalists. The surveys appear, on the surface, to make contradictory claims. But they're actually looking at the same picture from different angles – and choosing to emphasize different points. Neither is wrong, but they leave very different impressions with their audiences.

In the Knight-sponsored survey, 69% said "their trust in the news media has decreased in the past decade," with 4% saying it had increased and 26% saying their trust was unchanged. The political views of the respondents made a huge difference in their response. Ninety-four percent of Republicans and 95% of conservatives said their trust had decreased in the last decade. Compare that to 75% of independents; 66% of moderates; 42% of Democrats; and 46% of liberals.

Clearly, political views make a difference, and a majority of each group said they trusted "only some [news media], but not others."

Trust issues centered on inaccurate/misleading reporting and bias on the part of the news media. Or at least some of the news media.

Of course, it's hard to argue that point given Fox News and its conservative/right-leaning/Republican orientation and MSNBC with its liberal/left-leaning/Democrat orientation. But that's cable news. Most local news organizations attempt to present the news without bias or slant.

There are also significant insights on trust in the latest Digital News Report by the Reuters Institute for the Study of Journalism at Oxford University. They surveyed over 75,000 online news consumers in 38 countries in 2019; the US sample size was 2,012.

Overall, the top "brand for news" in terms of trust was local TV news at 30%. Fox News came in at 29%; NBC/MSNBC came in at 25%, CNN and ABC News at 22%, CBS News, regional/local newspaper and Yahoo! News tied at 20%.

While overall trust in media came in at 32%, 50% reported "trust in news I use." Twenty-five percent had trust in search engines for news; and just 14% had trust in social media for news.

What can you and your news organization do to help build trust in news media? Be accurate. Don't make mistakes. Even little ones. Don't do anything to get a news story that you wouldn't tell the audience about. In fact, tell them. Transparency in reporting and news operation is one of the most important things that you and a news organization can do. Bring the audience into the news gathering process. Follow the guidelines of the Radio-Television Digital News Association (RTDNA) and Society of Professional Journalists' (SPJ) Codes of Conduct that follow.

● ● ● ● ●

Ethical Decision-Making Starts at the Top

Ethical decision-making is easier if it's clear that the news organization you work for cares and values that approach. Having a written code of ethics or guiding principles is a good start. You'll find the RTDNA Code of Ethics and Professional Conduct and the SPJ Code of Ethics at the end of this chapter. A good organization should subscribe to one of these codes or have developed its own. Critically, it should reinforce that code through actions.

Writing for the RTDNA *Daily Communicator*, News Director Treena Wood at CKWX-AM in Vancouver, British Columbia, noted that her station had been successful by adhering to internally developed guiding principles. Number 1:

> *First, we get it right. Nothing goes to air or online before it's independently confirmed. We wait, make phone calls, put out the emails, gather the evidence, and get our facts straight before rushing to get something out there, no matter what everyone else in the media is doing. No one remembers who got it first, but everyone remembers who got it wrong.*

● ● ● ● ●

Issues in Media Law

A few words about media law in a chapter on ethics is not a substitute for a media law course. Still, a few words seem appropriate.

We are still guided and most often sheltered by the First Amendment to the Constitution:

> *Congress shall make no law respecting an establishment of religion, or prohibiting the free exercise thereof; or abridging the freedom of speech, or of the press; or the right of the people peaceably to assemble, and to petition the Government for a redress of grievances.*

We may consider the First Amendment to be a bedrock of our society – and it certainly is as far as the news media is concerned, but it has always been controversial. If it wasn't controversial, it wouldn't have been required as an amendment to the Constitution; it would have been included in the original. And it remains controversial.

The Freedom Forum's annual First Amendment Survey in 2019 found more awareness of what the First Amendment is about. Seventy-one percent could name at least one First Amendment right – although 16% thought it included the right to bear arms. Of concern, the survey found that 29% thought the First Amendment went too far. That was up 6 points from 2018. Seventy-two percent agreed that it was important for the news media to act as a watchdog on government.

Note that we're talking about the *first* amendment – the first individual liberty stipulated by the founding fathers is designed to restrict federal or state limitations on individual liberties.

Without freedom of speech and freedom of the press, there is the real potential of converting journalism into someone's or some group's version of public relations.

As it is, freedom of speech and freedom of the press are not without their limitations or consequences. Freedom of speech does not include the right to yell "fire" in a crowded theater – one of the classic examples of limitations. Someone also cannot incite people to riot.

In addition, the US Supreme Court has found that broadcasters (unlike print journalists) may be regulated based on a scarcity of channels (licenses for radio and television stations), and that scarcity allows for "content-neutral" regulation of radio and TV. As an example, tobacco companies have always been free to advertise cigarettes in newspapers and magazines, but Congress banned cigarette advertising on radio and TV starting in 1971.

Clearly, different technologies are treated differently. While the Supreme Court has upheld regulations and restrictions on broadcasting, the Court has recognized full Constitutional protections for the internet since 1997.

It's also critical to understand that the media possess no rights beyond those afforded to every American. The freedom to speak and publish views is no greater for CBS or your local hometown newspaper than it is for you.

At the same time, the fact that you're able to make whatever controversial statements you wish . . . and publish those thoughts in whatever publication you create or can convince to run them, doesn't REQUIRE any medium to publish or air those views. That would, after all, infringe on someone else's constitutional rights.

But expressing those thoughts can still have consequences. That's true for both individuals and for the media. The three legal areas where the media are most likely to get into trouble include *libel, entrapment* and *invasion of privacy.*

There appears to be a widespread belief that these are potential problems most often of concern in investigative reporting. That's probably not the case. When the news media spend a lot of time on investigative work, part of that time frequently includes meeting with lawyers to go over scripts and documentation to ensure that the station or news outlet is on solid ground. That doesn't preclude lawsuits; anyone with money can file a lawsuit regardless of the merits or lack thereof. The point is that the material is typically thoroughly vetted. Stations probably more often get into potential trouble in the day to day reporting when oversight might not be as carefully provided.

The distinction between libel and slander is in the delivery. Libel involves written (published or broadcast) and slander involves spoken (but not including broadcast). In either case, it generally includes the false or malicious publication of material that damages someone's reputation or relationships with family, friends, co-workers or neighbors. Obviously, including someone's name is a form of identifying an accused individual, but identification can also be done by picture or a description that may single out a particular individual.

Truth is the best and, most often, an absolute defense against libel. In journalism, there's never a good substitute for being right and being able to prove that you're right. That's the gold standard, and that's what you should be prepared to argue based on the journalistic work you do. The one place where truth may not be enough of a defense is if someone can show malice. In other words, a statement may be true, but if the person can show that you, as a reporter, were out to get someone for personal gain, then truth may not be an adequate defense.

Opinion may be used as a defense against libel. That's most often the case in things like critical movie or restaurant reviews. This defense is also known as fair comment. There is a clear line that's drawn. In a restaurant review, for instance, saying that you thought the beef burgundy was bland or overcooked is fine. That's opinion. Saying that the kitchen is dirty and the place is a breeding ground for rodents is only okay if you can prove the truth of that statement.

Privilege is another defense against libel. That issue involves statements made by people testifying in court or speaking at a government public hearing, for example. Those are okay as long as you, the reporter, don't take sides in the case.

Consent may be a defense – where the person who feels injured in fact agreed to the publication of the material.

Public officials have a harder time arguing that they have been libeled. They must argue that not only was the material false, but that the reporter or news organization either knew it was false and broadcast it anyway or exhibited a "reckless disregard" for the truth. Public officials include not just politicians but also actors, sports figures, celebrities and so on. The issue of publishing or republishing, reposting and linking have also raised new issues associated with developing and evolving notions of defamation liability.

Entrapment is another potential area of legal trouble. In arguing entrapment, the injured party is arguing that the libelous behavior only happened because the reporter or news organization induced the person to do something he or she would not have otherwise done. For instance, if you simply walked up to people and asked them to do something that would be considered libelous – like a crime or performing an embarrassing act – that could well be considered as entrapping the person. Don't do that.

Invasion of privacy can be pretty complicated. Let's say you're on public property – a public sidewalk for instance – and you see an accident on the street. You can take pictures of that scene, and you're not invading anyone's privacy. There is no reasonable expectation of privacy on a public street. What if something happens in someone's front yard? Can you take and use pictures of that from the public sidewalk? Yes. Still no expectation of privacy. What if you're on that sidewall and see something happening inside a house? No good. Just because the curtains may not have been closed doesn't mean that the people inside still don't have a reasonable expectation of privacy. Generally, if you're on public property, anything you shoot that's outside or also on public property is fair game, and you're not invading someone's privacy.

What about the use of drones? Be careful here. There are federal and state laws already on the books and in the works on the use of drones, and you better know what they are before attempting to shoot video of something with a drone. See more on the use of drones in Chapter 14.

The use of ever more powerful technologies has added to privacy concerns. Telephoto lenses, parabolic microphones, camera-equipped drones and "public" online places have all raised increasing questions about public spaces and expectations of privacy.

Related to all this, if you walk up to someone on the street, camera or notebook in hand, and ask a question, you do not need a signed release in order to use that material. You have what is called *implied consent*. They see the notebook or camera and spoke with you. They have, in effect, given their consent.

If you have any concerns about the legality of any action, check with competent and appropriate legal counsel.

●●●●●

The Radio-Television Digital News Association (RTDNA) Code of Ethics and Professional Conduct

Guiding Principles

Journalism's obligation is to the public. Journalism places the public's interests ahead of commercial, political and personal interests. Journalism empowers viewers, listeners and readers to make more informed decisions for themselves; it does not tell people what to believe or how to feel.

Ethical decision-making should occur at every step of the journalistic process, including story selection, news-gathering, production, presentation and delivery. Practitioners of ethical journalism seek diverse and even opposing opinions in order to reach better conclusions that can be clearly explained and effectively defended or, when appropriate, revisited and revised.

Ethical decision-making – like writing, photography, design or anchoring – requires skills that improve with study, diligence and practice.

The RTDNA Code of Ethics does not dictate what journalists should do in every ethical predicament; rather it offers resources to help journalists make better ethical decisions – on and off the job – for themselves and for the communities they serve.

Journalism is distinguished from other forms of content by these guiding principles:

- Truth and accuracy above all
  - The facts *should* get in the way of a good story. Journalism requires more than merely reporting remarks, claims or comments. Journalism verifies, provides relevant context, tells the rest of the story and acknowledges the absence of important additional information.
  - For every story of significance, there are always more than two sides. While they may not all fit into every account, responsible reporting is clear about what it omits, as well as what it includes.
  - Scarce resources, deadline pressure and relentless competition do not excuse cutting corners factually or oversimplifying complex issues.
  - "Trending," "going viral" or "exploding on social media" may increase urgency, but these phenomena only heighten the need for strict standards of accuracy.
  - Facts change over time. Responsible reporting includes updating stories and amending archival versions to make them more accurate and to avoid misinforming those who, through search, stumble upon outdated material.
  - Deception in newsgathering, including surreptitious recording, conflicts with journalism's commitment to truth. Similarly, anonymity of sources deprives the audience of important, relevant information. Staging, dramatization and other alterations – even when labeled as such – can confuse or fool viewers, listeners and readers. These tactics are justified only when stories of great significance cannot be adequately told without distortion, and when any creative liberties taken are clearly explained.
  - Journalism challenges assumptions, rejects stereotypes and illuminates – even where it cannot eliminate – ignorance.
  - Ethical journalism resists false dichotomies – either/or, always/never, black/white thinking – and considers a range of alternatives between the extremes.
- Independence and transparency
  - Editorial independence may be a more ambitious goal today than ever before. Media companies, even if not-for-profit, have commercial,

competitive and other interests – both internal and external – from which the journalists they employ cannot be entirely shielded. Still, independence from influences that conflict with public interest remains an essential ideal of journalism. Transparency provides the public with the means to assess credibility and to determine who deserves trust.

■ Acknowledging sponsor-provided content, commercial concerns or political relationships is essential, but transparency alone is not adequate. It does not entitle journalists to lower their standards of fairness or truth.

■ Disclosure, while critical, does not justify the exclusion of perspectives and information that are important to the audience's understanding of issues.

■ Journalism's proud tradition of holding the powerful accountable provides no exception for powerful journalists or the powerful organizations that employ them. To profit from reporting on the activities of others while operating in secrecy is hypocrisy.

■ Effectively explaining editorial decisions and processes does not mean making excuses. Transparency requires reflection, reconsideration and honest openness to the possibility that an action, however well intended, was wrong.

■ Ethical journalism requires owning errors, correcting them promptly and giving corrections as much prominence as the error itself had.

■ Commercial endorsements are incompatible with journalism because they compromise credibility. In journalism, content is gathered, selected and produced in the best interests of viewers, listeners and readers – not in the interests of somebody who paid to have a product or position promoted and associated with a familiar face, voice or name.

■ Similarly, political activity and active advocacy can undercut the real or perceived independence of those who practice journalism. Journalists do not give up the rights of citizenship, but their public exercise of those rights can call into question their impartiality.

■ The acceptance of gifts or special treatment of any kind not available to the general public creates conflicts of interest and erodes independence. This does not include the access to events or areas traditionally granted to working journalists in order to facilitate their coverage. It does include "professional courtesy" admission, discounts and "freebies" provided to journalists by those who might someday be the subject of coverage. Such goods and services are often offered as enticements to report favorably on the giver or rewards for doing so; even where that is not the intent, it is the reasonable perception of a justifiably suspicious public.

- Commercial and political activities, as well as the acceptance of gifts or special treatment, cause harm even when the journalists involved are "off duty" or "on their own time."
- Attribution is essential. It adds important information that helps the audience evaluate content and it acknowledges those who contribute to coverage. Using someone else's work without attribution or permission is plagiarism.

- Accountability for consequences
  - Journalism accepts responsibility, articulates its reasons and opens its processes to public scrutiny.
  - Journalism provides enormous benefits to self-governing societies. In the process, it can create inconvenience, discomfort and even distress. Minimizing harm, particularly to vulnerable individuals, should be a consideration in every editorial and ethical decision.
  - Responsible reporting means considering the consequences of both the newsgathering – even if the information is never made public – and of the material's potential dissemination. Certain stakeholders deserve special consideration; these include children, victims, vulnerable adults and others inexperienced with American media.
  - Preserving privacy and protecting the right to a fair trial are not the primary mission of journalism; still, these critical concerns deserve consideration and to be balanced against the importance or urgency of reporting.
  - The right to broadcast, publish or otherwise share information does not mean it is always right to do so. However, journalism's obligation is to pursue truth and report, not withhold it. Shying away from difficult cases is not necessarily more ethical than taking on the challenge of reporting them. Leaving tough or sensitive stories to non-journalists can be a disservice to the public.

A growing collection of coverage guidelines for use on a range of ethical issues is available on the RTDNA website – www.rtdna.org.

Revised Code of Ethics adopted June 11, 2015
Reprinted with permission.

●●●●●

The Society of Professional Journalists Code of Ethics

Preamble

Members of the Society of Professional Journalists (SPJ) believe that public enlightenment is the forerunner of justice and the foundation of democracy. Ethical journalism strives to ensure the free exchange of information that is accurate, fair and thorough. An ethical journalist acts with integrity.

The Society declares these four principles as the foundation of ethical journalism and encourages their use in its practice by all people in all media.

Seek Truth and Report It

Ethical journalism should be accurate and fair. Journalists should be honest and courageous in gathering, reporting and interpreting information.

■ Journalists should:

- ■ Take responsibility for the accuracy of their work. Verify information before releasing it. Use original sources whenever possible.
- ■ Remember that neither speed nor format excuses inaccuracy.
- ■ Provide context. Take special care not to misrepresent or oversimplify in promoting, previewing or summarizing a story.
- ■ Gather, update and correct information throughout the life of a news story.
- ■ Be cautious when making promises, but keep the promises they make.
- ■ Identify sources clearly. The public is entitled to as much information as possible to judge the reliability and motivations of sources.
- ■ Consider sources' motives before promising anonymity. Reserve anonymity for sources who may face danger, retribution or other harm, and have information that cannot be obtained elsewhere. Explain why anonymity was granted.
- ■ Diligently seek subjects of news coverage to allow them to respond to criticism or allegations of wrongdoing.
- ■ Avoid undercover or other surreptitious methods of gathering information unless traditional, open methods will not yield information vital to the public.
- ■ Be vigilant and courageous about holding those with power accountable. Give voice to the voiceless.
- ■ Support the open and civil exchange of views, even views they find repugnant.
- ■ Recognize a special obligation to serve as watchdogs over public affairs and government. Seek to ensure that the public's business is conducted in the open, and that public records are open to all.
- ■ Provide access to source material when it is relevant and appropriate.
- ■ Boldly tell the story of the diversity and magnitude of the human experience. Seek sources whose voices we seldom hear.

- Avoid stereotyping. Journalists should examine the ways their values and experiences may shape their reporting.
- Label advocacy and commentary.
- Never deliberately distort facts or context, including visual information. Clearly label illustrations and re-enactments.
- Never plagiarize. Always attribute.

Minimize Harm

Ethical journalism treats sources, subjects, colleagues and members of the public as human beings deserving of respect.

- Journalists should:
  - Balance the public's need for information against potential harm or discomfort. Pursuit of the news is not a license for arrogance or undue intrusiveness.
  - Show compassion for those who may be affected by news coverage. Use heightened sensitivity when dealing with juveniles, victims of sex crimes and sources or subjects who are inexperienced or unable to give consent. Consider cultural differences in approach and treatment.
  - Recognize that legal access to information differs from an ethical justification to publish or broadcast.
  - Realize that private people have a greater right to control information about themselves than public figures and others who seek power, influence or attention. Weigh the consequences of publishing or broadcasting personal information.
  - Avoid pandering to lurid curiosity, even if others do.
  - Balance a suspect's right to a fair trial with the public's right to know. Consider the implications of identifying criminal suspects before they face legal charges.
  - Consider the long-term implications of the extended reach and permanence of publication. Provide updated and more complete information as appropriate.

Act Independently

The highest and primary obligation of ethical journalism is to serve the public.

- Journalists should:
  - Avoid conflicts of interest, real or perceived. Disclose unavoidable conflicts.

■ Refuse gifts, favors, fees, free travel and special treatment, and avoid political and other outside activities that may compromise integrity or impartiality, or may damage credibility.

■ Be wary of sources offering information for favors or money; do not pay for access to news. Identify content provided by outside sources, whether paid or not.

■ Deny favored treatment to advertisers, donors or any other special interests, and resist internal and external pressure to influence coverage.

■ Distinguish news from advertising and shun hybrids that blur the lines between the two. Prominently label sponsored content.

Be Accountable and Transparent

Ethical journalism means taking responsibility for one's work and explaining one's decisions to the public.

■ Journalists should:

■ Explain ethical choices and processes to audiences. Encourage a civil dialogue with the public about journalistic practices, coverage and news content.

■ Respond quickly to questions about accuracy, clarity and fairness.

■ Acknowledge mistakes and correct them promptly and prominently. Explain corrections and clarifications carefully and clearly.

■ Expose unethical conduct in journalism, including within their organizations.

■ Abide by the same high standards they expect of others.

The SPJ Code of Ethics is a statement of abiding principles supported by additional explanations and position papers (at spj.org) that address changing journalistic practices. It is not a set of rules, rather a guide that encourages all who engage in journalism to take responsibility for the information they provide, regardless of medium. The code should be read as a whole; individual principles should not be taken out of context. It is not, nor can it be under the First Amendment, legally enforceable.

Revised Code of Ethics adopted by SPJ on September 6, 2014
Reprinted with permission.

● ● ● ● ●

Summary

Get the facts right and behave like a responsible and caring human being.

● ● ● ● ●

Exercises

A. The preambles to the two codes both deal with the public, but they approach that point a bit differently. How are they different, and which do you prefer and why?

B. The RTDNA Code of Ethics and Professional Conduct notes three broad principles, but the SPJ Code of Ethics includes four principles. How do those three and four principles differ? Are the two codes really saying the same thing in different words, or do they differ in meaningful ways?

2

The Business of News

A s this is written, 705 TV newsrooms are producing news for those 705 stations and running that news on an additional 393 stations. A total of 1,098 stations. Most – but not all – of those stations have seen a general decline and aging of the local TV news audience. Still, the business side of local TV news is strong and growing.

The Big Picture

At a time when the news landscape is changing as rapidly as it is, it's increasingly critical for prospective news people to understand the business context within which news happens.

There is no evidence that fewer people are consuming news . . . or that they're spending any less time doing so. But few industries have seen so many dramatic changes over the last decade or so. Survival in this environment makes it especially critical that you understand the new ground rules of the news business along with the signs to watch for as we head into a foggy future.

The point is that news doesn't just rain down from the sky, and its continued existence – to say nothing of continued employment – depends heavily on companies making money by supplying news and information.

In 2018, The Knight Foundation contracted with Deb Wenger (University of Mississippi) and me to conduct a study and analysis on the future of local news. We were to focus particularly on local TV news, but in a competitive market, you really need to look at all the players.

Newspapers

In 2019, in one of the largest newspaper acquisitions ever, GateHouse purchased Gannett. The enlarged Gannett (the combined company is using the Gannett name) now owns 260 daily newspapers and more than 300 weeklies. It has a total US circulation approaching double the second-largest newspaper chain. But in the last 15 years, the company has shut down 5 daily newspapers and closed or merged dozens of weeklies.

That's the word from the best study I've seen recently on newspapers: "The Expanding News Desert," produced by Penelope Muse Abernathy at the University of North Carolina in 2018. The report notes that more than one in five papers has closed in the last 15 years, and it talks of the rise of "ghost newspapers" – papers that are "mere shells, or 'ghosts,' of their former selves." The report estimates that between 1,300 and 1,400 communities that had their own papers in 2004 now have no coverage at all.

The newspaper economic problems are simple to define: As Newsonomics' Ken Doctor has noted, newspaper viability is dependent on boosting circulation/subscriber income from the roughly 35% of newspaper revenue that it currently takes in to 60 to 70% of total revenue. But as newspapers continue to lay off staff and cut content, it becomes increasingly hard to convince the dwindling subscriber base to pay more and more money for the ever-shrinking newspaper.

In the decade since the last recession hit, newspapers have shed 26,300 newsroom employees – 46.1% of total employment. "The combination of less content, smaller print products, inferior mobile products and finally doubling the price of subscriptions and single copy [sales] have caused deeper losses in circulation," notes Doctor. He points out that the problem isn't readership; the combined print and digital readership "has never been higher." It's the loss of advertising.

●●●●●

Radio

Financial analyst BIA/Kelsey reports that there are 29 all-news radio stations in the US. There are 438 stations that say they're news/talk, but many of those are almost all talk and have few – and in many cases no – reporters. The median number of news employees at US radio stations has remained at one for decades. As it is, a third of all radio news directors aren't even full-time station employees. The average number of news people at non-commercial stations is 3.3 but the median (typical) number is two, and 41% of non-commercial radio news directors are not full-time employees of their stations.

Total radio advertising revenue is now slightly higher than total newspaper advertising revenue. That's not because radio has grown but because newspaper has fallen. Radio advertising and listenership have both largely held steady. Nielsen Media Research reports that, overall, news/talk/information is the most popular single radio format with 9.6% of all listeners.

Podcasts appear to be getting more popular, but most are free and advertising, while growing, is nowhere near the level required to actually support the medium.

● ● ● ● ●

Online

Most online news is produced by legacy media: newspapers, magazines, television stations and radio stations. But what about online-only news sources? How do they fit into the picture? Are they making money? Are they having an impact?

In our study of dozens of markets across a wide range of sizes, we found that commercial TV and newspapers dominate local news online.

Of the 22 markets initially analyzed (excluding New York City and Washington, DC, with its three national newspapers), newspaper websites came out on top in 14 of the markets, and television websites came out on top in 8.

Of the 37 smaller markets analyzed, numbers 25 to 205, television websites came out on top in 23, newspapers came out on top in 13, and radio came out first in one.

The point is that while we have relatively new, successful national online news sites, that really hasn't been the case on the local level.

Online-only websites are making a mark, but it's primarily a major market phenomenon. Of 153 online-only websites analyzed in 56 markets, only 26 sites reached at least 5,500 visitors a day. Three more sites came close. Of those 29 online-only websites, 18 are located in five of the seven largest markets in the US: New York, Los Angeles, Chicago, Philadelphia and Washington, DC. Several have been shut down since this analysis was done. Ownership complained that the sites weren't financially feasible – and those were among the most successful in audience reached. The few successful exceptions in smaller markets prove that stand-alone online news sites are possible, but the numbers strongly suggest that we're a long way from stand-alone news websites as a major factor in local news.

There are a growing number of successful statewide online only news sites. Most are non-profit and at least partly supported by foundation grants. Foundation grants tend to be temporary, and it's unclear whether there's enough reader support to keep most of them going. Their long-term success probably depends on their ability to successfully execute the public radio model of listener (in this case, reader) support. It's simply too early to know.

Hyperlocal news platform Patch is reportedly looking at alternatives to traditional advertising support like user payments. That might include payments for inclusion in local calendars, for instance. Patch says that it's profitable, and owner Hale Global is quoted as saying in 2019 that the 1,227 local sites produced over $20 million in ad revenue. But that's under $17,000 average per local website.

●●●●●

TV

In late 2018, the Pew Research Center found that 31% of American adults say they follow local news "very closely." Not surprisingly, that tracking of local news directly correlates with age. Just 15% of 18- to 29-year-olds said they followed local news closely, up to 42% for those 65 and older. Blacks and Hispanics were higher than whites, and the higher the education level, the LESS likely that someone followed local news closely.

The younger the adult, the more likely that their preferred source of local news was online . . . from 60% for 18- to 29-year-olds down to 14% for those 65+. Conversely, the older the adult, the more likely he or she preferred to get local news from TV . . . from 26% for adults 18 to 29 up to 51% for adults 50 to 64 and 65+. Note that after combining online and TV, there isn't much room left for other media.

And there's a pretty strong resistance to paying for local news. Just 7% of young adults, 18 to 29, said they paid for local news in the last year . . . to 9% for those 30–49 . . . up to 15% for those 50 to 64 and 29% for those 65+.

Much of the news online comes via social media. Because of that, media outlets are spending more of their time and resources on social media, particularly Facebook and Twitter, but the revenue picture in social media is fuzzy at best. Right now, media outlets derive most of their digital dollars from website advertising, but the audience is mostly on social media, and most of the social media revenue just goes to Facebook and Google.

Among media outlets, TV stations dominate social media. Excluding the skewed markets of New York City and Washington, DC, we found the median social media share for all TV was 85.5%, and the median share for all newspaper was 11.7%. With one exception, radio social media share ranged from 3.3% in Montgomery, Alabama, to 10% in Chicago.

Stations and station groups are also looking at ways to make money on what's called OTT – over the top. OTT involves streaming channels or services that go directly to an audience without going through a station broadcast or cable or satellite systems. Hulu, Roku and Disney+ are all examples of OTT/streaming providers. Anyone, of course, can produce OTT content, but TV stations have the advantage of equipment, expertise and a relationship with potential sponsors in order to make money. Salt Lake City's KSL-TV joined with local Chevy dealers and Ski Utah to produce a video series that helped parents teach their kids to ski. Nexstar is experimenting with a paid video-on-demand subscription (SVOD) service in San Francisco . . . looking toward creating some sort of paid or free OTT product wherever the country's largest station owner has a facility.

Consulting and research firm Magid released a streaming landscape study recently that found age as a critical divide. Those 45+ still prefer (linear) TV, but 44 and under prefer streaming platforms. The company also reports that cord-cutting is accelerating. Those are people dropping cable or satellite for TV and viewing video OTT. That video includes getting TV channels directly over the air as well as through a variety of streaming services.

Financial analyst BIA/Kelsey projects that local OTT advertising will be up 43% from 2018 to 2019 to $857 million . . . and rise to $2.13 billion by 2024.

At this point, there may be more questions than answers about where OTT is going. At a recent conference on OTT, the CEO of Scripps' co-owned Newsy news network is quoted as noting there are, "no standards, no regulation and no real consensus [in the] industry on where we need to be going." And there's no consensus about how to measure the audience and value the product.

Nevertheless, OTT will become increasingly important to local TV stations, and that means they need to figure out what kind of content viewers will want to see – not when the station wants to air it (like linear TV) – but when the audience decides it's interested. The traditional newscast is probably not the answer. And if the competition is Netflix and binge watching, local TV news needs to be producing the kind of compelling storytelling that can compete with that.

As this is written, TV news employment is at its second highest level ever. Why? TV news continues to make money, and stations, and the companies that own them, continue to invest in news.

The business of news, then, is very definitely about revenue and expenses.

● ● ● ● ●

The Scope of Media Use

Media research and consulting firm SmithGeiger reports that adults 18 to 54 spend 11 hours and 1 minute with screens – per day. 7:06 goes to TV – split into 2:42 watching live TV; :52 watching time-shifted TV; and 3:30 with streaming TV (like Netflix, Roku, Hulu, etc.). Smartphone is next at 1:48 per day; computer at 1:18; and tablet at :47.

Part of the difficulty of peering into the future of news is that there's a lot we don't really know . . . even though we frequently pretend that we do. But let's start with what we do know. Media use is the number one life activity for the average American adult. Even more than sleeping. Way more than work. After all, we don't work seven days a week, but we do consume media every day. Depending on whether you believe more in Nielsen or eMarketer, we spend somewhere between 11:27 and 12:09 hours per day, respectively, interacting with media. And right there you have a sense of the problem.

According to eMarketer, digital accounts for 6:35 of that total; TV is 3:35; radio 1:20; newspapers 0:11; and magazines 0:09.

According to Nielsen, 4:59 is digital; 4:27 is TV; 1:42 is radio; :19 is other.

Total media time is about half an hour apart, but digital estimates are more than an hour and a half different, and TV differences are nearly an hour.

So when eMarketer made a big deal about time spent with mobile passing time spent with TV, that's based on their estimates – but those estimates don't agree with Nielsen's.

So who's right? I have always thought that Nielsen's methodology is much more sound, but people will believe whatever suits their purposes.

● ● ● ● ●

Media Use Is More Complex Than It Used to Be

A few short decades ago, media use was a lot simpler. There were morning and afternoon papers, four television stations, a bunch of radio stations and magazines, and that was about it. Today, we have fewer newspapers but more of everything else. And more choices beyond that – most notably the internet. Same number of hours in the day, but a staggering fragmentation of options – most shouting, "watch me," "listen to me," "read me."

And we do. And since we still only have 24 hours in a day, we seem to cope by piling on. The assumption had generally been that as new media came along, it displaced older media. Not today. Perhaps led by the computer, which really taught us how to multitask, we are more and more using two or more media at the same time. Not just young people, but almost everyone. In our last Middletown Media Study, over 30% of media use involved two or more media at the same time. Much of that involved two or more different uses of a computer (e.g. email and software), but much of it either involved the computer and another medium (most often TV) or two or more other media.

● ● ● ● ●

It's Hard to Measure Media Use

There are a lot of reasons why it's so hard today to measure media use. The use of two or more media at the same time is part of the problem. You can observe that complexity (as we did in our research), but it's nearly impossible to ask someone about it. We looked at 17 media in our research. If we asked people about each possible pairing, it would take

136 questions. And that wouldn't get at three or more media at the same time, and, yes, people do that, too.

Part of the problem relates to the staggering number of media choices. It's hard enough to keep all the choices straight much less remember which ones you used and for how long. How accurately could you reconstruct your media life – even from yesterday, much less a broader question like whether you're using a given medium more or less than you used to or more or less than another? Unfortunately, much of what we hear about media use we get from questions like that via phone surveys. It's interesting data, and it may help us see developing trends, but, as we proved in our observational studies, it's strikingly inaccurate.

The biggest problem in these self-reported surveys is that we're simply not very good at estimating how we use our time. Another part of the problem relates to media bias. The fact is, we've been conditioned to understand that some media use is generally "good," and some media use is generally "bad." We know the answers, and it undoubtedly biases our responses.

In the first Middletown Media Studies, when we compared phone survey, diary and observation, we observed that people used 130% more media than they said they did, but the discrepancies weren't consistent from one medium to the next. People weren't far off on their estimation of how much time they spent with print media, but they underestimated their TV use by 160%.

In Middletown Media Studies II, we called people after we observed them and asked whether, on the day they were observed, (which, in most cases, had been the day before), they read the newspaper, listened to the radio, used the computer, went online, watched TV . . . and, if so, how much? We had just observed them, which means they should have been extremely conscious of their media use. Even so, they substantially overestimated their use of newspapers and the computer but underestimated their TV use by almost 50%. It's not that survey research doesn't work, it's that there are serious limitations to asking people about behavior, especially when some of that behavior is considered "good" and some is considered "bad."

The situation is further complicated by a lack of standards for judging internet use. Internet use was initially measured by "hits" until advertisers (who are the real reason audience is measured at all) understood that the numbers were largely meaningless and easy to manipulate. We moved to page views, which is still in use. Some argue that time spent online is a better measure, although, from an advertising standpoint, it tends to undervalue the brief but frequent time spent with search.

Cross-checks on internet usage have found major discrepancies between the numbers reported by the websites themselves and the numbers that outside, independent companies were able to measure. Not surprisingly, the websites themselves always reported far higher usage than that reported by outside, independent companies.

Why are there such differences in some of the estimates? There are a variety of reasons, but one of the biggest problems is that many of the surveys are conducted online. That's a huge problem if you want accurate numbers.

How big a problem? Pew reports that 10% of Americans don't use the internet at all. The Federal Communications Commission (FCC) reports that 6% of the US population don't have access to high speed internet, but a 2019 study by NPD Connected Intelligence found that 31% of US homes do not have broadband.

In the midst of falling TV ratings, an uptick may be in sight. Nielsen has announced that it will start including out-of-home viewing in local markets in the fall of 2019 and nationally in 2020. Everyone has known that there's a meaningful out-of-home TV audience (bars, restaurants, hotels, other people's homes, etc.), but that audience has never been included in the ratings. Nielsen started working on the project in 2008. Coincidentally or not, that's just after our Middletown Media Studies showed that nearly 10% of TV viewing took place outside the home.

● ● ● ● ●

Ratings

There are some who argue that *ratings* is a dirty word, synonymous with the worst pandering to the lowest common denominator. But ratings are just numbers, and people in the business who say that they don't pay attention to ratings – or care how many people watch or listen to the news – are fools or liars. The business is about informing, perhaps enlightening, and definitely engaging the audience. But if no one is out there listening or watching, then newscasters are just talking to themselves.

There are two critical terms to define in order to understand ratings: *rating* and *share*. Both are percentages. In television, rating is the percentage of homes watching a TV program of all the homes that have a television set (that's estimated at just over 96% of all homes in the US). In radio, it's the percentage of people listening to a particular station of all the people who have radios. In essence, it's a competitive measure of how a TV program or radio station is doing against all the choices in life: eating, sleeping, working, watching another station and so on.

For example, in TV, a rating of 5.4 means that 5.4% of all the homes that *could* watch that program had that program on. If we're looking at a local station, it's 5.4% of the station's local market. If we're talking about a network program, then it's 5.4% of the country. What's going on with people in the rest of the 94.6% of the homes? Some are watching other channels; some are listening to radio instead; some are reading; some are sleeping; some aren't home and so on.

The other term is share. It's also a percentage, but it's a competitive measure against competitive media. A TV program that has a 5.4 rating, for example, might well have a 16.1 share, for example. That would mean that – of the homes that have TV *on* – 16.1% are watching that particular program.

In radio, it's the percentage of people listening to a particular station as opposed to the percentage listening to other stations.

So if you know exactly what people are watching or listening to, then share will always add up to 100%. Ratings, in contrast, will never add up to 100% simply because there will never be a time when everyone (or every home) is watching TV or listening to radio at the same time.

By the way, despite all the hype around streaming and various digital platforms, the *Washington Post* noted that of the 50 most-watched shows on all platforms in 2018–2019, all but six were on broadcast TV.

It's also possible that the importance of ratings will become a thing of the past. Networks and station groups are working to get away from ratings and instead base their ad sales on impressions: how many people are reached on whatever platform they're watching. The reason is simple. As more and more watch on streaming services, traditional ratings aren't capturing those people. But networks and stations know how many there are, and they can be added to the traditional TV audience to determine the total number of people reached. NBC is leading the way in this now.

●●●●●

Where the Programs Come From

TV stations get their programming from three sources: (1) Network, assuming they're affiliated with a network, like ABC, CBS, Fox, NBC, CW, and so on; (2) syndicated programming, like the daytime talk shows, some game shows and some off-net, older network shows and older episodes of current network shows; and (3) local programming, almost all of which is news.

The network programming includes the prime time lineup in the evening as well as most sports and some daytime shows. There was a time when the networks paid the stations to run network programming (really, to run the commercials in the programs), but that time is long gone. Today, almost all stations pay the networks for the programming the networks produce. It's called "reverse compensation," and that compensation comes primarily in the form of stations paying the network a portion of their retransmission revenue. That relationship is not likely to change anytime soon, but more and more stations are re-evaluating their syndicated programs.

Most stations pay for syndicated shows through a mixture of barter and cash. Barter means they give up some of their commercial time to the companies supplying the syndicated programs (barter) in addition to paying cash to the syndicator for the programming itself. As that programming has become more and more expensive, in both time and cash, stations are starting to look at creating more local shows to replace costly syndicated ones. That's part of what's behind the steady increase in the amount of local news that stations produce, but stations are also starting to look into other local information/entertainment programs. Producing TV news is expensive because it's so people-intensive. But once a station has a news department, the *incremental* cost of running *more* news is fairly low. That's part of why the average TV station that runs local news is now running a record amount: 5.9 hours per weekday.

●●●●●

Where the Money Comes From

Nexstar Broadcasting reached a milestone in the first quarter of 2019. It reported that the company took in more money from retransmission fees than from advertising. "Retransmission" is the money cable, satellite and telco companies pay to broadcasters to include those local channels on the cable or satellite system. Of course, the networks want a share of that money as well – commonly around 50 to 55% or so. Local station revenue from retransmission is now estimated to be 40% of total station revenue. That's more than double the percentage when the last edition of this book came out.

And while Nexstar didn't end the year with that ratio (advertising came out on top), it highlighted how the industry's revenue model has changed in just the last few years. And it's not just Nexstar. Scripps reported retransmission revenue up 21%; Meredith reported a 16% increase. And even though more than half that revenue winds up going back to the networks, it's still a huge gain for local TV.

The last edition of this book noted that retransmission revenue was $2.4 billion in 2012 and was estimated to be $8 billion in 2016 and to hit $12 billion by 2022. In fact, retransmission revenue for 2019 hit almost $11 billion.

TV still generates most of its income from advertising, and for stations that run local news, half of total station revenue comes from news. Station websites have become increasingly profitable, and 2019 estimates put digital ad revenue at 7.2% of total station ad revenue.

In 2020, with the current coronavirus pandemic and local advertising down substantially, it's hard to tell where things are going. Between a record-setting presidential campaign and the Olympics, 2020 should have been a bonanza for TV. Political advertising will still come through, but the Olympics has been pushed back to 2021, and the near-term future of business in this country is far from clear.

Dave Lougee, the CEO at Tegna, one of the largest TV group owners, said that over a two-year cycle (which means it includes political advertising), the company takes in more money from the combination of retransmission and political advertising than from TV advertising in general. Lougee spoke with Harry Jessell at TVNewsCheck. What that means is that TV has become less dependent on car advertising. Lougee said that auto used to be more than 30% of total business (which meant that if auto dropped, stations got hurt). Today, auto is right around 10%.

● ● ● ● ●

The Predicted Demise of TV

When TV was first publicly introduced at the RCA pavilion at the 1939 World's Fair in New York, a *New York Times* article dismissed it with this now-famous critique:

> *The problem with television is that people must sit and keep their eyes glued on a screen; the average American family hasn't time for it.*

The irony is that the author was dead wrong then . . . but it's possible that the prediction is now starting to come true.

Over the decades, pundits have predicted the demise of each of the three major legacy networks: ABC, CBS and NBC. In 1986, media observers noted that the new Fox TV network couldn't possibly succeed because there just wasn't room for another network.

In 1983, ABC and Westinghouse sold their Satellite News Channel to CNN, in essence ceding that there just wasn't room for a cable news competitor to CNN. So when Fox announced the start of Fox News Channel in 1996, experts again predicted that it couldn't possibly succeed.

In the 1990s, there was a widespread expectation that the number three and, certainly, the number four news stations in TV markets would either go out of business or at least get out of the local news business. Today, all of the top 80 markets and 83% of the 150 biggest TV markets have three or more separate, English language newsrooms producing local news. Only two markets in the top 100 don't make that cut.

For nearly 20 years, media critics have written about the impending demise of the TV "upfronts." The upfronts involve the summer sale of a portion of the advertising for the networks' upcoming TV season starting in the fall. Despite the annual predictions of disaster, *Variety* reports that the nation's five English-language networks (Disney/ABC, CBS, Fox, NBCUniversal and Warner Media) gained between 12% and 15% on the value of the advertising and increased volume by 3 to 4% for the 2019–2020 season.

Certainly, not every venture in television has been successful, but this list of inaccurate predictions of the demise of TV should serve as a warning. The disappearance of TV has been predicted since before the medium even got started. Its continued expansion and even existence has always been met with skeptics whose regular pronouncements and expectations of imminent failure have gone unrealized. The lesson to take away is to be careful about predicting the future – especially the future demise of television.

● ● ● ● ●

A New Model for News?

Back in 2000, quite a few of us traveled to Tampa, Florida, to examine the "next big thing" in news. It was called convergence, and, in this case, it involved a new building housing the Media General co-owned *Tampa Tribune* newspaper, WFLA-TV and combined website TBO.com. Many hailed this convergence and cooperation of media as the future of news. I was fascinated by the concept, and I was firmly convinced that this was the best model for journalism education. I still believe that last part for reasons not particularly relevant to this text. But as I wrote after visiting, I didn't see much real convergence actually taking place in Tampa, and it wasn't clear that it was ever going to happen on a widespread, commercial basis. It didn't, and in 2012, Media General sold off all its newspapers and became just a local TV and digital company. In 2016, Nexstar purchased Media General. That was the same year the *Tampa Bay Times* bought the competing *Tribune* . . . and shut it down.

There are at least some "converged" news operations, perhaps most notably the *Deseret News* and co-owned KSL-TV and radio in Salt Lake City. But convergence did not become the new model in news, and there are actually fewer cooperative ventures between TV stations and newspapers today than a few years ago – and the trend is down rather than up.

There are a variety of reasons why convergence didn't develop the way many expected. Probably the two most important are the internet and the FCC.

Although newspapers and TV stations competed against each other in newsgathering, they never really competed for audiences. The decisions to read the paper or watch the news on TV were largely independent of each other; most newspaper consumption took place in the morning, and prime TV news time was in the evening. Convergence seemed to make sense. Until the internet. Everyone competes head to head online, so while the convergence of jointly owned stations and papers might grow, convergence among stations and newspapers without common ownership is not likely, and the widespread use of newspaper paywalls makes this form of convergence less and less likely in the future.

There was also an expectation that the FCC would loosen its rules against new jointly owned, co-located newspapers and TV stations. At least some in the business thought that the combination of newspaper and TV would lead to a more profitable operation. The subtext actually involved the far more profitable TV station propping up a declining newspaper. But although the FCC tried to change its policies, a federal appeals court refused to allow it. Today, most combined newspaper and TV groups have split the two media apart.

●●●●●
The New TV Newsroom

Today, more and more TV stations – maybe even most – are "digital first." But considering that pretty much everything in TV is digital, what does that really mean? From a practical standpoint, a TV newsroom proclaiming that it's "digital first" means that the station puts out the news on the first and fastest channel available. Most often that's social media or online streaming – or both.

Some will argue that that represents a recognition that more and more people get their news first (if not primarily in the case of younger people) from social media and online. That's certainly an influence, but what's more likely at play is a new understanding of news consumption. As my research partner, Deb Wenger demonstrated in our research on the future of local news for the Knight Foundation, there's no evidence that breaking news first online or, in particular, on social media undercuts the audience on traditional TV. What appears more likely is that the more news that's going on (in all platforms), the more people watch. Putting it out on social media doesn't cannibalize the audience. Chapter 4 goes into this area in far more depth.

As General Manager of Digital, Kurt Christopher is responsible for the business side and monetization of digital for the Hubbard TV stations in Rochester and Albany, New York; Albuquerque, New Mexico; Austin, Texas; and Duluth and Minneapolis, Minnesota. That includes responsibility for company products and website apps . . . and for maximizing the business side of digital including increasing traffic, quality content and whether the websites are set up to capture maximum audience.

The business is growing, but that growth is primarily fueled by digital agency: the buying and selling of ads not only on Hubbard's websites but any website. They work with national clients to handle digital marketing. "That's the fastest growing part of digital for Hubbard," says Christopher.

For the most part, the TV stations handle their own websites. That's where there's a "constant battle" between online and social media. "Social media is the juggernaut," notes Christopher, "and it's had a massive impact in how [online] content is consumed. People don't use the [station] homepage nearly as much as they used to."

Christopher says people see an article and click on it and then bounce out. "That's the toughest issue for us – the behavior change," he says. "People don't visit us as a brand [as much] anymore – we're just a feed service. So what we try to do is get people to go from one article to one more, and it's been tough."

The issue is making money. Stations make money on their own website. Live feeds and streaming on Facebook Live engage an audience but produce no revenue.

"We want people to consume news on the website, but we need to keep up the engagement [in social media] for the traffic," notes Christopher. "If we don't engage with people, we get pushed down in the feed [on Facebook]."

In the old days, Christopher says everyone wanted to buy ads on the station homepage. Now, some advertising buys specifically exclude the homepage.

Article pages always ruled overall, but now that most of the traffic comes from news aggregators or social media, almost all the traffic goes straight to the article pages. "No one bookmarks the homepage anymore," says Christopher.

The company has gotten more and more into OTT – over the top – and each station has an OTT channel. The sales side buys and sells ads based on the interest in the addressable aspect of it. By addressable, it's the idea that they can sell ads based on the characteristics of the specific audience that can be reached. At least that's the idea.

"But we've found that the exacting technology needed is still playing catch-up," notes Christopher. "When you're targeting for ads, you need information from the TV. As TVs become smarter, we're getting better data, but it's not as reliable as it needs to be."

Scale is a major concern. "With cord-cutting and live streaming," notes Christopher, "viewers can do really well with a good OTA (over the air) signal and streaming. Addressable TV advertising inventory will only grow with the streaming segment. Advertisers also want the precise targeting of digital on TV – and the technology and scale of that is still a ways off."

●●●●●

So Where Are We Going?

First, let's focus on the parameters for the debate. It's really not whether there's a future for news. Every reasonable measure of how people spend their time – as well as what they say they're interested in – makes clear that people have a huge and, if anything, growing appetite for news and information.

The debate is about which media will supply that news and what form that news consumption will take.

The bottom line on the future is that we really don't know who the winners and losers in the news field will be. No one knows. Not for sure. Some of that is because we really can't see into the future, and some of that is because we're much too early in another media evolution to know with certainty how it will come out. Besides, news consumption is permanently evolving, so we're talking about predicting the future that now appears possible – not the future we have yet to imagine.

As we try to figure out where we're heading, let's start with a few more things we know based on what people do and what people say they want.

- The internet has clearly led to a greater demand for user control and convenience, but it's not clear who's going to supply that or how.
- There's a lot of loyalty to established, traditional media. That will likely translate into the present established brands dominating the news and information fields in the future, regardless of platform.
- Newspaper's triple problems of aging consumers, rising production costs and a shrinking advertising base (especially classified) will lead to radical changes in newspapers in the next 10 years. Some will cut back on the days of publication; some papers may become boutique subsets of their websites; many won't make it at all.
- Just because something is new doesn't mean people will care. People will adopt new technology to the extent that it allows them to do what they now do better, easier or more cheaply. Plenty of new efforts and ideas won't measure up.
- Progress and change always happen faster when looking back on it than when you're living it. Wholesale media changes have not happened yet and will not happen overnight. Partly that's because change doesn't happen that way. Partly it's because we're not dealing with a vast dissatisfied group of consumers desperately searching for wholesale changes. When asked what their choices are for news delivery, they give answers that largely mirror their present use. In other words, they're generally fairly happy with what they have, and that will affect how quickly change happens – or doesn't.

So what predictions can we make for the future of local news?

- In the end, it will come down to money . . . as it always has.
- The newspaper revenue model is unsustainable for almost all newspapers. The exceptions will be a handful of papers of record and a handful of papers supported by the good will or vanity of extremely wealthy patrons. As we appear to be entering the next recession, we already see increasing signs of newspaper carnage. The newspaper landscape is probably changing forever.

- Local TV is almost certain to remain profitable for at least the next decade – aided by increasing retransmission revenue, increasing political revenue and industry consolidation.
- There are no guarantees, and local TV news must improve. Local TV news shines in crisis – whether natural or self-inflicted. But it must be better and more relevant day in and day out.

In the end, if local TV stations can transform into local news and information services, they still have multiple advantages over the rest of the field: revenue streams are expanding, they know video, they have regulators seemingly ready to make consolidation easier, and they are poised to get a new transmission standard, ATSC 3.0, that will allow them to offer better quality mobile reception, more multicasting opportunities and new business models to strengthen their overall revenue potential.

In the end, this we know for certain: For the foreseeable future, people will want to see and hear and read news and information, and those who want to provide it must learn how to tell stories in pictures and words. The rest is detail.

• • • • •

Summary

News is a business, and its survival depends on a business model that enables it to take in more money than it costs to produce news. TV still dominates the media jungle – both in time spent overall and in where people get most of their news, but the internet is rapidly catching up. And the amount of TV news being produced keeps growing, year after year. Measuring media use is difficult, and that difficulty, coupled with problems in methodology and media bias, sometimes leads us to misleading or inaccurate media use numbers. Still, it's clear that we're in a period of significant change.

Young adults get more news from the internet than TV; more and more people generally are getting news online. Although there are a variety of new efforts in news delivery, so far the traditional players are the leading suppliers of news, and it's clear that news consumption is not shrinking, even though it is fragmenting.

More and more people are getting news and information on mobile devices, but it's too early to know how that will affect the industry.

• • • • •

Key Words and Phrases

Profit . . . revenue . . . expenses . . . advertising . . . cable and satellite carriage . . . retransmission fees . . . market area . . . network, syndicated and local programming . . . rating . . . share . . . media use and location . . . smartphones . . . paywalls . . . news aggregators . . . OTT

● ● ● ● ●

Exercises

A. Make a list of the TV stations, radio stations and newspapers in your market area. Which stations run news, and how much do they run? Do they produce their own news or get it from somewhere else? If somewhere else, where? Make a list of all the online media in your market area that produce *local* news. Characterize the kind, detail and amount of local news that they run.

B. How have the news media in your market area changed over the last 5 or 10 years? Who's running more, and who's running less? Check on length of newspapers and number (and size) of pages; TV newscasts added or dropped; TV stations that have started news departments or terminated them; radio stations that used to run news and now don't, and ones that now run news but didn't before. Compare broadcast-based and print-based news websites. Are there new online news and information websites in your area? If so, who's doing them and how do they compare with websites from traditional media companies? Which local news websites have paywalls and how do those paywalls work?

C. Make a list of the TV stations in your market area that run news on another medium (list all the media that each is on).

D. Make a list of all the cooperative ventures that the TV, radio stations and newspapers in your market area are involved with.

E. What are the local stations doing on mobile? Are they using apps? How do those work, and do they charge for them?

F. Keep a 48- or 72-hour diary of your own media use. All media. How did that come out? How does that compare to what you thought it would be?

3

• • • • •

News

Although this book focuses on writing, it takes as a given the reader's acceptance of the basic tenets of broadcast journalism: to be accurate, fair, clear and interesting. Accurate because no manner of clever word weaving compensates for wrongful injury to the people we cover or the self-inflicted damage of a correction that could have been avoided. Fair if we are to be trusted. Clear because without clarity what we do has no meaning. Interesting because it really doesn't matter what we do if no one's out there listening and watching.

• • • • •

What Is News?

There are common characteristics or values that make up the typical news story:

1. **Importance or significance**. Some stories are news because they involve events that have a meaningful impact on people. War, famine, an outbreak of a dangerous disease are all significant on a global basis. A zoning decision or a school board election could be an important event in a small town. Generally, for an event to be significant or important, it should have a meaningful impact on a meaningful percentage of the audience. A fatal car accident on a lonely stretch of road may be a disastrous event for the people involved and the family, but it's not a news story based on significance or importance. On the other hand, the story may well be considered news based on human interest.

2. **Prominence**. Some people – by virtue of who they are by birth or deed – make news no matter what they do. The president, a major Hollywood or sports star and British royalty all make news by doing almost anything at all. Or nothing. Some people acquire temporary prominence – their 15 minutes of fame – by some extraordinary action – good or bad. The person who rescues a family from a burning home and the newly

accused serial killer both achieve a measure of prominence. Every area has its local prominent figures and characters, but few people rise to the level of prominence such that we recognize who they are by name alone.

3. **Conflict**. War is obvious, but conflict can just as easily be over ideas like abortion, charter schools, separation of church and state, any election and most crimes. If there were no "other side" or "opposing view," then many of the stories we cover could simply be calendar listings rather than news stories.

4. **Human interest**. Some stories are just interesting. Yes, that includes the newscast filler of the waterskiing squirrel, but it also includes the wide range of stories that describe what we do with and to each other – like a daring water rescue in a faraway city or a child's battle with a ravaging disease or that fatal accident noted earlier. CBS's Steve Hartman provides us with extraordinary stories that report on the human condition.

Some people consider *impact* – as in having a strong or significant effect on a (large) group of people – as a separate characteristic of news; some view it as a part of the earlier list.

A story only needs to be strong enough in one of those four characteristics in order to be newsworthy, but many stories include more than one. The remaining two characteristics are relevant to every story – either positively or negatively.

5. **Time**. Time factors into all stories. A story is most newsworthy when it happens, but news ages quickly. Absent a new development, news generally has a life cycle of no more than 24 hours. A major event that breaks on the 6 p.m. news is likely to be on the 11 p.m. news and probably again on the next morning's newscasts. The story might get on the noon news but would not likely air on the next day's 5 p.m. newscast, and it certainly wouldn't (or shouldn't) be repeated on the next day's 6 p.m. news. But that's only the case if there are no new developments. New developments restart the news cycle. Along with that overall life cycle, absent new developments, a news story typically becomes less newsworthy with each succeeding newscast. So time figures into every story or potential story as either an ally – if it just happened – or an enemy – as it ages. What about an old story that a journalist just learned about? Those are trickier. If the story isn't too old, and if it has other strong values, the standard 24-hour life of the story will exist. But because the story is old (even if new to the reporter or audience), the story must be stronger in other categories to get on the air at all.

6. **Proximity**. Again, all stories involve proximity since all stories are based somewhere geographically. As with time, proximity is either a help or a hindrance. Geographically, the closer the story is to the

audience, the easier it is for the story to be considered newsworthy by other standards. Conversely, the farther away a story is from the audience, the higher the story must score in other categories to be considered newsworthy. The arrest of a small-town mayor for drunk driving will be a huge story in that small town. It might well be a small story in the nearest large city. A state or two away, the story will likely get no attention at all.

For a story to make it on the air, it must have one or more of the first four values in sufficient quantity to be worth telling, and it must pass separate tests for time and proximity.

● ● ● ● ●

Balancing News Values

There's no absolute scale. There's no way to assign numbers for every case and call something news if it exceeds some total score. Worse, reasonable people will always disagree on *how* important or interesting a story is. Part of the discrepancy is just human judgment. Part of it involves the background and interests of different people. Older people may find any story on Social Security to be extremely important, while younger people may be largely indifferent. Because the general audience is a diverse group, the people deciding what news is should have a similar diversity, otherwise the news organization may miss stories that a significant segment of the audience really cares about.

We put those definitions of what is news into practice in the day to day decisions of exactly what news to cover and how. That takes us to another list: the types of news stories that we broadcast.

● ● ● ● ●

Types of Stories

From a newsroom coverage and story assignment standpoint, stories break down into six categories.

Breaking News

More and more loosely defined, this is hard news that the station and the audience are just learning about that day. Breaking news has become the bread and butter of TV newscasts. Usually handled by live reporting, there's no way to plan for the specific event; it's simply what a station reacts to, preferably with a plan for responding, generally, to breaking news. Real breaking news will inevitably alter newscasts and coverage plans a station made earlier in the day.

Examples:

■ A surprise political resignation
■ A seven-car pile-up on the interstate
■ A triple murder
■ A flash flood or tornado or earthquake
■ An unexpected major business development

If a station knew about the event ahead of time and could plan for coverage, then it isn't breaking news. Note that with rare exception, all competing stations are likely to learn about breaking news at just about the same time. They may react differently, but breaking news is seldom a secret or exclusive, so stations differentiate themselves on breaking news not by whether they have the story on the air. All are likely to have it. The difference comes in how each station handles the breaking news.

Planned Event Reporting

While some stations will label almost everything breaking news, much of what stations cover they knew about in advance. Calling it breaking news may work from a promotion standpoint, but it's certainly not an accurate portrayal. Planned event reporting includes coverage that comes out of a city council or school board meeting, a court case, or a scheduled news conference. Anything that you knew in advance was going to happen.

Advancing an event would also be included in this category. That's when a station does a news story before (in advance of) a school board meeting or any planned event. Ongoing coverage of an event also goes here – even if the original event was breaking news. For instance, hurricane coverage is breaking news, but the inevitable series of follow-up stories are really planned events because you know in advance that you're going to continue coverage.

Examples:

■ A story on the top agenda item on the evening school board meeting
■ A story on the scheduled report issued by the city council or the state legislature
■ A story on the scheduled local appearance of a prominent politician, actor, sports figure

A news organization reacts to breaking news, but planned event reporting – as the name makes clear – is planned. As with breaking news, all competing stations will normally know about the same planned events.

Enterprise Reporting

Breaking news may be a station's bread and butter, but enterprise reporting, day in, day out, is commonly what separates the top stations from the also-rans. Enterprise reporting combines the hard news values you'd find in a breaking news story or a planned event, along with station exclusivity. It's a story a news person comes up with by virtue of being observant, creative or maybe just lucky. The key is that other media don't have the story. A hallmark of enterprise stories involves learning or discovering something that people didn't know, realize or expect.
Examples:

■ The discovery that a major local business is in serious financial trouble and about to lay off workers
■ The discovery that a major public works project is way over budget and well behind schedule
■ The discovery that a new principal at a local high school has established some really unorthodox approaches to education that really seem to be turning students around (or failing miserably)

Because these stories are exclusive to the station that came up with them, they're more promotable, and they make a difference in where the audience turns for news. Some will argue that *all* reporting should be enterprise reporting. Sure, in that perfect world that none of us lives in, maybe that's true. In the meantime, if you're looking for a job in this business, your "reel" of stories should be primarily – if not exclusively – breaking news and enterprise stories.

Investigative Reporting

Real investigative reporting is enterprise reporting on steroids. Typically, this is where you learn something that others didn't know – and that at least some people would rather you *not* know. Most often seen during sweeps or ratings period, this is the most time-consuming and therefore most expensive reporting there is. Anyone can make accusations. The key to good investigative reporting isn't making accusations or raising questions, it's about "proving" something.
Examples:

■ Proving that a local politician has been accepting bribes
■ Proving that a local nursing home has been abusing patients
■ Proving that a company is knowingly selling an unsafe product

More and more, stations are working to build their *brand* around investigative reporting. The RTDNA research, conducted in 2015 and again in 2019, shows that no area of TV reporting has grown as much and increased in station emphasis as much as investigative reporting.

Special Segment Reporting

For the most part, these are usually either planned event reports or enterprise stories about a specific topic. They can be either harder news topics or softer features, but their existence is scheduled and built into various newscasts. Health and consumer reporting are probably the two most common. Stations also run what are sometimes called "franchises" – special segment reports that commonly air weekly.
Examples:

■ Daily health report – especially done by a doctor employed by the station or an outside company
■ "Mr. Food" or other cooking segment
■ Pet or child adoption segment
■ "On Your Side" or other consumer reporting segment

Features

Features had largely fallen out of favor over the past decade, but we might just see a revival. They're typically non-timely stories about who we are and what we do to and with each other. Commonly, these stories have strong human interest aspects and frequently involve the secondary aspects of earlier breaking news or planned events.
Examples:

■ A follow-up on how a family is coping now that the primary breadwinner is out of work due to a plant shutdown
■ A profile of someone who has overcome an obstacle
■ A story about search and reuniting
■ The story of someone with a bizarre hobby or collection

"I'm looking for stories that haven't been told before," says CBS' Steve Hartman, the top network feature reporter today. "Stories that aren't clichés. Stories that aren't copying other people's deeds."

Why a possible revival? Because features – by virtue of their timelessness – have a better chance of going viral than a lot of run of the mill news of the day. Feature stories can also live on a station's website a lot longer than the typical news of the day.

Stories can also cross lines to incorporate aspects of more than one category. The recovery and rehabilitation of a veteran who fought in Afghanistan is a feature although it obviously has a timely aspect to it. In fact, many if not most stories cross boundaries at least to some degree.

●●●●●

Where Story Ideas Come From

Stations get story ideas from a variety of places:

- **Social Media** like Facebook, Twitter, Instagram, blogs, Pinterest, etc.
- **Wire services** like the Associated Press
- **News releases** from government, businesses and organizations
- **Agendas** from governmental or quasi-governmental organizations
- Scheduled **news conferences**
- **Follow-up notes** from previous stories
- **Other media**, including newspapers, books, magazines, radio, cable, other television stations and so on
- Story idea **services and consultants**
- **Reporters** and other news people who have seen something, talked to someone or just had an idea
- **People who call** the station with information, tips or stories

One of the first places newsrooms look for story ideas is inward. What's trending on a station's website? What's getting the most clicks. Where are people posting the most comments . . . and what are they saying? Are they asking questions that haven't yet been answered?

The wires supply a steady stream of news and information all day. Most of that news is national or international, but some involve state and local news. Stations are always looking for state, regional, national or international news that has local implications. A US military plane that crashed on the other side of the world could have been made in your community. Or maybe the same kind of plane is flown at a military base in your area. Or the crew flying that plane could have been stationed in your community not too long ago.

News releases tell us what some organization or company or government agency would like us to run a story on. Maybe that's a worthwhile story like a new program to help feed poor people or a local business expanding and adding new jobs to the community. Maybe the information ties in with another story a reporter is working on. Maybe within the press release is information on a more interesting story. Maybe the information simply gets you thinking about a story idea. Most news releases contain little real news, but that doesn't mean that they can't inspire terrific news stories.

Agendas tell us what's slated to come up at various government or organization meetings. Some of the topics may clearly be newsworthy. Others we may need to call on to gather additional information. Remember that a meeting agenda doesn't tell you what old or new business might come up . . . and that could be the most interesting news of all.

News conferences commonly tell us information that we probably should have found out already by good reporting. But sometimes that's not possible, and the news conference also tells us when we'll have access to people that we may want to question – even if those questions have nothing to do with the topic of the news conference.

Every time we work on a story, we're talking with people who should be giving us information that we can use for other stories. Sometimes those stories relate to the one we're working on, and sometimes they're completely different. Or maybe we just want to remember to follow-up on the original story that we did. If the story was meaningful enough to put on the air the first time, maybe we should keep track of it to provide progress or follow-up reports.

We constantly monitor other media to see what they have and to compare what and how we did with the competition. A good, timely story that we didn't have might force us to play catch-up. An interesting feature might be worth putting aside to do on our own in a few months or so.

There are a number of private services that supply story ideas – and news consultants do that as well.

We'd also find a lot more stories if we just opened our eyes and our minds. What's going on behind that new construction fence? Why is a school teacher moonlighting as a waitress at a local restaurant? Why does it take so long to register your car or get a new driver's license? What are the issues your neighbors are concerned about or service people are talking about? We all probably walk through a dozen good story ideas every day. Too often, we're too busy with less important issues to see them. **Too often, our outside-of-work personal interactions are limited to other news people. You'll pick up no story ideas there; get to know real people who live and work and play in the community.**

For seven years, Steve Hartman told amazing stories in a feature called, "Everybody Has a Story." At the end of each story, the person profiled threw a dart at a map of the US, and Hartman and his photographer would travel there and randomly pick a name out of a phone book. Hartman did a story on the first person who agreed to see them. "There was always a life lesson," notes Hartman. "Not only does everybody have a story, but everybody has a story worth telling." That's a lot easier said than done, but part of the point is that good, meaningful stories are lurking almost everywhere.

Sometimes people call in great story ideas, but it's rare. More than rare. Mostly, people who call feel abused and want to get even; people misunderstand something or how the system works, but they want the station to fix it; people try to get someone in trouble. Worse, there seems to be a rule requiring every unbalanced person in America to call their favorite television station at least once a day. On the other hand, there was a very strange woman who called a large television station in the Midwest to complain that a US congressman was having sex with her underage daughter. The woman was probably unbalanced, but her underage daughter really *was* having sex with a US congressman. That award-winning story is part of why we listen.

●●●●●

The Assignment Desk

The assignment desk is the nerve center of the newsroom. Commonly overseen by the assignment manager or managing editor, the assignment desk monitors police, fire and emergency frequencies on the scanners; regularly checks the wire services; makes regular calls to police, fire and hospitals (among others) to find out what's going on; maintains the future file or daybook to keep track of scheduled events for the day, the week, the month and the year; frequently handles the logistics of pairing photographer and reporter (assuming they're separate); and makes sure events are covered, people are where they should be, even whether crews are getting time off for meals.

The assignment desk works with producers, managers and others to make sure that everyone is on top of events of the day and how the newsroom is going to deal with them. It's a great job for people who require constant stimulation and truly enjoy juggling lots of balls at the same time.

There are good stories and there are good TV stories. Know the difference; use both and assign the right people to each type of story and recognize where in the newscast each should go. On the assignment desk, you're always looking for a good lead story – a story that affects the most people or is, itself, most affecting.

TV still makes its mark in breaking news. If you're thinking about how much resources to put into a breaking story, you're almost always better off rolling big and rolling early. You can always scale back later.

●●●●

Morning and Afternoon Meetings

In order to determine how to deploy news people and what stories to run on the day's newscasts, most stations have a morning meeting – usually starting around 8:30 a.m. to 9:30 a.m., running no more than a half hour or so. The morning meeting sets the agenda for what the station plans to cover that day and determines, in large measure, what will air on the afternoon and early evening newscasts, and even on the multiple stations that many newsrooms program for – assuming that breaking news doesn't alter the landscape.

Who runs the morning meeting varies from station to station. Commonly, it's the news director or assistant news director, managing editor or executive producer. In other words, one of the top managers in the newsroom. Sometimes it's the assignment manager or assignment editor. Some stations rotate the person in charge.

Who attends the meeting varies as well. Some stations require everyone who's working in news at that hour to attend and participate; others require only a small group of managers, assignment editors and producers – with reporters welcome but not required; others are somewhere in between. In some cases, everyone is required to propose an idea; in other places, reporters simply wait to be handed an assignment.

Who isn't there? The morning producer is likely done for the day, and the morning show is already over or nearly over. The noon producer may listen in, but the noon show is already set unless a reporter will cover something in the morning that might offer a live shot possibility for noon. The (late) nightside producer and crew aren't in yet. The point is, the meeting is primarily about the afternoon/early evening newscasts.

As stories are discussed and accepted or rejected, producers of the various afternoon/early evening newscasts are likely to claim stories for their shows. Generally, it's not a battle of equals, with the 6 p.m. producer commonly getting first shot because that's likely to be the newscast with the largest audience. Even that varies, however. And when a newsroom handles the news on multiple stations, it's likely that there's a primary station and a secondary one or ones.

In order to determine what to cover, stations – implicitly or explicitly – ask two fundamental questions:

1. What's important?

2. What are people talking about?

A station commits its resources in response to the answers to those two questions. When a single story is the top answer to both questions, then you have a clear lead story for the day. More often, the answers are different and less definitive.

Commonly, stations have a second assignment meeting in the afternoon, usually around 2:30 or 3 p.m. This smaller meeting involves the "nightside" crew – afternoon/evening assignment editor, 9 p.m., 10 p.m. or 11 p.m. producer, nightside reporters and, perhaps, others. The concept is the same as the morning meeting, but the target is the late evening newscast. At some stations, the afternoon meeting includes a late review of the early evening newscasts and an assignment desk handoff from the dayside assignment editor to the nightside assignment editor.

Note that the earlier description is far more applicable to medium and large newsrooms. Smaller shops go through the same processes – but with fewer people who frequently double-up on the roles they play. And while we're clearly in the digital age, dry erase white boards remain a common way to keep track of the day's assignments.

● ● ● ● ●

Innovation in TV News

There are plenty of critics who argue that local TV news today looks a lot like it did 40 or 50 years ago. On the surface, there's an element of truth to that. Over those years TV news has moved from one news anchor to (usually) two, added more news, goes live a whole lot more, the technology has gotten lighter, better and (relatively speaking) less expensive, and the faces on the air are a lot more diverse.

But it's still news, sports and weather; it's still readers, voiceovers (VOs), voiceover with sound on tape (VO/SOTs) and packages, and a lot of what local TV news covers is the same old stuff.

There's actually a lot of innovation at TV news stations, it's just that most of it doesn't involve the traditional TV newscasts. There are some experiments on-air – perhaps most notably Denver's KUSA-TV's blow-up and complete redesign of the 6 p.m. news, but that's very much an exception.

Most of the innovation is on the digital side – online and with social media. And there's lots of experimentation there.

When Deb Wenger and I studied the future of local news for the Knight Foundation, we found that top stations – the ones holding or even growing their on-air audience – had three characteristics:

1. They put a premium on enterprise and investigative reporting.
2. Transparency. They tended to bring the audience into their decision-making process and show the audience how they did what they did – and why.
3. More audience listening and engagement. They used their website – and especially social media – to have conversations with their audience. And listen.

● ● ● ● ●

Following the News

At least part of how we learn what news really is . . . is by consuming it. If you're interested in going into the news business, you should be reading newspapers and magazines, listening to radio news (especially

NPR), watching local and network television news and consuming news online. If you don't follow news on a regular basis, it will be pretty hard for you to determine whether something you hear about or come across is actually news or just life as usual. We're not surprised when we run across someone who is crazy about sports who says that he or she wants to be a sports reporter or sports anchor. Someone who wants to be a news reporter or news anchor needs to have the same passion for news.

●●●●●

Summary

The basic tenets of broadcast journalism – or any kind of journalism – involve a news person being accurate, fair, clear and interesting. What we call news isn't simply random facts, it's material that contains one or more of four basic news values: importance, prominence, conflict and/or human interest . . . and passes additional hurdles of timeliness and proximity. From a station coverage standpoint, those news stories break down into six categories: breaking news, planned event reporting, enterprise reporting, investigative reporting, special segment reporting and features.

Ideas for those stories come from a wide variety of sources and are discussed at the morning and afternoon meetings, where the afternoon and early and late evening newscasts are planned in response to two underlying questions: What's important, and what are people talking about?

●●●●●

Key Words and Phrases

Accurate . . . fair . . . clear . . . interesting . . . importance or significance . . . prominence . . . conflict . . . human interest . . . time . . . proximity . . . breaking news . . . planned event reporting . . . enterprise reporting . . . investigative reporting . . . special segment reporting . . . features . . . the assignment desk . . . future file or daybook . . . morning and afternoon meetings . . . social media

●●●●●

Exercises

A. Watch or listen to a local or network television or radio newscast and evaluate how each story measures up in terms of accurate, fair, clear and interesting. Check facts to see if the stories were correct. If the story involved something controversial, how were the different sides treated? Does treating people fairly mean giving everyone the same amount of time and space? Did you understand all of the stories? Were the stories interesting to you? Even if they weren't, do you think others might find the stories interesting? If so, who?

B. Watch or listen to a local or network television or radio newscast. Do you think all the stories were really newsworthy? Might others think so? List each value or characteristic of news and score or explain whether each story scored high or low in that category. Why was each story on the air?

C. Watch a local or network television newscast and determine what type of story each item was. Do you notice any organizational plan in the sequence of those stories? How does each story answer those two fundamental questions that stations ask to determine what to cover?

D. Talk to people (preferably including people who are not just like you) and come up with a story idea – that's NOT a profile of someone. Make a couple of calls to see if it's really a story. Explain why it's worth covering and what values make it a story.

E. Which news values do the following scenarios exemplify?

1. A local factory that employs 1,500 people will shut down in 90 days.

2. Two local teens who were drag racing collided, and one of the cars hit and killed a pedestrian.

3. A local business announced that it had received an award from the company's headquarters (in another state), recognizing the local business for its "service excellence."

4. The Labor Department reports that the local consumer price index rose 1.5% last month in the local area.

5. Scientists at a local university say that the community is not prepared for the possibility of an earthquake that might hit the local area sometime in the future.

6. A local city council member has just announced her resignation in order to spend more time with her family.

7. The weather service just announced that a major storm with wind gusts as high as 60 miles per hour may hit the local area tonight.

8. The Food and Drug Administration has just announced a recall for packages of fresh chicken manufactured by The Very Best Company. One of your local supermarket chains carries the brand, but other stores do not.

9. The State Environmental Protection Agency released a report that says the local water supply has 65 ppb of Pb.

10. Local police announce that because of a shortage of manpower, they're going to stop responding to non-injury traffic accidents.

11. Charity Navigator notes that a local group that raises money for veterans spends 33% of its income on administrative and fund-raising expenses.

F. If you're putting together a local newscast, on a scale of 1 (lowest) to 5 (highest), which stories in Exercise E are the most newsworthy?

G. Rank the stories in Exercise E that you'd run in a local newscast from most important to least important.

4

●●●●●

Digital First

Most TV news operations now declare that they're "digital first." But what does that mean? It means that, generally, news gets posted on the first available platform . . . which usually means social media or the station website or both. If that breaking news happens just before a TV newscast, then the newscast might get first shot. But even then, there's likely to be a posting to social media (and/or push alert) to let the audience know what's coming.

It's not that stations see social media and the web as being equal in importance to TV; it's more that stations have seen the futility of trying to hold news until the next TV newscast, and **there's evidence that breaking news on social media or the web doesn't take away from TV viewing.**

That last research comes from an extensive evaluation of social media and Nielsen ratings by my research partner, Deb Wenger (University of Mississippi). In a study we did for the Knight Foundation, she found that sharing content on Facebook does not cannibalize the newscast audience. Analysis of Facebook engagement data and Nielsen ratings indicates a significant correlation between days with higher levels of social engagement and higher newscast ratings. However, cause and effect is not clear, and the driver for both may simply be the day's news events. In other words, if it's a busy news day, more people will get news on social media AND more people will watch TV news.

On the one hand, posting news on social media doesn't cut into the broadcast audience. And on the other hand, more and more, information *from* the website may well drive the news day. What's trending online – what has been most read and reacted to online – likely plays into (if not dictates) what the day's news coverage will look like.

So digital first really isn't simply about the posting of stories, it's also about influencing – if not determining – the coverage of the day's news.

From a station standpoint, social media isn't an end in itself because stations make little to no money on social media. Facebook and Google, combined, take in 60% of all internet advertising revenue. Add in Amazon, and it's 70%. Consequently, the station emphasis is on moving the audience to the station website or TV itself. That's where stations make money.

The RTDNA research says that social media drives about 50% of the traffic on station websites, and for many stations, it's a lot higher than that.

Another thing we found in our Knight research is that more social media posting doesn't correlate with more engagement. A number of stations with staggering numbers of social media posts had remarkably small engagement numbers. Social media success comes with posting quality and appropriateness – not volume.

At KSNV-TV, the NBC affiliate in Las Vegas, Nevada, Rebecca Lewis says everything gets posted to the website first – then social media. That's the directive from station owner, Sinclair Broadcast Group. Lewis is Digital Executive Producer, heading up the station's six-person digital team. It's actually a hybrid team, handling both digital and helping or handling the assignment desk. Lewis says that hybrid model is becoming more and more common across the country. The combination makes sense, Lewis says, because of the emphasis on breaking news on social media, and the desk puts them closer to it and helps get material on social media and the web faster.

● ● ● ● ●

Why Social Media?

Social media involves a station reaching out to members of the audience. That reaching out could include efforts at gathering news and information, such as pictures or news tips or crowdsourcing, or it could mean promotional efforts to boost newscast or website audience, or it could mean efforts at building a dialog with the audience to bring them into the decision-making process.

Reporters find that when they post to social media about a story they're working on, potential sources may find them and help supply additional perspectives and information that they might not otherwise have picked up.

It's not simply that television and radio stations are doing more with social media these days, it's also that – at least in the case of TV – they're doing something different. At TV news operations, social media is about connecting with and having conversations with the audience. Radio, in contrast, looks more like television did a few years earlier, where most of the efforts really were just promotional.

In its most recent study, in late 2018, Pew Research Center found that almost as many Americans say they prefer to get news online (37%) as prefer to get it on TV (41%). Notice, that the combined figure (78%) doesn't leave a lot of room for everyone else.

Pew also found that local TV stations still top the list of where US adults turn to the most for local news. Radio comes in second; newspapers third; online fourth.

In looking at just social media, according to the Pew online research, 43% of US adults get news on Facebook; next comes YouTube at 21%, then Twitter at 12%, Instagram at 8%, LinkedIn at 6%, Reddit and Snapchat at 5%, WhatsApp at 2%, and Tumblr at 1%.

The point is that if a station is going to move people from social media to the station website or on-air, then the station needs to be active on the social media where people hang out.

A lot of the activity involves the use of Facebook Live. Some stations use Facebook Live to run events and news conferences, provide mini-reports from the field or just show a reporter setting up gear. Some are even using Facebook Live to operate a virtual live TV channel, showing news and sports events (and other things) that appeal to a niche audience or the station was unable to broadcast because of on-air programming commitments. So now stations are live streaming on two platforms: Facebook Live and their own website. Increasingly, it's the same material on both sites. The live streams may come from the regular field cameras the reporter or photographer uses, but it's even easier to live stream from a smartphone.

Digiday reports that NPR has learned several things experimenting with Facebook Live. First, don't go live just because you can. "Hovering around" has no meaning; showing something with real content does. Second, the audience has a real interest in meaningful live reporting. Third, while video quality is important, it's less important than strong content. Fourth, whatever you do should be about engagement and deepening the loyalty of the audience.

● ● ● ● ●

Measuring Engagement and Driving Traffic

Everything is measured in social media and online, and that allows stations to see instantly what works in terms of audience reaction and engagement and what doesn't – and respond immediately. According to TVNewsCheck, Gray Television uses CrowdTangle to gauge Facebook performance and a mix of Social News Desk, Google Analytics and Google Data Studio to determine engagement and clicks on links.

Sinclair also uses CrowdTangle and other analytics to measure how the station is doing compared to competitors.

WNYW-TV (Fox) in New York uses Share Rocket for station metrics, and the station holds a daily social media meeting to talk about the metrics. Fox also tracks audience response because the company figures that if something is successful (engaging) for one of its stations, there's a fair chance it'll work elsewhere, too.

The goal is always to drive traffic back to the station's digital properties and the TV because that's where the money is.

Metrics can help stations learn about their audience for specific targeting . . . as well as what kinds of stories and story approaches resonate with the audience.

All of this means that stations have to bring social media content into the workflow. That also means that stations need to use integrated tools that work across multiple platforms – otherwise, they're spending time doing the same basic job over and over for each platform.

● ● ● ● ●

What It Means on the Ground

John Morris, Vice President for Content Development and Innovation at WPVI-TV, has spent most of his career at the ABC-owned station in Philadelphia.

He says management of station social media accounts (mainly Facebook, Twitter, Instagram – as well as experiments with up-and-comers) is left to the digital teams. When a digital producer creates content for the website, that person is also responsible for posting, or scheduling that post, to the social platforms. "We are all also working with some social automation that scrubs our site for well-performing posts and will send them to Facebook and Twitter," Morris notes. The digital producers are responsible for writing headlines that work well for the various social platforms.

"Anchors and reporters are responsible for their own social accounts," notes Morris, "with station oversight and guidelines."

"There are stations and groups that will post live social media metrics in the center of the newsroom so talent can see who is doing well and who is not," he says, but WPVI doesn't do that. "We do seek out and praise the high performers and have conversations with the poorer performers."

Social media and online have meant that station reporters now have additional social expectations and digital obligations. "They are responsible for sending in a script written specifically for the website," notes Morris, with the soundbites transcribed, added information that may not make the broadcast version, story-relevant links and photos that they may have taken along the way. They also are given a daily expectation of how to share information on social platforms. As you can imagine, these added responsibilities are not in place of any of their traditional work, they're in addition to it, and that makes for a busy day. The station doesn't stream newscasts on social media. They consider that "premium" content and want people to watch on the station website where they can monetize a live stream. A big event that everyone's covering, though, will go on Facebook Live, and anchors and reporters will use it to talk about developing stories, and weather anchors will use it to interact with the audience.

If reporters and anchors are live on Facebook, they use their phones. "We don't stream to Twitter," Morris notes. "I haven't found that it's worth the effort."

The station also has "a very strong belief" that teases and promotions on social are "deadly content." "Followers not only hate them," says Morris, they get angry. All of our social content, even if it's pointing ahead to a newscast must contain usable information and something that someone is likely to share. A post that says, 'Coming up at 6, I'll tell you about the cure for cancer' is not an acceptable post. Morris says Instagram is a challenge that they use in a few ways. "We are dabbling more and more into Instagram TV to share short video-rich stories, mostly light, lifestyle content." They also do "feel good about your city" posts with photos and videos of our region that either we have taken ourselves or users have sent in. "Trying to use Instagram for hard news has been a struggle," he says. "While it may be where the young eyeballs are, those eyeballs don't have any interest in looking at a crime scene or a mug shot."

The eight digital teams at the ABC O&O stations talk and share ideas daily via Slack and weekly over the phone. "We have lively conversations about the 'next big social platform,'" says Morris. "Right now it's TikTok; once it was Snapchat. We are split over the value of being on those platforms. The pro argument is that is where young people are, and if you can make them aware of your existence now with platform appropriate content, even if it's not news, you are preparing them to come to you when they do seek out news. The con argument is that there is no evidence that being on a non-news platform with non-news content, being seen by a non-news audience will convert any of that crowd to become YOUR audience, and in newsrooms that are strapped for resources, there are better uses of time and money."

Rebecca Fisher at KSNV-TV says she has a weekly phone meeting with Sinclair and she talks to the members of her team informally, usually Wednesday when everyone is there. Sinclair provides station goals – in this case, a 22% increase in page views from 2019 to 2020 . . . to 4.5 million per month. She views that as doable.

The importance of social media has made the social media manager probably the fastest growing position in TV news today. The issue certainly isn't whether social media is important, the question is how to handle it. Some stations and media companies are handling their own social media efforts, and some are using software specifically designed to deal with social media. Probably the most widely used service comes from a company called Social News Desk.

Newsroom computer systems have also reacted to the increasing need to post material on multiple platforms. Today's newsroom computer systems operate on what they commonly call a story-centric basis. The idea is that newsroom material is being produced for on-air as well as online and social media, and the computer system works to make it relatively fast and easy to post and format material for the various platforms in use.

TV consolidation has also meant that stations have access to more and more material than ever before. They always had access to feeds from their own network (assuming they're an affiliate) and from news services like CNN and AP (assuming membership), but now they have a huge supply of material from other stations within their company (like Nexstar and Sinclair) and easy access to material anywhere online as well. That poses the challenge of understanding copyright laws and what online material is available to post and what is not.

Matthew Seeman, Digital Content Producer at KSNV-TV in Las Vegas, starts his day at 5:30 a.m. He checks in with the morning executive producer and then starts posting material online and on social media from overnight. The afternoon/evening digital content producer left at 11:30 p.m. the evening before. Seeman uses TweetDeck to monitor Twitter accounts from the station staff, competitors, police/fire, newsmakers, NBC, etc. He says he frequently gets police news faster from Twitter than from police directly. Then he checks RSS feeds for news. RSS stands for Really Simple Syndication. It's a web feed of whatever news and information you subscribe to . . . aggregated for easier information collection.

More and more, the notion in the industry is that everyone needs to be involved with social media. That's part of what the 2019 RTDNA Survey found. When asked what they were doing that's new in social media, the top answers from TV news directors were organization and strategy. That involved laying out specific guidelines on minimum posting requirements, especially by anchors and reporters.

Univision 41 in New York City says it's had particular success in connecting with its audience using WhatsApp, and a lot of stations use Instagram to bring people "behind the scenes."

●●●●●

Think Mobile

Today, the primary access to social media and the internet is via the cellphone. In 2019, eMarketer reported that the amount of time spent on mobile (226 minutes per day) passed the time spent with TV (216 minutes per day).

While these numbers don't match what Nielsen reports (which I consider better research), the point remains: mobile is huge and continues to grow even as time with TV continues to fall. And the latest Pew Research Center figures (2019), found that 57% of adults often get news on mobile devices – versus 30% on desktop or laptop computers. **Stations need to make sure that they have a strong presence on mobile and that what they're doing in mobile looks good and works well on the small screen.**

As we first reported in the Middletown Media Studies, the time spent with TV is also frequently time spent with mobile. A lot of people use both devices at the same time: on the phone, looking up things related to what they're seeing on TV, texting/messaging friends about what they're seeing, etc. Smart broadcasters will find multiple ways of engaging the mobile audience in connection with what's on TV news (like polling or choosing between or among choices/ideas/solutions/etc.).

Today, a reporter with a mobile phone and Facebook Live (or other software) can be on social media and connecting with the audience from just about anywhere in a matter of moments.

●●●●●

Apps

Apps – short for applications – generally involve software programs designed to run on mobile devices – phones and tablets. At this writing, over 93% of TV stations have at least one app. Most stations have at least two. The bigger the staff, the more likely that the station has one or more apps. In TV, almost all apps are free.

It's common today for TV stations to have two or more apps, but KSNV-TV in Las Vegas is down to one . . . and they say they send out the fewest number of alerts of any station in the market . . . but have the highest returns on those alerts. The station says they found that people got annoyed with too many alerts and cancelled the app. Now, they issue no notifications unless it's something major.

The percentage of radio stations with apps is now 63%, and the typical number of apps for a radio station is one. Non-commercial stations were more likely to have apps than commercial stations, but non-commercial stations tended to have fewer apps per station than commercial stations.

●●●●●

OTT (Over the Top)

Stations and broadcast companies are devoting more and more time and energies on what's called OTT – over the top. As noted in Chapter 2, OTT involves streaming channels or services that go directly to an audience without going through a station broadcast or cable or satellite systems.

Anyone, of course, can produce OTT content, but TV stations have the advantage of equipment, expertise and a relationship with potential sponsors in order to make money.

Primarily because of Netflix, some surveys put prime time viewing to OTT ahead of what's called linear TV – TV viewing via antenna, cable, satellite or telco. That's why stations are putting more and more content on OTT, and it's paying off. News and sports viewing via OTT rose 65% from 2018 to 2019.

Along with what individual stations are doing, broadcast companies are creating their own OTT services:

- Tegna's Premion
- Sinclair's STIPP and CompulseOTT
- Syncbak's SBTV
- NewsON
- CBSN (each CBS-owned station will have its own operation . . . at this writing, New York, Los Angeles, Boston and San Francisco are up and running)
- TownNews
- Brightcove and Ooyala
- ATV Broadcast
- Akamai
- ViewLift
- VDMS
- Local X (NBC's new local OTT)

There are already stations running as much as 18 hours of streaming content (OTT) per day. KSAT-TV in San Antonio built a digital set in the middle of the newsroom and, at this writing, streams an open-ended 9 p.m. news program.

WCPO-TV in Cincinnati is doing a lot of experimenting with streaming and a variety of streaming content. KLTV in Tyler, Texas, streams news and information all day long.

There are people who believe that the time will come when local stations are just streaming and not broadcasting. We'll see.

● ● ● ● ●

A Final Note

This chapter is about the concept of "digital first," what that means and some of what you need to know. There's a lot more detail on software and what you can do with it later in this book, especially in Chapters 17 and 18.

• • • • •

Summary

Digital first means sending out information to your audience using the fastest and best platform possible. Commonly, that means news goes on social media and online before it goes on air. Along with that, what the audience is reacting to online and on social media frequently determine what the day's news coverage will include.

• • • • •

Key Words and Phrases

digital first ... mobile ... apps ... Crowdtangle ... Social News Desk ... Google Analytics ... Share Rocket ... OTT ... streaming ... TweetDeck ... RSS

• • • • •

Exercises

A. Look at a station's website and Facebook page *before* a newscast. Compare the major local stories on the web and Facebook to the major local stories on the air. Is the station holding back stories from online in order to break them on the air, or are they operating on a digital first basis? Give concrete examples.

B. Look at a station's website and Facebook page first thing in the morning, and note the top local stories and what's going on in those stories. Compare that to the 5, 5:30 or 6 p.m. newscast that day. Does it look like the station is updating or advancing the top local stories on TV compared to online? Can you tell if the station is using what's going on online to inform what the station covers and reports on later that day?

C. Take a look at the websites for the ABC, CBS, Fox and NBC stations in your area. What live streaming are they doing? How do you connect to their live stream? How do you connect to the stations' Facebook Live streams? Are they streaming newscasts? News events? Sports? Weather?

5

•••••

Research, Collecting Information and Bites

In the news business, we're always in search of information. The internet has become our go-to source for background, data and general information. It's also a major source of rumor and misinformation. The point is – be careful!

•••••

Some Basic Terms and Concerns

It's not a big deal, but there's a difference between the internet and the World Wide Web (or web). The internet is the infrastructure that allows computers to communicate with each other. The web is the network (or web) over which that communication takes place. Email is not a part of the web – even though you probably access your email via the web. Email is, however, sent over the internet.

The URL is the address of a website. It stands for uniform resource locator. The end of the basic address – after the period but before any slashes – is the domain. The domain indicates either the type or the purpose or the geography of the website.

.com is commercial or business

.edu is education

.gov is government

.int is international

.mil is military, the US Department of Defense

.net is networks (as in internet network, not TV)

.org is short for organizations – usually non-profit, but it doesn't have to be

Sites that end in. gov are official US government websites. That doesn't necessarily make the information correct. Government and government agencies can be self-serving and just plain make mistakes, but at least you have a source that should be worth citing.

Sites that end. edu are education sites, like a university. But many schools make their system available to faculty, students, staff and alumni. A site marked .edu might be an official university site or the personal site of a clueless freshman.

Sites ending in .org are often owned by non-profit organizations, but that's not a requirement, and a number of for-profit businesses operate .org websites. And non-profit doesn't necessarily mean unbiased or authoritative, anyway. Many non-profits also advocate for a variety of causes. Again, this is useful information to know, but nothing about a .org at the end of a URL guarantees accuracy or unbiased information.

Sites ending in .com are commercial sites. But that doesn't mean those sites can't contain good, unbiased material. Most news sites – newspaper, magazine and broadcast – are .com sites because they sell online advertising.

As the internet has grown, so have the online suffixes. Many are additional commercial endings, and many denote country of origin, or at least licensure, like .ca for Canada, .mx for Mexico and .au for Australia. Then there's the relatively new domain, .vegas.

● ● ● ● ●

Research and the Web

The internet has certainly revolutionized news. Start with research and news gathering. A staggering amount of material that was once available only in reference books or courthouses is now readily accessible to everyone online. Census data, health statistics, proposed legislation and legal rulings are examples of such factual material. The federal government, states, counties, cities and even towns and villages are all making much of their data available online. Keep in mind, though, that older material hasn't always been digitized, and organizations and governments frequently don't make all current data available online, either.

Unfortunately, the widespread democratization of the web means that anyone and everyone can make information available online. The greatest research challenge today remains separating accurate, reliable data from random, self-serving opinion. Or even spoof sites. You can't be too careful about where information comes from, and, given the potentially anonymous nature of the web, that's even more true for online material than other sources.

A few years ago, the Woolshed Company, based in Australia, released a video showing that it had produced at least eight fake videos to "explore the phenomenon of 'viral videos and shareable content.'" Those fake videos were viewed 205 million times and made it onto countless news websites and on-air. The videos showed amazing feats and fascinating encounters, but they were all fake.

The internet is a great tool, but it's not a substitute for critical thinking, checking with sources and other research. Research generally involves collecting information, locating people, and confirming information you already have. There are search engines (like google.com), subject directories (like yahoo.com) and restricted subject area search tools (like findlaw.com). The quality of your research depends on where you go, the quality of your questions and the evaluation of both your information choices and the material itself.

Through email, the internet also allows journalists to conduct interviews online. Be cautious. First, there's no substitute for a face-to-face interview. You get to see the person you're talking to; you get to know if there's anyone else present during the interview who might influence the answers; you get to see the body language of how that person reacts to you and your questions; you get to hear the nuances of how someone answers a question; and, you get to know with reasonable certainty that the person you're talking to is the person you think you're talking to.

Most of those things are lost in email interviews – starting with the certainty of whom you're interviewing. Consider email interviews as a last information-gathering resort, and note in the story that you received the answer via email.

Still, it's a great way to follow up with someone you interviewed in person or on the phone to get quick clarification on a point. Again, face-to-face is always first choice; apps like Zoom, FaceTime and Skype are second choice (at least you can see to whom you're talking), phone contact is third choice, but email can be a useful way to reach a hard-to-pin-down, busy person. It's a great way to set up an interview. It may also be your only choice to reach someone far away. And having a paper trail of information can be useful. Just recognize the drawbacks and act accordingly.

● ● ● ● ●

Interviewing

When we cover events, we're interviewing people, and we're capturing the sound of the event itself. When we go to the scene of an accident, the aftermath of a storm, the meeting of the city council . . . we collect information by listening, by observing and by questioning. And in both radio and TV, we capture the sound of the events and the accompanying comments on those events. More and more, all media, including radio, are also collecting the pictures of those events. That used to be just the province of TV, but as coverage has expanded to Facebook Live and (other) online streaming, everyone seems to have a camera and is in search of pictures to go with all the sound.

We'll deal more with pictures later. Let's start with sound . . . and with interviewing.

We gather much of our information – along with radio actualities and video bites – through interviews, so how well we do in the field and on the phone determines what we have to work with later on. As with many things in life, the more interviews you conduct, the better you'll tend to get. Bites and actualities are the same thing: the actual sound of someone in the news. It might be a statement from the mayor, the argument of conflicting protestors or an interview with a young kindergartner. It involves sound that we can clearly understand and that tells some part of the story. In radio the term is *actuality;* in TV it's *bite.* Otherwise, they're the same.

An interview is any exchange during which the news reporter or writer collects information. In radio, interviewing is most commonly done on the phone. That's not nearly as good as doing it in person, but it's efficient and inexpensive. Even in television, we conduct many interviews on the phone. After all, our calls to set up interviews are in many cases interviews themselves. We need to know that the prospective interviewee really has something to say, will say it to us and can say it well.

We also deal in mass interviews. Those include news conferences at which a speaker or speakers take questions. We also conduct interviews in groups – some newsmakers call them packs – in which we question a city council member, the police chief, a hospital spokesperson and so on.

Along with actualities and bites, we also collect natural sound. Called variously *natural sound, nat sound, background sound, ambient sound* and possibly a few other terms, it's the sound of real life captured by the microphone. It might be the chatter of children in a playground, the sound of traffic on the highway or an explosion.

●●●●●

Conducting Successful Interviews

Understanding What Makes Good Bites

Most bites on radio and television probably aren't worth putting on the air. Most bites involve a simple recitation of facts that the reporter or anchor could usually say better, clearer and in half the time.

Good bites – the best bites – generally fall into one of four categories:

1. Personal account. These are the bites in which people tell us what they saw, heard, felt, smelled or tasted. Note the response of the senses. These are the first-person accounts of what happened, told best by people who have an emotional stake in the outcome. These are the bites from people who survived the earthquake, searched for the missing child, got fleeced by a con man, ran the marathon and so on. Their

firsthand account of having been involved cannot be duplicated by the writer or reporter. These people bring their passion and feeling to the story because it's their story.

2. Witness account. Sometimes as strong as personal account, these are the stories of people who saw or felt what happened. They witnessed the fire; they saw the accident happen; they heard the cries for help. Although usually missing the personal involvement, these bites can be just as strong because they can supply us with a sense of what happened that we, as writers or reporters, would have to cite as sources to explain.

3. Personal opinion. Everyone has an opinion, and these bites can be good if they're short and to the point. This is the person reacting to news of a tax hike, the election outcome, the demolition of a city landmark, the construction of a new highway or shopping center. Man-on-the-street (MOS) reaction stories fall into this category. Remember that these may or may not be informed opinions, and they should not be presented as representative of a larger group unless you actually have real survey data to back that up.

4. Expert opinion. There are experts on just about everything, and most places have several on any given topic. That puts the onus on the reporter to locate people who not only know the subject well but can also speak about it clearly and succinctly. Keep in mind that in many cases, different experts see the same data or circumstances differently. Don't limit yourself to one interpretation or viewpoint because you've located someone who speaks in good sound bites or who may share your own perspective. Aggressively seek out a diverse group of experts from which to draw.

From a *content* standpoint, weak bites fall into two categories:

1. Hard data. A recitation of numbers or facts is almost never a good bite. Rarely can someone we interview express numbers or facts as clearly and succinctly as we can. Invariably, they hem and haw, they stumble and restate, they give us too much data or too detailed data. Talk to people and collect that information, but it's almost always better to include relevant hard data in the reporter track or anchor script, rather than letting weak and tedious bites on the air. The fire chief may tell us it was a three-alarm fire that took firefighters two hours to get under control, but the better bite comes from the sweaty, soot-streaked firefighter telling us that he had to run for his life when he heard the roof start to go.

2. Anything not well said. Even if you talked to the right people, not everyone has something compelling to say or is capable of saying it well. Bites can confuse the audience just as easily as they can enlighten. Just because you recorded someone for a story doesn't mean you

should burden the audience with the material. Don't punish the audience with a long, tedious bite because it took someone a long time to explain the situation. Children and teenagers can be especially difficult to get good bites from.

"Kill the babies," says former NBC reporter Don Larson. He's referring to a producer he knew who had trouble getting rid of bites she had worked so hard to gather. They became "like her babies." Be ruthless. If the bite won't really mean something to the audience, don't use it.

Former NBC national correspondent Bob Dotson also argues that the quality of a sound bite has nothing to do with length but whether it's something that will stick with the audience. "Robert Frost used to say that a good story starts with a lump in the throat," says Dotson. The whole point of sound bites, then, is to add texture to a story or pound home a point.

"I'm looking for [bites] that are emotional," says Wayne Freedman, a reporter at KGO-TV in San Francisco. "I don't want facts, I want emotions. I want somebody to tell me how they feel. The story is about the *people* in the story."

And make sure that the people you talk to for stories represent the broad spectrum of your audience . . . and that they don't all look a lot like you. That applies to the experts that you choose to talk with as well as the random people you interview on the street.

Plan

This is the most important part of a successful interview. Going into a major interview on an investigative story will obviously require extensive planning, but you should plan for *every* interview you do. Why are you interviewing this person? What are you after? What would make this a successful interview? How does – or might – this interview fit in with others? If you can't answer those questions, how will you know what to ask? If you can't answer those questions, how will you know when to end the interview?

Inexperienced reporters commonly conduct long interviews. That's frequently because they don't know what they're after, and **if you don't know where you're going, it can take a long time to get there.** That creates two problems. You use too much time conducting an overlong interview, and then you use too much time going through the whole interview to figure out what you have and what to use. Time is too precious for that.

Even on breaking news, there's planning to be done. Take a house fire, for example. You've got a few minutes in the car on the way. Think about what kind of story it's likely to be. Who do you talk with first? Who's next? Who comes after that? What are the human elements you're after?

The answers matter because people leave and memories and emotions fade. Resist the temptation in the earlier example to start with the fire chief. If you talk to the chief at all, do so at the end. First are the people who live there. They're most involved in the story, and depending on damage and injuries, they may leave. Remember, the best bites are personal accounts, and this is where you get them. Next come the neighbors. They're potential witnesses, and they're readily available. Soon, they won't be. Talking to them when they're outside watching is usually easy. Once they go into their homes and shut the doors, you'll have a harder time convincing them to talk. Then interview the firefighters. Pick the dirtiest ones first. They're the people with the greatest personal involvement in the fire. Remember what makes for good bites. The hard data that the fire chief may be able to supply also belongs in the story, but you're almost always better off incorporating it into your script.

Keep in mind how people think and what's important to them. In fires or natural disasters, after people and pets, the next greatest loss involves personal items – especially pictures. We have insurance for furniture and clothing and other largely meaningless possessions. The real value lies in the stuff of our lives that can't be readily replaced. But if you didn't plan or think about these things, would you watch for and see them? When you see people picking through the rubble after the fire or earthquake or tornado, think about what it is they're really looking for.

Listen

After planning, listening – really listening – is the second most important skill for successful interviewing. It's the most critical skill you *must* develop to be a good interviewer. Don't simply hear; listen to every word.

Generally, the biggest impediment to listening is our inability to cope with silence. Especially with beginning reporters, we're frequently so concerned about what we're going to ask next that we're not listening closely enough. We're worried that the person will stop talking, and we won't know what to say, so we focus inward on ourselves and what we'll ask next instead of focusing outward on the people we're talking to.

If it will help you to focus on the people you're interviewing, make a few notes of topic areas and put them in your pocket. Use that short list as your security blanket to enable you to focus on the people you're interviewing. All your attention and energy must go toward these people. If you pay enough attention – to what they have to say, how they say it, what they don't say and body language – they'll tell you where to go next in your interview. In most cases, the best question to ask next comes logically out of the previous answer. Remember that ideally, an interview is just a conversation between two people in which the person being interviewed does most of the talking. The ability to listen and focus on the person or people you're talking to will make all the difference in the success of your information gathering. Planning may be step one, but if you don't listen, you won't know whether that planning worked out for you.

Technical Concerns

In broadcast we generally record our interviews, and you must record high-quality sound and pictures. The audience will notice technical flaws before they notice anything else, and *all* of the audience will notice. You must get it right.

In radio, much of the listening takes place in a car, so you're already competing with road noise, traffic and other people for the listener's attention. People will not strain to hear or understand an actuality; they will not turn up the volume and quiet down the environment. If the technical quality of the actuality isn't good, people will simply miss it. Having tuned out the actuality, they've now tuned out the story and the newscast. If the technical quality of an actuality isn't on a par with that of the newscaster, don't put it on the air.

Television offers a little more flexibility – but not much. It's easier to understand people when we see their lips moving, so that gives us a little more leeway. A really compelling (or self-incriminating) bite that proves a story can always be supered on the screen to make sure the audience understands. But again, technical quality matters, and the typical bite for television should be crystal clear.

Natural sound that runs under a reporter track doesn't have to rise to the same standards, but if you want to bring the natural sound full – and you should, as part of the story – then that, too, needs to be high quality.

In radio, listen to the environment, and make sure there are no distracting noises that will ruin the recording. The same goes for TV, and you also need to think about focus, framing, light and color – among other things.

Always check your equipment in advance. Make sure you have everything; make sure it's working; and make sure you know how to operate it. There are rules in this business that say that everything you don't check is likely to break or fail.

Make the Interviewee Comfortable

In breaking news stories, you interview people where and when you can. In other cases location can make or break an interview. The more comfortable the people you're talking with, the more open and forthcoming they're likely to be.

People are usually most comfortable in their own homes, so that's frequently a good place to conduct interviews. Offices pose more of a challenge. That desk they're sitting behind serves as both a physical and a psychological barrier. Equipment noise can make an interview unintelligible. Try to avoid having to contend with those kinds of obstacles. Look for a couple of comfortable chairs or another site. In radio, a conference room may work. In television, look for an interview site with a background that helps tell the story. Offices make common but boring backgrounds.

Watch out for the phone. Once a phone starts to ring, the interview is over – at least temporarily. The ringing makes that spot in the recording unusable, and the distraction derails everyone's train of thought. Try to get the phone turned off (both desk phone and cell phone), have phone calls held or move someplace where there's less chance of a distraction, such as outdoors.

Remember that many of the people we interview are nervous about the whole process. They're worried about how they'll look, what they might say, how they'll sound and whether they'll do a good job. Nervous people give poor interviews. Make them comfortable, and make them comfortable talking with you. The more they talk before the interview, the more comfortable they're likely to get. But *don't* talk about the interview subject until you're actually recording. Talk about the weather, talk about sports, talk about pictures on the office wall – talk about anything *except* the subject at hand. Generally, you'll get good, animated, responses to your questions one time and only one time. If you're not recording when they first say it, you've lost the moment. The second time around, the life will be sapped out, and the person will say things like, "Well, like I told you before. . . ." But since the audience didn't hear it before, that kind of comment should not be used on the air.

Ask Questions That Deliver What You're After

Questions that start with *Do, Are* and *When* are fine as long as answers like *Yes, No,* and *Yesterday* are what you're looking for. And they may be. If you're after hard data and concrete information as background for your story, questions that start with *Do, Are* and *When* may be the fastest way to get it. But if you're after usable bites to put on the air, it would be dumb luck if those questions generated worthwhile answers.

If you're after bites, ask people to *Explain* something. Ask *Why* or *How come.* Ask people to *Describe* what they saw, heard, felt, smelled or tasted. Those are most likely to produce good bites.

Again, the issue comes back to planning. If you know what you're after, it can help frame your questions so that you get what you need.

Unless you're attending a White House news conference and have one chance to ask the president something, don't ask complicated, multipart questions. Don't make speeches. Generally, don't share your personal experiences. Train yourself to be brief and direct. The more straightforward you are, the better the responses are likely to be.

The fewer words you use in your questions – delivered cleanly and crisply – the greater flexibility you have in putting together the story.

A one- or two-word response to a question commonly won't work for a bite. But sometimes it can – if you asked the question in about the same amount of time. It is possible to make a quick series of tight questions and answers into a bite. Given the difficulties in interviewing young children and teenagers, this approach may be your best shot at usable bites with difficult groups or individuals.

Generally, start with the easiest, least controversial questions and end with the hardest. First, the more comfortable someone is talking to you, the more likely that person is to respond – even as the interview may move to touchier subjects. Second, even if the interviewee is so offended by a tough question that the interview is terminated, at least you have something. Third, most controversial decisions made sense to someone at the time they made them. So you're better off starting with questions that take the interviewee back before the critical moment you actually want to ask about.

Use Silence

That same silence that you're uncomfortable with (see the earlier section entitled "Listen"), generally works the same way for the person you're interviewing. You can use that as a technique. After an answer that may seem incomplete, don't say anything. Just look at the person expectantly, as if to say, "Where's the rest of the answer?" Frequently, that's when the person, uncomfortable with the silence and/or perhaps sensing your lack of understanding, will blurt out the real story. It's not about tricking someone; it's about searching for the truth. If they just look back at you and smile, they know about the technique. In that case, just move on.

Maintain Strong Eye Contact

Don't stare at interviewees, but do engage them. Strong eye contact demands that someone look back at you. It says you're interested and involved. It says you care. It also helps to take someone's mind off the equipment, and in the case of television it increases the odds that the person you're interviewing will look back at you and not directly at the camera.

It's hard to maintain strong eye contact if you're reading questions from a pad of paper or a cellphone. If you need that kind of preparation because it's a complex story with lots of data you must refer to, then you do it. Otherwise, you're always better off acting like a real person asking questions, rather than reading from a prepared script.

Learn to Respond Inaudibly

Almost everyone in the business learns the importance of this the hard way. You need to respond to the person you're interviewing, or the person will stop talking. But if you respond out loud, you'll ruin the audio. Many interesting interviews never made it on the air because constant *uh huh, uhhh, okay, I see* responses by the interviewer simply made the audio unusable. Maintaining good eye contact helps. Nodding is all right, but mindlessly bobbing your head up and down could make it appear that you're agreeing to some sort of outrageous comment the person is making. Facial expressions can help a lot. Just make sure you respond silently.

Follow Up and Clarify

Any time the person you're interviewing uses a name that you (and/or the audience) don't know, a technical term that you don't understand, or a peculiar phrasing that isn't clear, you have an interruption in the flow of information. In all likelihood you can't use that material on the air because the audience won't understand.

If this happens in a live interview, you must interrupt and clarify the point right then. Otherwise, you've lost the audience, who will be puzzled over what they don't understand. In a recorded interview, you can wait until the person finishes the sentence or thought and then go back for an explanation.

This is another critical reason to listen. If you're not paying full attention, you'll miss the problem spots in an interview, and you won't hear the kinds of statements that require follow-up questions to make sure you – and the audience – understand. If you don't understand something, there's no way that you're going to be able to make that clear to the audience.

Maintain Control

Never hand over the microphone to someone else. This is *your* interview, and you have to remain in charge. It's up to you to maintain the technical quality; interviewees who take the mike from you will commonly not use it properly on themselves and will almost never hold the mike in a way to pick up your comments or questions. Without the microphone you have no way to interject to clarify; you're completely at someone else's mercy. If you give up the mike, you're no longer conducting the interview. Whoever has the mike is the person who's in control.

Ask for More . . . Twice

In an important interview, it's frequently a good idea, at the very end, to ask whether there's anything you missed, any ground not covered. In most cases the answer will be no, but sometimes people will come up with pertinent material. Occasionally, it's something useful for the story at hand. More likely, if there's anything at all, it's an interesting, related point. While it may not belong in the story you're working on, it may be a great story idea or nugget for a future story. Make note. You should always be collecting future story ideas.

Finally, after you shut off the equipment, watch for a sigh of relief. The interviewee survived. If you see this happen, ask again whether there's anything you missed. "Well," the person might say, "of course I can't really say much about such and such." Now comes the dilemma. Technically, of course, you're still on the record, you're just not recording. But what is the perception of the person you're talking to? We're back to ethical decision-making. If you're talking to a politician, he or she knows the rules, and, absent a clear understanding, everything is on the record. Not so with others. In any case, your job as a reporter is to convince them to let you turn your equipment back on and talk about this unexplored area. If you work at it – and care about the outcome – most of the time you'll succeed.

Make Notes Afterward

No camera or recorder will register every nuance you may have seen or noticed. Telling details such as the weakness of a handshake, an odor of stale cigars or the chill of a drafty room can make or break a story. Pay attention to these things, and make notes right away. Later, in the rush to air, it's easy to forget, and then they're lost forever.

Examples of Questions that Work . . . to Produce Bites

Can you explain that to me?

Tell me about X.

Why did you think that?

What did you do next?

What were you thinking when you did that?

How do you think X felt about that?

So now what?

Where do you go from here?

Commonly, the best questions are follow-ups to what the interviewee has just said. That's why it's so important to listen. Those follow-ups can be as simple as:

Why?

Then what?

And did that work?

KARE-TV's Boyd Huppert, one of the country's top local reporters, says he never likes to ask someone for an interview. Too formal and potentially off-putting. He likes saying, "Can I ask you something/" And his favorite: "Can you help me with something?" Most people want to help if they can.

● ● ● ● ●

Beyond the Interview

Being Human

The toughest interview is the "grieving widow" – the person (widow or otherwise) who has just suffered a loss. It might be a fatal car accident, a drowning or a devastating loss from a tornado. How do we talk to the person in grief? Should we talk to that person at all?

In some respects the answers vary depending on the particulars and the particular reporter. Without question, some people in grief will be highly offended at the notion of speaking to a reporter. But others find the experience cathartic or an opportunity to publicly memorialize a victim. Don't prejudge how *you* think someone should behave. It's really not up to you to pre-censure what someone should or should not say.

But be a human being first. *Without* a recorder or camera aimed and running, offer the sympathy any human being would extend to another at a time of loss. Offer to talk if the person would like to. Make yourself available. If people are interested or willing, they'll say so. If not, you wouldn't have gotten a usable bite anyway. In either case you'll be able to sleep better at night.

Never ask victims of tragedy *how they feel*. If you don't know the answer to that question already, find a different career.

A Closing Thought

One advantage that we have in this business is that we do record our interviews. That means the audience gets to hear exactly what someone sounds like, and it means that our quotes are completely accurate.

It also means we get a chance to learn from every interview we conduct. **Don't just listen to your interviews for good bites; listen to learn about interviewing and yourself.** How were your questions? Did you listen completely? What can you learn to make the next interview better?

● ● ● ● ●

Summary

Bites and actualities involve the actual sounds of people in the news. We call them *bites* in TV and *actualities* in radio, but otherwise, there's no difference. Natural sound is the actual sound of life (traffic, kids on a playground, and so on). Beyond making sure the technical quality is high and the sound clear, the best bites involve personal account, witness account, personal opinion and expert opinion. Generally, weak bites involve hard data and anything not said well. The quality of our bites and actualities depends heavily on the quality of our interviews. This chapter contains a dozen points for better interviewing: (1) Plan; (2) listen; (3) get the technical side right; (4) make the interviewee comfortable; (5) ask questions that deliver what you're after; (6) use silence; (7) maintain strong eye contact; (8) learn to respond inaudible; (9) follow up and clarify; (10) maintain control; (11) ask for more – twice; and (12) make notes afterward. Be human, and remember that a good interview is generally just two people having a conversation – with the interviewee doing most of the talking. Never ask victims of tragedy how they feel.

● ● ● ● ●

Key Words and Phrases

Bites . . . actualities . . . nat or natural sound . . . personal account . . . witness account . . . personal opinion . . . expert opinion . . . plan . . . listen . . . the use of silence . . . strong eye contact . . . follow up and clarify . . . maintain control . . . ask for more

● ● ● ● ●

Exercises

A. Come up with three solid story ideas (no profiles allowed) based on interviewing people *not like you*. That means no college or graduate students. Find out what their concerns and interests are . . . and what stories they think the media have ignored. Write two paragraphs on what they had to say, include their name and a way to reach them – either phone or email – and a third paragraph based on your research that either determines that the proposed story idea is valid – or that it's not. And why.

B. Watch one of the Sunday morning talk show like *Face the Nation* (CBS), *Meet the Press* (NBC) or *This Week* (ABC). What did you notice about the interviewing? What worked and what didn't? Make a list of the three best questions the interviewer asked. What made them good?

C. Watch a *60 Minutes* or *CBS Sunday Morning* piece that's primarily an interview. What did you notice about that interview, and how did it compare to the Sunday morning talk shows in B? What were the best questions the interviewer asked? Why?

D. Record at least one of the interviews in Exercise A. Pick out the best bites from the interview you conducted and evaluate the questions you asked that elicited the best answers. What do you notice about those questions? Make a list of your three best and three least effective questions. Explain why each question made the list.

6

●●●●●

Readability

This chapter is really about writing copy that's going to be read out loud – either for TV/video or radio/audio. We'll discuss writing for online in another chapter.

Information that's going to be read out loud also means that people must understand the material just by listening. That's a critical difference from almost all other forms of writing.

Broadcast news writing involves not only the basic elements of all good writing – but a number of special conventions and peculiarities of its own.

Broadcast copy must be easily readable. Because breaking news and the nature of the business may result in last-minute changes in reading assignments, there are basic rules to give any announcer a fighting chance to convert words into meaningful and readable copy.

●●●●●

Broadcast News Writing

Writing for the ear is special – not better or worse than its print or online counterparts – but different. Think of how many times you've found yourself rereading material only moments after your first journey through it. Perhaps your mind wandered. More likely, the material simply wasn't well-written, well-organized, or logically presented. The written word can perhaps tolerate those lapses; the spoken word cannot. As with music or plays or films, the broadcast audience gets one chance and one chance only to understand what's being said. The wrong word, the right word in the wrong place, too much information too quickly, words mismatched with pictures – all can result in an audience lost in information. In broadcast, you cannot afford even a momentary loss because the newscast continues, and the words and stories keep coming. Every time viewers or listeners must stop to sort things out, they miss even more.

Beyond writing for the ear, the broadcast writer must think about how words sound together. Are they easily readable? Can the announcer read the words with proper emphasis without gasping for breath? How much meaning can be inserted with inflection rather than text? Does the sound of the words match the story those words tell? How do the words blend with accompanying video?

- - - - -

Writing for the Ear vs. Writing for the Eye

Broadcast copy differs from print and online in two critical conceptual points. First, it's designed to be read aloud; second, it's written to be understood by people who only get to hear it. Those two points, flip sides of the same coin, lead to virtually all of the rules about writing broadcast copy. Broadcast writing isn't different from print or online for its own sake, it's different because it's produced and consumed differently. This chapter focuses on the first of those differences: reading out loud.

Today, essentially all newsrooms use some sort of computer system, and that system dictates some of the stylistic rules.

Every computer system is just a little bit different, and all are customizable, so there are even some differences within the same software. The first challenge on the job is to learn how to use the station's software. It's basically just a word processor and archive library within a newscast environment. More and more stations are integrating that newsroom writing and producing system with character generators for automatic supers and desktop audio and video editing.

- - - - -

Rules of Readability

Although every station does things a little differently, and newsroom computer systems tend to dictate technical form, these are the general guidelines accepted in the industry. The whole point of these rules is that anyone should be able to pick up any piece of copy and read it well.

Newsroom Computer System

The computer ensures that everything is typed. Most stations double-space, although many computer systems display single-spacing on the terminal but double-space or 1.5 spacing on printed scripts and prompter copy.

See more on today's newsroom computer systems in Chapters 15 and 17.

The Slug

Each story must have a slug – a heading that separates that story from all others that day. Usually written in either the upper left or across the top of a page, it includes a one- or two-word name for the story, the writer's last name or initials, the date and the time of the newscast the story is being written for. In most TV newsrooms (and large radio operations), newscast producers or assignment editors determine the slug for each story. Again, newsroom software dictates exactly how all of these things are recorded.

```
FBI arrest
Smith
1/12/20
6 pm
```

The Printed Word

Use paragraphs, indenting the first word of each. Radio copy normally goes across a full page and runs three and a half to four seconds a line, depending on type style and margins. TV copy goes on the right side of a split page and runs one to two seconds a line, depending on type size.

Radio
The FBI today arrested one of its 10 most-wanted criminals.

TV	
Video	Audio
	The FBI today arrested one of its 10 most-wanted criminals.

Note that most newsroom computer systems don't show the split screen when you're writing, but the concept remains. Newsroom computer systems time copy automatically, adjusting the projected time for different readers based on reading speeds entered into the system. Even so, view that time as approximate; there's no substitute for having the person who's going to read the copy on the air time it exactly.

Hyphenation

Don't hyphenate or split words from one line to the next. Doing so increases the chances for unnatural hesitation or mispronunciation.

INCORRECT: He went in search of the corporate head-
          quarters.
CORRECT: He went in search of the corporate headquarters.

Fortunately, most newsroom software won't allow this mistake in copy.

Do hyphenate some words within a line for the sake of readability. Words like *pre-disposition* and *anti-missile*, although not grammatically correct, are much easier to read correctly with hyphens. Be especially careful with prefixes that create double vowels, such as *pre-eminent.* But don't overdo it. Words like *cooperate* and *coordinate* we recognize easily and don't need to hyphenate.

Abbreviation

Don't abbreviate. Not everyone understands what a given abbreviation stands for, and some, such as *St.,* can stand for different things (Street and Saint). Exceptions are *Mr., Mrs., Ms.* (pronounced "miz") and *Dr.* We see them so often, day in, day out, that we have no trouble reading them. Incidentally, *Dr.* in broadcast usually refers to medical doctors, including physicians, dentists and chiropractors. *PhDs* should not be called doctor without making clear their area of expertise.

Symbols

Don't use symbols. Symbols such as %, & and $ are too easily missed, require translation and, in the case of $, come out of sequence in how it's read.

INCORRECT: ... 40% ...
CORRECT: ... 40 percent ...

Some experienced anchors will use the dollar sign in copy (*$4-thousand*). That's what they're used to, and it works for them. But it's safer to use the word instead (*4-thousand-dollars*).

Initials and Acronyms

Almost everything uses initials or an acronym these days, but don't presume that the audience will remember and understand them without some help. In almost all cases, use the full name in the first reference with initials or acronym thereafter. A few will work for first reference, like FBI and CIA. Don't make up your own initials or acronyms for a group in an effort to shorten the name. For many organizations there are no shortcuts.

When initials are to be used, place dashes between the letters:

N-C-A-A   I-R-S

When the letters are to be read as an acronym, use all caps without dashes:

OPEC   MADD

OPEC is unusual because it's one of the few acronyms that's preferable to the full name. More people are familiar with OPEC than the full, formal Organization of the Petroleum Exporting Countries.

Names

Generally, write names the way people are known. If the governor is known as *Joe* Smith rather than *Joseph*, use *Joe*. But don't use names that only family and close friends use; if you're unsure, stick with the formal name. Nicknames present more of a problem. Ultimately, the issue is less one of right and wrong than of consistency. Stations should establish a set form – and make sure everyone knows what it is – for any problem name.

Generally, don't use middle initials or names. That's because few people are popularly called by their middle name or initial. Two exceptions: when someone *is* popularly known by his or her middle initial or name:

```
Michael J. Fox
Mary J. Blige
Ruth Bader Ginsburg
```

or when someone with a fairly common name has been charged with a crime or is involved in something controversial. In that case the middle initial or name (and perhaps even an address) helps to isolate the individual from others with similar names:

```
Police charged John S. Smith of State Street with
yesterday's robbery at the First National Bank.
```

Numbers

Minimize the use of numbers in broadcast copy. Numbers are hard to take in and understand when we only get to hear them, so always try to use a word description (e.g., *almost all*) instead of the number. When you must use them:

- Write out all numbers one through nine. One, two, three, four, five, six, seven, eight, nine. A single digit is too easily lost on a page, and 1, 2 and 5 can look a lot like I, Z and S.
- Use numerals for numbers 10 through 999.
- Use names for thousand, million and so on. You can't expect an announcer to count the digits of a number to figure out what to say.
- Newsrooms are split on numeral and word combinations. Some stay with the same form listed earlier – mixing numerals and words as appropriate (e.g., one-thousand, 22-thousand). Others use only numerals when they're connected to a word by a hyphen (e.g., 5-thousand).

- Write out *a hundred* or *one hundred* to prevent an announcer pausing or stumbling over the decision of which way to pronounce it.
- Ordinals may be written as numerals or words (*2nd* or *second*).
- Write out fractions in words (*one-half, two-thirds*).
- Numbers below 1.0 such as .4 (in economic reports, for instance) should be written as *four-tenths of a (or one) percent*. Above 1.0, the use of *point* is fine (e.g., *one-point-two percent*), but round off when possible.
- Write numbers coming next to each other in contrasting style (e.g., *the score was 162 to 140, fourteen points shy of the record*).
- Write years as numerals (e.g., *1999* or *19–99, 2021 or 20–21*).

For TV, always think about ways to visualize numbers through graphics, but don't use TV graphics as a crutch for countless and usually meaningless numbers. The audience is not interested in wading through a sea of charts and graphs. Graphics involve a better way of demonstrating numbers that are still best rounded off and held to a minimum.

Look at all the numbers in this copy – which went on the air on a large market TV station:

PROBLEM: So far this year, calls to the I-R-S telephone assistors are producing wrong answers 30-point-8 percent of the time. That's worse than last year, when the error rate was 28 percent. The I-R-S says it's trying, but of its five-thousand assistors, 15-hundred are new to the job, and tax questions can be tough to answer.

And broadcast copy can be tough to follow, especially in a short story with four complex numbers, most of them not essential.

BETTER: So far this year, calls to the I-R-S are producing wrong answers more than 30-percent of the time. That's slightly worse than last year. The I-R-S says it's trying, but that nearly a third of its telephone assistors are new this year.

Note that part of the solution above involves the substitution of words that express relationships (*a third*) instead of actual numbers.

Ages

Generally, we report ages only when they're an important or interesting part of the story. Newspapers and the web can give ages quickly and easily (e.g., *Mary Smith, 41, was injured . . .*). In broadcast, we have to tell the audience that *Mary Smith is 41 years old.* Since it's so much more cumbersome in broadcast, think about whether the age really adds something to the story.

UNNECESSARY: `The accident injured 41-year-old Mary Smith.`
NECESSARY
AND
INTERESTING: `The driver of the car was nine years old.`

An exception: If the story includes information about someone's death (e.g., in a traffic accident), then we usually do include the age. That's because the story serves as something of an obituary, and we always give the age in an obituary.

Emphasis

Broadcast copy is to be read aloud with meaning transmitted through both words and inflection. Indicate emphasis through underlining or capitalization or whatever a given newsroom computer system provides:

`The mayor says he will` <u>`not`</u> `run for re-election.`
`The mayor says he will NOT run for re-election.`

Indicate pauses with dashes (—) and ellipses (. . .), with spaces before and after the dashes or ellipses. But don't use either where a period should go. And double-spacing after all periods makes for cleaner-looking and easier-to-read copy.

CORRECT: `The mayor shouted - then grabbed his chest.`
CORRECT: `The mayor shouted ... then grabbed his chest.`

Pronouncers

Every word that might be mispronounced, especially a name, should have a pronunciation guide immediately after it in parentheses.

Watch out for easily mispronounced names such as Lima (LEE ma), Peru and Lima (LI ma), Ohio. Indicate emphasis by capitalizing the emphasized syllable or, if you're writing in all caps, by putting an apostrophe after the emphasized syllable:

`LIMA (LEE' MA), PERU AND LIMA (LI' MA), OHIO`

Note: A pronouncer is not a substitute for the correct spelling. Names and places on scripts frequently wind up being supered (the words superimposed on the lower third of the TV screen) and used as keywords for computer searches somewhere down the line. All too often, phonetic spellings have been supered on the air because the writer never used the correct spelling or didn't make clear which spelling was correct and which was phonetic. Be careful.

Wherever possible, avoid words with the same spelling but different pronunciations and meanings. *Suspect, read, wind* and the like can all be dangerous to an announcer who hasn't been able to pre-read copy.

Spelling

Spell correctly. Any word that's misspelled is likely to be mispronounced on the air. And remember that between computers and closed captioning (for the hearing impaired), some of the audience gets to see all of your spelling.

• • • • •
Summary

Broadcast writing is different than traditional print or online because there's an announcer reading it out loud, and the audience only gets one chance to hear the material. Although newsroom computer systems frequently determine style, there are generally accepted universals in writing broadcast copy. Use paragraphs, be careful with hyphenation, generally don't use abbreviations, symbols, middle initials or ages. Use numbers sparingly, and learn how to write them properly. Indicate emphasis to determine how copy is to be read, and use pronouncers for unfamiliar names. Spelling counts.

• • • • •
Key Words and Phrases

newsroom computer systems . . . slug . . . paragraphs . . . hyphenation . . . abbreviation . . . symbols . . . initials and acronyms . . . names . . . middle initials . . . numbers . . . ages . . . emphasis . . . pronouncers . . . spelling

• • • • •
Exercises

A. Write each of the following words or phrases correctly based on standard broadcast writing:

NCAA	2-thousand	422	Dr. Jones
17th	10,000	alot	point-7

8-percent	persons	says	fortitude
male	will not	deceased	tuna
2	one hundred	34	19-95
one-half	point-five	$55	FCC
Houston St.	Mrs. Smith	ACLU	998
halibut	John A. Church	1600	3RD
can't	seperate	female	goldfish
sattelite	2-hundred	english	1/3
IU	N-C-double-A	kids	U-S
989 point-3			

B. The following sentences have errors and/or words, phrases or means of expression not acceptable for broadcast writing. Make them acceptable.

1. Their are alot of rules for writing broadcast copy that you must understand.

2. Fore instance they're about 8 rules for writing numbers including things like how to deal with numbers and phrases like 6.4% and 3/4 and 200,000.

3. Many of these rules are about readibility – so that the announcer won't have to struggle thru your copy in order to figure out what you meant when you talk about a $2.46 pay rise per hour for workers in Nassau Co., NY or a new record low temperature of -27 in Albany.

4. Goverments, goverment agencies, and political organisations like O-P-E-C and the IRS may work to muddy our language and the meaning of words, but your job is to simplify and clarify with in the rules of writing for broadcast writing.

5. It really doesn't matter whether your reporting the news from Lima, Peru or Lima, OH – you've got to seperate the facts and make things clear.

C. Re-write the following story using a proper slug, and correct any errors you find:

According to sources inside the Teamsters union, 4 labor leaders are being investigated for misappropriation of funds. The amount of money involved hasn't been disclosed, although its believed to be almost $1,000,000. The names of the 4 have been witheld as the FBI investigation continues.

7

• • • • •

Words

For the most part, it doesn't matter whether we're writing for broadcast, the station website, social media or anyplace else. Good writing has nothing to do with word length or complexity. **Good writing – including broadcast news – involves choosing words that convey a meaning that's accurate, a tone or feel that's appropriate and, wherever possible, a sound that matches the meaning.** Those second and third points are true in all genres, but especially important when writing for the ear. This chapter focuses particularly in writing for broadcast.

First, get it right. You have no better friend than the dictionary. You can't have too many of them, and they should be handy whenever and wherever writing is possible. Beware the thesaurus. This potentially useful tool can mislead writers into substituting longer and more complicated words of only approximate similarity to the original. Meanings must be precise, not approximate. A *ship* is not a *boat; burglary* is not the same as *robbery*. If you don't know the difference, you're already potentially in trouble.

Second, use words whose primary meaning and feel match what you're trying to say. When the audience gets only one chance to understand what's being said, we can't defend our word choice because the fourth or fifth definition matches our intended meaning. The audience simply doesn't have the luxury of thinking over what we're trying to say. Use words the same way people most commonly do.

Third, think about sound. It's called *onomatopoeia* when the sound of the word matches its meaning. Words like *buzz* and *cuckoo* are the most obvious, perhaps, but even the use of soft or hard sounds to describe soft or hard issues or events can strengthen your writing. *Weed killer* is almost always better than *herbicide*. Same length (in syllables), same meaning, but *weed killer* is universally understood, easier to pronounce and has a far more graphic and harsh feel.

• • • • •

Keep It Simple

Use simple words expressed in simple ways. Not simplistic, but simple. Broadcast news is *not* written for 12-year-olds; by and large, children neither watch nor listen to news. It *is* written for a large, diverse audience. There's nothing wrong with using a big and, perhaps, not universally known word if it's the most appropriate. But use such a word only in a context in which its meaning is clear. Don't make the audience's ability to understand a line dependent on knowing the definition of an obscure word.

OBSCURE: The suspect will be arraigned later today.
CLEARER: The suspect faces court arraignment later today.
BETTER: The suspect faces formal charges in court later today.

• • • • •

Keep It Conversational

Informal Words

Use informal words – not slang or colloquialisms but informal. Broadcast news is a blend of written and spoken language. The way we tend to write is commonly too formal, but the way we commonly speak is a bit too casual. Broadcast writing is written the way we *would* speak if we could plan it out well. It's what we *wished* we had said – after we were less eloquent extemporaneously.

A word you're unlikely to hear in spoken English is rarely appropriate for broadcast. Only newspapers refer to legislators as *solons* or talk of people being *feted* – no normal person would do that. And only journalists call a *fire* a *blaze* or use the word *some* to mean *about*. Normal people don't do that; you shouldn't either.

Contractions

Use contractions; that's how we speak. But be careful about contracting the word *not*. If the meaning of the sentence hinges on the audience hearing the *n't*, you probably should not contract it.

RISKY: The senator says he isn't running again.
BETTER: The senator says he is not running again.

The riskiest contraction is *can't* because the difference between the positive *can* and the negative *can't* rests solely on the ability of the announcer to pronounce the *t* sound clearly. Generally, don't take the chance.

Formal Terminology

Avoid formal terminology like *male, female* or *juvenile*. Other than police and the military, most people don't talk that way. With rare exception, use *man/men, woman/women, child/children* or *kid/kids*. Avoid pretentious or oblique terms. Generally, in broadcast, people do not *pass away*, nor are they *late* – they just *die*.

People . . . Not Persons

Although grammatically correct, the use of *persons* is, at best, stilted. One *person* is right, but more than one should be *people*.

•••••

Keep It Clear

Common Usage

Use words in the same context in which they're normally used. Almost every word conjures up an image in the minds of the listeners and viewers – an image based on the *common* usage of the word they're hearing. You can play with words for effect, and it's wonderful if you can pull it off. But if you're not careful, you'll just confuse – as did the following examples used on the air by some large-market TV stations:

PROBLEM: Governor Smith's popularity isn't looking very
    nice. In fact, it's on a downhill slide.
PROBLEM: Ministers in town are crying for a citizen
    review board to keep an eye on police.
PROBLEM: A house subcommittee has fattened the governor's
    tax package to support the next two-year state
    budget.

In all three cases the writers used words in ways that just don't compute. We don't refer to popularity as *nice*. Popularity may be *up* or *down* or perhaps a few other things – but not *nice*. Ministers in town may be *asking for, arguing for, demanding,* perhaps even *pleading for,* but not *crying*. It's also not likely that *all* ministers are involved, as the wording of this sentence suggests. And the word *fattened* just doesn't make sense. People get *fat;* animals may be fattened up; there can be fat in a budget. But we're just not used to hearing about a tax package that's *fattened*.

BETTER: A new survey says Governor Smith's popularity is heading down.

BETTER: Some local ministers say we need a citizen review board to keep an eye on police.

BETTER: A house subcommittee has tacked on more taxes to the governor's tax package. It's all part of figuring out how the state will cover the next two-year budget.

All those "better" examples use common words and terms the way we expect to hear them used.

PROBLEM: Today people are spending a lot of money on new-fangled gadgets for their home. The latest is an electronic brain which does all the housework. All you have to do is push a button.

The oven can be started from telephone beeps. The furnace can be turned on from a button on the TV screen.

About two thousand homes have this stuff in them nationwide.

The problem in this copy, which also went on the air, is that turning on the oven and furnace may be this unmarried, male reporter's idea of housework, but it doesn't match the way most of the audience think of it. That electronic brain doesn't sweep, vacuum, dust or do dishes – all of which are part of what most people think of when you say housework.

BETTER: This could be the gadget-lover's heaven on earth ... an electronic brain for the ultimate in remote control. Telephone beeps can start your oven ... a button on the TV screen can turn on the furnace.

More and more homes have this Star Wars stuff in them nationwide.

The pictures in TV are more likely to amplify the problems of a poorly selected word than compensate for it. Not only does the word have to be accurate and logical, it also has to blend with the picture the audience is seeing, which may further limit the writer's choices. Words that fight with what viewers see can wind up canceling out both, leaving a bewildered audience.

Technical Terms

Technical terms are fine for technical publications; they don't work in broadcast. It's true that some technical terms do creep into everyday lexicon; however, unless the term has not only crept in but firmly implanted itself, it must have an explanation. Problems in scientific terminology tend to be obvious. Watch out for legal terms. *Certiorari* means various things depending on who's asking for or granting it. It means nothing to most people in the audience.

And don't invent your own terminology.

> **PROBLEM:** Researchers have discovered a body chemical that lures the cold virus away from its targets inside a nose – where a cold starts.

By the time the audience figures out what a *body chemical* is in this copy (which went on the air), they've missed the rest of the line. Sometimes the shortest way to say something isn't the best. Here, what the reporter means is a chemical found naturally in the body.

> **BETTER:** It isn't a cure, but researchers have discovered a chemical that can help fight the common cold. The chemical – which is found naturally in the body – can lure the virus away from its targets inside a nose – where a cold starts.

Definite and Indefinite Articles

Watch out for the definite article *the*. This innocuous-sounding word can get you in a lot of trouble if misused. Frequently, *the* acts to single out a specific thing or person.

> **PROBLEM:** Police arrested a man for the robbery last night.
> **PROBLEM:** Police arrested the man for a robbery last night.

Both examples have problems created by the word *the*. In the first example, if the audience isn't familiar with last night's robbery, the line raises as many questions as it answers: What robbery? Use *a* instead of *the* when the described person or thing is not specific or when referring to something you have not yet mentioned in a story. The same applies in the second example. What man? *The* may also indicate *the one and only* – as it does in the examples above. There's a good chance more than one robbery took place last night, and more than one man may have been arrested.

> **BETTER:** Police have arrested a man for robbery.

Notice that *the* can frequently be omitted when it precedes a plural noun – as in the above example, in which we say *police* rather than *the police*.

By the way, with rare exception, pronounce *a* as "*ah*" and pronounce *the* as "*thuh*." Those are the more informal ways to say the words, and they're how we usually say them when we're not paying attention to our pronunciation.

● ● ● ● ●

Keep It Tight

Don't write phrases when words will do:

Wordy and Weak Phrases	Tighter and More Direct Words
subsequent to	after
prior to	before
in an effort to	to
for the purpose of	to
in order to	to
is of the opinion that	believes
due to the fact that	because
with the exception that	except
in the near future	soon
at this point in time	now
being that	since

● ● ● ● ●

Make It Powerful

Use Strong Nouns and Verbs

Use nouns and verbs that say something, not just take up space. If the meaning or feeling of a phrase depends mostly on adverbs and adjectives, your writing is lazy. Rewrite.

Weak: The noisy crowd did not like the speaker.
Better: The crowd jeered [or booed] the speaker.
Weak: Dozens of motorists were left stranded by a blizzard.
Better: A blizzard stranded dozens of motorists.

See Chapter 8 for an explanation of writing in the punchier, preferred, active voice rather than the weaker, passive voice.

Avoid Weak Qualifiers

Avoid meaningless qualifiers that weaken the copy. Words like *somewhat*, *fairly* and *very* rarely add anything to copy.

PROBLEM: Smith's corporate wallet was somewhat emptied
    tonight. A federal court fined the defense contractor
    five million dollars ...

In this example, used on the air, the use of *somewhat* makes a bad sentence even worse. What does a *somewhat emptied* corporate wallet look like? Stay with stronger terms that people know.

BETTER: A federal court says Smith double-billed the
    government ... and will have to pay five million
    dollars in fines ...

• • • • •

Get It Right

Grammar

There's simply no excuse for writing that's ungrammatical.

NOT ACCEPTABLE: If you want to lose weight ... clean out
    your kitchen! A group of women were left in untidy
    and clean kitchens ... along with a batch of
    cookies. The group ate less cookies in a clean
    kitchen! Experts say ... one possible reason is
    that a chaotic environment makes people feel out of
    control.

The experiment may be valid, but the grammar in this story, that went on the air, is not. *A group* is singular, so it should be *A group of women was.* . . . Given the awkwardness of that phrasing, it would better (and grammatically correct) to say, *Women left in* . . . And it's *fewer* cookies . . . not *less*. We're in the language business, and if we can't get that right, why would we think the audience would trust us to get the facts right?

Says

We use *says* all the time in journalism to convey someone's thoughts to the audience:

COMMON
USAGE: The mayor says he's against the plan.

The word has the advantages of being short, to the point, universally understood and neutral in meaning. The biggest disadvantage in broadcast is the constant repetition of the word. Look for places where a substitute will work. Some possibilities are:

acknowledge	concede	insist
admit	confess	maintain
agree	confirm	mention
allege	contend	narrate
announce	declare	pronounce
argue	demand	react
challenge	disclose	recite
charge	divulge	recount
cite	explain	relate
claim	grant	remark
clarify	indicate	repeat
reply	reveal	swear
report	speak	tell
respond	specify	testify

Substitute words say more – and might be better – if they're right. But keep in mind that substitute words that express more meaning than *says* also run the risk of being inappropriate. Some of the words in the preceding list have clear legal implications (e.g., *allege, claim, confess* and *testify*). If the possible substitute isn't completely accurate and appropriate, stay with *says*. Because we use the word all the time, we may get tired of it in broadcast copy; there's no evidence the audience shares that concern. Note that it's most often *says* and not *said*. More on that in Chapter 8.

Saying Too Much

Avoid words that convey editorial meanings. Words or phrases like *only*, *tiny*, and *so-called* are frequently pejorative and have no place in good broadcast writing except in direct quotes. Words like *finally* commonly imply that something took too long. Be careful. The audience rightly resents being told how to feel or what to think; stay with the facts.

One of the points that many of the great reporters make is that we work way too hard trying to manipulate the audience into feeling a certain way, instead of letting the audience feel the story – and come to their own conclusions.

Former network correspondent Deborah Potter says the audience is complaining, "Why are you shouting at me?" People just want to know what happened.

"Our writing is overstuffed and needs to go on a diet," she says. "You end up with stories full of emotion-laden adjectives like 'tragic' and 'terrifying' and 'horrible' and 'unthinkable' and 'unbelievable' and those kinds of words, all of which are designed to tell our viewers and listeners how they're supposed to feel about a story, but that eat up the time we could be spending on providing the detail that would allow our viewers and listeners to feel something."

Think

Write as if you had to defend every word you use. Is it the best choice possible? Is it the most accurate? Is it the most telling? Does it work with the video? From time to time we do have to defend every word to an irate listener or viewer – or in court. We'd be better off all the time if we thought that way before we started.

●●●●●

Common Problems

These are some of the many words and terms commonly misused, misunderstood or mispronounced.

accident: BE CAREFUL. Accidents happen all the time, but so do intentional acts. Don't predetermine cause by a haphazard word choice.

ad hoc: Means for a specific purpose only. It's redundant and wordy to say: *The governor has just created an ad hoc committee to study the issue.* In this case, leave off *ad hoc.*

admit: BE CAREFUL. Other than meaning to grant entrance (a usage that should be avoided in broadcast because of its awkwardness), the word means to concede or confess and implies an acknowledgment of wrongdoing. Generally, limit use of *admit* to legal and quasi-legal issues where it's clearly appropriate.

alleged: BE CAREFUL, and in general, don't use this word. See Chapter 8 and the crime and legal section of Chapter 21.

alumna, alumnae, alumni, alumnus: *Alumna* refers to one woman graduate or former student of a specific institution; *alumnae* is the plural for women. Use *alumnus* for one male graduate or former student; *alumni* is plural for men and should be used as the plural for a group of men and women.

among, between: Generally, use *among* when something is in the midst of more than two people or things; use *between* when something is in the midst of two people or things.

and/or: Don't use this stilted expression in broadcast copy.

as: See *because*.

average, mean, median: Take the numbers 2, 6 and 7; the *average* is the total (15) divided by the number of items being totaled (3). The *average* here is 5. The *mean* is the same as the *average*, but use *average* because it's more widely understood. The *median* is the middle figure in an ascending or descending series – in this case, 6. Generally, stick with *average* and write around the others.

because, since, as: *Because* shows a cause-and-effect relationship; *since* or *as* usually reflects a time relationship (one took place after the other), but the relationship is more indirect than cause and effect.

between: See *among*.

bi-, semi-: Unfortunately, depending on the source, *bi-* means either *once every two* or *twice a*. Those opposing meanings suggest that not using the prefix may be best in the interests of clarity. *Semi-* means *half* or *twice a*, but use the term only in a familiar context.

boat, ship: These terms are not synonymous. A *boat* is generally considered a small vessel, although ferryboats, PT boats and submarines are exceptions. *Ships* are larger, frequently oceangoing vessels.

bring, take: *Bring* involves transporting something to the speaker (here); *take* involves transporting it away from the speaker (there).

casualties: Includes dead and injured or sick.

cement, concrete: *Cement* and *concrete* are not the same. Cement powder is one of the ingredients in concrete.

centers around: Makes no sense; use centers *on* or revolves *around*.

claim: BE CAREFUL. *Claim* means to demand or assert a right (generally in a legal sense). Keep usage of this word in that context; it's not synonymous with *says*.

concrete: See *cement*.

consensus: General majority agreement, but not unanimous. The phrase *consensus of opinion* is redundant. Drop *of opinion*.

continual, continuous: *Continual* means ongoing at intervals; *continuous* means ongoing without stop.

convince, persuade: *Convince* generally means inducing someone to believe something; *persuade* involves inducing someone to some action.

cop: Slang for police, police officer. Better to say police.

crisis: Not every problem – or even every dangerous situation – is a crisis. Don't overuse. Plural is crises (KRI seez).

currently, presently: *Currently* means now. *Presently* means soon.

daylight saving time: Note that daylight saving time is singular. See Chapter 20 for more.

dialogue: An overused word that all too frequently replaces the simpler and more accurate *talk.*

die, kill: All people eventually die; some people are killed. Use *die* when death results from natural causes.

drugs: This word has taken on the meaning of narcotics (illegal, controlled substances) and should generally not be used as a synonym for medicine.

elderly: BE CAREFUL. This may be viewed as negative or simply inappropriate. As health care improves, the age at which people are "elderly" gets older. If you use the term at all, limit its use to over 70 or even 75.

emigrate, immigrate: *Emigrate* means to leave a country to settle elsewhere; *immigrate* means to enter a country from outside.

ensure, insure: Unless you're speaking about insurance, the proper word is *ensure* – to guarantee, to make sure of.

equal time, fairness: In broadcasting, equal time (passed by Congress) relates to political candidates only. Better called *equal opportunity*, it means that all candidates for the same office must be treated equally (outside of news), whether in opportunities to buy commercials or free appearances. The Fairness Doctrine, repealed in 1987, related to issues only. It said that stations must treat all sides of controversial issues in a reasonable manner – not equally, but reasonably.

execute: In the sense of dead, only governments, by virtue of law, can execute. Terrorists or individuals kill, assassinate or murder; they do not execute.

Fairness Doctrine: See *equal time, fairness.*

February: Although difficult to pronounce properly, there are two *r*'s in February. See also *library, hundred* and *nuclear.*

fewer, less: Both mean the same, but *fewer* relates to numbers and *less* relates to amount, more abstract ideas, bulk numbers and singular nouns and pronouns. Someone has fewer dollars, but less money.

figuratively, literally: *Figuratively* means like (as in a metaphor); *literally* means exactly, precisely.

firefighter, fireman: Although common in usage, use the gender neutral term *firefighter.* If you wouldn't say *firewoman* (and you wouldn't), don't say *fireman.*

flammable, inflammable: Both mean exactly the same thing – easily ignited – but use *flammable* because too many people think *inflammable* means the opposite of its correct definition.

gay: This word's only current usage relates to homosexuality, and it should be used as first reference.

ghetto: BE CAREFUL. This means a section of a city overwhelmingly inhabited by members of a minority group. The term also implies that a minority group has been forced to live in that section, so don't use this term lightly.

good, well: *Good* is almost always an adjective meaning well-done, worthy, kind and the like. *Well* is almost always an adverb meaning properly (except as an adjective meaning healthy).

gun: Acceptable term for any firearm.

half-mast, half-staff: What takes place in honoring the dead. *Half-mast* is for ships and naval stations; *half-staff* is on land.

Halley's Comet: Currently accepted pronunciation is HAL (as in pal) eez, not HAIL eez.

hang, hanged, hung: Everything hangs. People are or have been *hanged*; everything else has been *hung*.

hundred: Pronounced HUHN dred, not HUHN derd.

illegal: BE CAREFUL. Use this word only in reference to a violation of law – and with proper attribution. See the crime and legal section of Chapter 21.

immigrate: See *emigrate*.

impact: Don't use this word as a verb.

indict: Use this word only in its legal context of bringing charges. See the crime and legal section of Chapter 21.

inflammable: See *flammable*.

insure: See *ensure*.

irregardless: Not a word. Use *regardless* instead.

issue: Saying that something is a *controversial issue* is redundant; it wouldn't be an *issue* if it weren't controversial.

key: Another overworked word that only works, if at all, in the spirit of its original meaning of opening a lock.

kid, kids: Perfectly acceptable in broadcast for child, children.

kill: See *die*.

knot: See *mile*.

lady, woman: Use *lady* only in quotes and in formal titles (as in *Lady Marian*); otherwise, use woman, women.

less: See *fewer*.

library: As with February, there are two r's in *library*, and both must be pronounced.

literally: See *figuratively.*

major: Another overworked word.

majority, plurality: *Majority* means more than half; *plurality* means more than any other (as in the winner of a three-way race, perhaps).

massive: Another word worth resting.

mean, median: See *average.*

media: Includes all *media* and requires a plural verb (singular is *medium*). Use *media* rather than *press* unless you're specifically referring to print media only.

mile, knot: *Mile* is a measure of distance (5,280 feet), as distinguished from *knot,* which is a speed of one nautical mile (6,076.1 feet) per hour. See the weather section of Chapter 15.

none: Usually means no one or not one and almost always takes a singular verb.

NOW: National Organization *for* Women – not *of.*

nuclear: Pronounced NU klee ur, *not* NU kyu lur.

persuade: See *convince.*

plurality: See *majority.*

presently, currently: See *currently.*

press conference: Most broadcasters prefer *news conference* because *press* refers to print media only, although some argue that the term *news conference* elevates most of these gatherings beyond their substance.

rebut, refute: *Rebut* means to argue against with evidence; *refute* means to prove wrong. Don't confuse the two.

semi-: See *bi-.*

ship: See *boat.*

since: See *because.*

some: Means an unspecified number. Its use to mean *about* (e.g., *some one hundred years ago*) is classic journalese. Normal people don't talk like that. If you mean *about,* say *about.*

sources: An overworked, meaningless term that should be used more carefully. Don't use the word alone; it doesn't say enough to give any credence to a report or bit of information. Don't use with *unnamed.* The source does have a name, making the correct term *unidentified.* Even so, use some accompanying word or substitute phrase that provides more substance to the source (e.g., a *senior White House official* says. . .).

survey: BE CAREFUL. Don't use this word when there really hasn't been a formal survey.

take: See *bring*.

that, which, who: As pronouns, use *who* to reference people; use the appropriate choice of *that* or *which* to reference things.

toward: *Not* toward*s*.

unique: Means the one and only. No adjective modifying *unique* makes much sense. Things cannot be *more, less* or *very unique*.

viable: Means able to live. Much overworked term.

warn: Means to inform of possible trouble. Don't use the word when what's involved is really a statement and not a warning.

well: See *good*.

whether or not: Should almost always be just *whether*.

which, who: See *that*.

wide-ranging: Overworked phrase.

woman: See *lady*.

●●●●●

Summary

Choose your words carefully, making sure that they're accurate, are used the way most people use the word, and, if possible, have a sound that matches the meaning. Keep your word choice simple and conversational. Use contractions, but watch out for technical terms and words that may convey editorial meaning.

●●●●●

Key Words and Phrases

accuracy . . . tone . . . sound . . . simple . . . conversational . . . contractions . . . common usage . . . definite and indefinite articles . . . loaded words

●●●●●

Exercises

A. Write each of the following words or phrases correctly based on standard broadcast writing:

persons	male	will not
deceased	can't	female
kids		

B. The following sentences have errors and/or words, phrases or means of expression not acceptable for broadcast writing. Make them acceptable.

1. An unidentified man was hurt this morning when he was shot by robbers during a hold-up at Smith's Supermarket.

2. Certiorari was granted today in the case of Smith v. Jones by the State Supreme Court.

3. The superintendent of schools has stated that the air quality tests conducted in all of the districts 70 schools might be invalidated for 45 of the aforementioned schools.

4. Extensive rebuilding, reconstruction and renovation is what the building inspector said would be required for the dilapidated and run down housing project.

5. Last month the consumer price index took a 0.4% increase.

6. Although the 2 females and 1 male were searched for by members of the police department, but the men in blue weren't able to locate them.

7. The ruling by the state's highest supreme court has many local attorney's in the legal community here very displeased.

8. The govenor has decided to dulcify his critics by reluming the capitol dome.

9. The leader of Belize will travel to America to meet with members of Pres. Trump's administration over the new 6% import duty, according to the leader.

10. Being that there were 3 robberies last night, the police decided to elevate the number of units that would be driving around the apparently endangered area.

C. Record the first block of a radio or television newscast, and rewrite at least one story using fewer words and tighter phrasing – without sacrificing any important information.

8

•••••

Phrases and Phrasing

How well you piece all those appropriate, descriptive words together determines both the quality of the writing and how well
the audience understands it. Remember, in broadcast, the audience
gets only one shot at what you're saying. Phrases that are too cute or
simply don't work with the pictures may wind up merely puzzling the
audience.

You have a lot more latitude when you're writing for the web – where
the audience can see your words and take the information in at their own
pace. But here we're focusing on writing for the ear.

**After inaccuracy, the second greatest writing sin is creating con-
fusion.** And there are lots of ways to confuse the audience: a word or
phrase that's out of place or that doesn't mean exactly what it should, a
phrase that's awkward, even wordiness itself. If the audience has to stop
and think about what you mean, you lose them. Do it often enough, and
you lose them permanently.

•••••

How to Say It

Voice

Write in the active voice. If the subject of the sentence does something,
that's active. If something happens to the subject, that's passive.

PASSIVE: The First National Bank was robbed of two
thousand dollars this afternoon.
ACTIVE (AND BETTER): Robbers stole two thousand dollars from
the First National Bank this afternoon.
PASSIVE: The area was hit by a devastating winter storm.
ACTIVE (AND BETTER): A winter storm devastated [or battered]
the area.
PASSIVE: The car was driven by an escaped convict.
ACTIVE (AND BETTER): An escaped convict drove the car.

Passive: The bond issue was approved by the city council.
Active (and better): The city council approved [or passed] the
    bond issue.

The active voice is shorter, punchier, more interesting, more direct, and it's part of what broadcasting is all about. **Of all the writing skills you can master to improve and strengthen how you use the language, none compares to writing in the active voice.** And that's true whether you're writing for the ear or the eye.

There are occasional times when passive makes more sense:

■ When what has been acted on is much more important than what's doing the acting:

    The president was surrounded by the crowd.

■ When the cause is unknown or you want to avoid assigning blame:

    Union leader John Smith was shot this afternoon.

■ When active voice would be too awkward:

    The man was pinned between his own car and the
    guardrail.

Consider those the exceptions that prove the rule. Write actively.

Tense

Broadcasting's ability to be current in the news demands that we be current in our phrasing. First choice is present tense. Second choice is future tense. Third choice is present perfect tense. After that, it really doesn't matter.

Present: The city council votes on the sales tax bill
    today.
Future: The city council will vote on the sales tax bill
    later today.
Present perfect: The city council has voted on the sales tax
    bill.
Past: The city council voted on the sales tax bill today.

Note that present perfect's use of *has* and *have* makes the action sound as if it happened recently. Make sure you use it that way.

Remember, updating a story or looking to future implications of a past (tense) action will frequently allow you to use present or future tense:

Updated: The sales tax stays [or will stay] right where
    it is. The city council today rejected a bill that
    would have increased ...

Note that even though the action already took place (the vote came earlier), by focusing on the *outcome* instead of the vote itself, we can make the phrasing present or future tense.

Don't strain so hard to use present tense that the phrasing sounds awkward and strained.

Former network correspondent Deborah Potter says much of the news writing today is phony and doesn't sound like real people talking. "There's been a terrible crime committed against verbs in broadcast newsrooms across America," she says.

Potter offers her favorite example of this strange, new way of bullet-pointing the language:

```
Less resilient ... local business ... Dwight's
concession stand ... in the family ... three
generations ... sales this summer ... over
75 percent.
```

Potter notes that there are no verbs, just phrases. What happens, she says, is that an effort to sound more urgent simply winds up sounding awkward and largely unintelligible. Take this example that went on the air at a top 50 TV station:

```
A terrifying attack caught on camera.
Surveillance video showing a parking garage
attendant fighting off a man with a knife ... as he
tried to get some quick cash.
The car drove in with the license plate covered
early yesterday morning. The driver forced his way
into the booth, wrapping a shirt over his face. He
pulls a knife and demanded money the attendant
fought back. You can see him drop the knife and then
pick it up ... before he tried to get into the cash
register. He gave up and took [off] and now Miami
police need help finding him.
The worker is fine, but she quit her job.
```

No normal person talks like that, and the constant, seemingly random changes in verb tense make the information not only not conversational but also difficult to follow.

Clarity

As with words, use phrases the way people are used to hearing them. Twisting a phrase here and there can work, but if you're not careful, you'll only confuse.

PROBLEM: The General Assembly is putting a quick stop on legislation passed last year on strict handling of teenage drunken drivers.

Quick stops may apply to cars, but the audience that heard this copy read on the air probably never figured out what the reporter was trying to say.

BETTER: The General Assembly is back-pedaling on tough legislation passed just last year to deal with teenage drunk drivers.

Make sure you use phrases correctly. Things center *on* – not *around;* they revolve *around* – not *on.*
And watch out for mixed metaphors:

PROBLEM: And the race is on ... the battle over who gets your wireless plan nickels and dimes is at the front line.

Even giving the benefit of the doubt that the *front line* in this copy used on the air refers to a *battle*, neither refers to a *race*.

BETTER: Battle lines are forming in the war over who gets our wireless plan nickels and dimes.

Here, at least all of the references (*battle lines* and *war*) share a common theme.

Conciseness

Don't waste words or phrases; don't be redundant. There isn't time, and the more words you use to say something, the greater the chances for audience confusion.

REDUNDANT: The councilman argued for extensive rebuilding and renovation in the downtown area.
BETTER: The councilman argued for extensive rebuilding downtown.
WORDY: The car couldn't finish the race due to the fact that the engine in the car gave out.
BETTER: The car couldn't finish the race because the engine gave out.
or
The car couldn't finish the race ... the engine gave out.

Clauses and Phrases

Short introductory clauses and phrases work fine in copy written for the ear; parenthetical ones do not. With rare exceptions, a parenthetical phrase makes a sentence difficult if not impossible to follow because it requires the audience to remember what the writer was talking about before the phrase started.

INCORRECT: The U-S Forest Service, responding to criticism
　　from environmental groups, has agreed to review its
　　policies.

For the audience to understand this line, they must remember that the line started with the *U-S Forest Service* – which will review its policies. This is better handled:

INTRODUCTORY
PHRASE: Responding to criticism from environmental
　　groups, the U-S Forest Service has agreed to review
　　its policies.

Or

SPLIT UP: The U-S Forest Service has agreed to review
　　its policies. The decision comes in response to
　　criticism from environmental groups.

An audience that only gets to hear the information will find both of the above examples easier to follow and understand. These rewritten examples also put the verbs closer to the subjects; that, too, helps the audience follow what you're saying. News stories are not quizzes for the audience. Each sentence should take the listener or viewer from point X in knowledge, information, and understanding to point Y. That journey must be straight, clean and clear. Parenthetical phrases are side trips the audience can't follow when the journey is conducted by ear.

Positive Phrasing

Keep your phrasing in the positive. The issue isn't good news or bad news; it's whether you tell the audience what *is* going to happen or what's *not* going to happen. Negative phrasing is wordier and harder to understand.

NEGATIVE: The sheriff says they will not be charged until
　　tomorrow.
POSITIVE (AND BETTER): The sheriff says they will be charged
　　tomorrow.

NEGATIVE: There's no lack of demand for new single-family homes in Indianapolis.

POSITIVE (AND BETTER): There's new (or strong) demand for new single-family homes in Indianapolis.

NEGATIVE: ... But as reporter John Doe tells us, White House aides maintain any new proposal will not be announced before late January.

POSITIVE (AND BETTER): ... But as reporter John Doe tells us, White House aides say it will be at least late January before a new proposal is announced.

Pronouns

Watch out for pronouns. Pronouns are reference words and make sense only if the audience can instantly figure out what the pronoun refers to.

It's not clear who *he* is in the following:

An administration official complained that a network reporter asked unfair questions. He characterized the interview as nonsense.

Keep pronouns close to their antecedents, and look for ways to eliminate pronouns wherever you can. In the above example, using a name in line two should take care of the problem.

PROBLEM: He allegedly began molesting a seven-year-old girl three years ago. She's the daughter of some of his close family friends.

BETTER: Police say he began molesting a seven-year-old girl three years ago ... the daughter of close family friends.

In some cases a pronoun almost next to the antecedent may not be clear enough. The governing rule is that if you give the audience the slightest chance to misunderstand, that's what will happen. Also remember that singular institutions, businesses, and governments are *it* and not *they*.

NO: The company has been boxed in wherever they've turned.

YES: The company has been boxed in wherever it's turned.

That

Watch out for the word *that*.

■ Don't use the word where it's not needed.

WORDY: She says that she'll attend ...
BETTER: She says she'll attend ...

■ Do use the word when its absence sounds awkward.

AWKWARD: He feels the elephant will ...
BETTER: He feels that the elephant will ...

■ Do use the word to clarify paraphrasing, attribution and meaning.

UNCLEAR: The mayor reports firefighters who called in
sick will be let go.

That last sentence probably isn't what you mean unless the mayor is actually reporting those firefighters who called in sick.

BETTER: The mayor reports that firefighters who called in
sick will be let go.

The previous example helps keep the meaning clear. The next example points out a potential problem in attribution:

PROBLEM: The governor says his opponent is lying to the
voters and this is the dirtiest campaign ever.

This phrasing could easily be construed as you, the reporter, calling the campaign the dirtiest ever. Attribution is needed to make it clear that that's what the governor says. In this case, *that* indicates continued paraphrasing:

BETTER: The governor says his opponent is lying and that
this is the dirtiest campaign ever.

Time and Space Problems

Don't use words that require the audience to recall earlier material to figure out what you're saying. Words like *former* and *latter* (e.g., *in the latter case*) require the audience to remember not only what you said, but also the sequence in which you said it. The audience does not memorize copy and cannot follow these kinds of references.

Watch out for *here* and *there*. Think about both where you are and where your audience is before using those terms. Generally, do not use *here* or *there* unless it means the same thing for both the announcer and the audience:

No: Reporter Jane Smith says everyone here is up in arms
over the mayor's proposal.
YES: The new state measure will mean that people here
will pay twice as much for garbage pick-up.

The reason the first example above won't work is that the issue clearly applies to a city or town – where the mayor is. But the audience crosses political jurisdictions, and it's unlikely that people in distant suburbs or outlying towns care much about the proposal one way or the other. In the second example a statewide measure will clearly affect everyone "here" – assuming that you're not in a market that crosses state lines.

Reporters who are live in the field *should* use *here* to emphasize the fact that they're live and on location:

```
Police have surrounded the building here on the
lower west side.
```

● ● ● ● ●

What to Say

Titles and Identifiers

In broadcast copy, titles or identifiers go before names:

No: John Smith, State Attorney General, says his office
   will launch a new attack on illegal drugs.
Yes: State Attorney General John Smith says his office
   will launch a new attack on illegal drugs.

In almost all cases the title or description is really more important than the name itself, and what's important should come first. Putting the title or identifier first also avoids the same potential problem we have with parenthetical clauses and phrases.

Frequently, we paraphrase a long title to keep a sentence shorter and more to the point. An *associate commissioner of the state department of energy resources* should most often become *a state energy commissioner* or *a state energy official*.

Attribution

Attribution is the term we use to describe the concept that we generally cite (or attribute) the source of information that we put on the air, noting either the person or the organization that supplied that information. We don't just tell people, for instance, "There has been a new outbreak" of some disease. We tell them, "The Centers for Disease Control reports a new outbreak. . . ." We don't just tell people, "John Doe has committed a crime." We tell them, "Police say John Doe committed a crime." Attribution qualifies statements and puts them into proper context. It makes clear the source of our information; it protects us in controversies and legal disputes.

In broadcast copy – written for the ear – put attribution before the statement. Although there are occasional exceptions to this, most of the exceptions you hear on the air are examples of a writer opting for effect over responsibility.

UNACCEPTABLE: Busing doesn't work, according to Senate candidate Jane Smith.

ACCEPTABLE: Senate candidate Jane Smith says busing doesn't work.

Attribution after the fact forces us to think back and, perhaps, reevaluate the material. After-the-statement attribution confuses the audience, causes listeners to miss the next few words during the reevaluation process or just angers them because you made a ridiculous statement without making clear at the beginning that the statement should have been taken with a grain of salt.

Attribution is always needed when someone is accused of a crime, but avoid using the word *alleged*. It's a weak crutch that no one uses in normal speech; it won't necessarily keep you out of legal trouble; and you can almost always work around it by attributing information to police, a prosecutor or an indictment.

WORKS: Smith allegedly entered the bank armed with a shotgun.

BETTER: Police say Smith entered the bank armed with a shotgun.

or

Police charge that Smith entered the bank armed with a shotgun.

Part of why the last two sentences are better is that they also make clear who's making the accusation. That's better reporting.

Make sure you use the attribution at the appropriate spot:

No: Federal and local authorities are looking for two men who allegedly held up a Chicago bank today.

This is wrong because federal and local authorities are looking for the two guys who actually did it. No need for *allegedly* or any other qualifier here.

YES: Federal and local authorities are looking for two men who held up a Chicago bank today.

Don't use attribution for the wrong thing:

WRONG: Police arrested Jane Doe for the alleged murder.

Wrong again. In this example the issue isn't whether a murder took place, it's whether Jane Doe did it. You don't need attribution for an arrest. That's a fact, and someone was either arrested or not. It's not the *crime* that requires attribution, it's the link between a crime and a suspect. If there is a question about whether a crime actually took place, then you'll have to attribute that, too:

Yes: `Police say it was a brutal murder.`

Otherwise, use attribution in reference to suspects, not crimes. And use it often. **Every statement that links an identifiable individual – no matter where in the story that person is identified, no matter whether the identification is by word or picture – requires some form of attribution.** One qualifier at the beginning won't protect you. For more detail on this, see the crime and legal section of Chapter 21.

Attribution is also needed when you're dealing with anything that might be considered controversial, especially if it's changeable.

Risky: `The company will not relocate any of the laid-off`
`workers.`
Better: `A company spokesman says there are no plans to`
`relocate any of the laid-off workers.`
Risky: `The store will no longer accept credit cards.`
Better: `The store says it will no longer accept credit`
`cards.`

In both of the previous cases it's possible that the business involved will change its mind. Without attribution, you're the one making the statement instead of the company, and you don't know what the company might do.

Don't overdo attribution. If the governor's news secretary says that the governor will hold a news conference later today, it's usually fine to say:

`The governor will hold a news conference later`
`today.`

If the governor has a tendency to cancel these things or the news secretary is unreliable, then it might be safer to say:

`The governor has scheduled a news conference for`
`later today.`

Avoid making statements about someone's state of mind.

No: `The governor believes we need to build a new prison.`
Yes: `The governor says we need to build a new prison.`

No: The governor wants to build a new prison.
Yes: The governor says she wants to build a new prison.

The fact is, you really can't know what the governor believes or wants – only what he or she says. Limit your reporting to what you know. And use attribution where there's any reasonable possibility that the statement might be wrong or questioned in the future.

Quotations

Generally, don't quote. Few statements are so strong that we need to quote them, and we'd obviously much rather have the actual bite of the person making the statement. In most news stories, based on your phrasing, the audience will know you're either quoting or paraphrasing, and the distinction isn't significant as long as the point is accurate and fair. When a *short* quote (the only kind you normally ever use) is necessary, you do have to make clear that you're quoting.

```
    The governor said [pause] ...
    In the governor's words [pause] ...
    The governor said, and I quote ... (Reserve this
    more cumbersome phrase for particularly
    controversial quotes.)
```

In TV, if a direct quote of more than a few words is worth using, it's frequently worth supering the quote on the screen. In that case, make sure the script and the super go together precisely. You cannot ask the audience to read words on the screen while the announcer says something else.

Obviously, in copy written for the web, you do use quotes. See more on social media and online in Chapters 17 and 18.

Numbers

Generally, avoid numbers when substitutes are possible. Think about the story. If it's about a 3% hike in real estate taxes, then the figure obviously must be used. That's what the story is about. But if the story is that 98% of the city high school students failed a reading test, then the first reference should say *almost all*. Think about the point of the story.

When numbers must be used, try to round off if appropriate: *986* should usually be *nearly* or *almost a thousand, 103* should usually be *just over a hundred* or *a little more than a hundred, 8.4* should usually be *almost eight and a half, 52 of 74* should usually be *more than two-thirds*.

Never force the audience to perform mathematics to understand what you're talking about. And notice that none of the above examples uses *about* or *approximately*. Rather than those vague words, use more descriptive ones: *nearly, almost, just over* and *more than* all say more.

If you don't know the exact number, then *about* is clearly preferable to *approximately*. The words mean exactly the same thing, but *about* is much shorter.

Race

Use identification of race only when it's clearly part of a story, and never use racial epithets except in quotes. Race is clearly relevant to the story:

■ when it's part of a specific description of a person being sought by law enforcement,
■ when race is a central or significant issue of the story, such as some stories on politics and voting patterns,
■ when its absence would make the story less clear or meaningful.

A physical description of someone wanted by police should *always* include race in radio writing. Use race in television writing unless you have a picture, in which case there's no reason to include race at all. Also make sure that a physical description is sufficiently detailed that it has meaning. Saying that police are looking for two white men, or black women, or Hispanic men won't allow anyone to make an identification. That lack of description becomes nothing more than a race story. If you're talking about a hate crime, that may make sense; if not, leave it out.

There are lots of "minority" groups, and there are few if any communities where minority equals only one group, so don't use *minority* as synonymous with black or Hispanic or any other single group. Be aware of the impression you leave with the audience – by both the words that you choose and the pictures that you run.

There are leaders who are black and Hispanic and so on. But no one person speaks for any community, and unless you characterize people in your community as "white leaders" (and you don't) don't characterize minorities that way.

Make a conscious effort to ensure that the only time the audience sees or hears from minority groups isn't when it's a story about minorities. Minorities pay taxes; they're lawyers, doctors and experts in any number of areas that we cover. Make sure the audience sees and hears those voices in stories that have nothing to do with race.

And diversity isn't just racial. It's religious, political, economic and so on. Again, make sure the diversity of your audience is reflected in the diversity of voices – and sources – in the news.

●●●●●

What You Didn't Mean to Say

Dates

Where you place words in a sentence can alter the meaning significantly. Misplacement of the date presents one of the easiest traps to fall into. Notice the difference:

OPTION 1: `The State Supreme Court today agreed to review ...`

OPTION 2: `The State Supreme Court agreed to review today ...`

In Option 1 the State Supreme Court decided today that it will review a case some time in the future. In Option 2 the State Supreme Court agreed to review the case *today*. Make sure that what you say corresponds with what happened.

Unintended Meanings

Make sure you say what you mean, and watch out for meanings you didn't intend.

PROBLEM: `Luckily, only two of the 27 people who came down with the disease have died so far.`

Medically, this may be correct. But both *luckily* and *only* are highly judgmental and have no place here. The families of those two people who died will find little luck in this. And don't make the audience do the math.

BETTER: `Two people are dead so far ... another 25 are still fighting the devastating disease.`

Then there was this interesting gem, which went on the air:

PROBLEM: `A Cleveland elementary school is teaching its kids how not to be the target of a crazed gunman. They're teaching the kids terrorist training....`

In addition to the awkwardness of the negative lead in this story, the words conjure up an image of hundreds of little Rambos stalking the halls of some Cleveland elementary school, learning how to be terrorists.

BETTER: How's this for a sign of the times? A Cleveland elementary school is giving its kids anti-terrorist training.

Consider this next sentence. It came at the end of a real story about a kid going to the White House based on a letter of suggestions he wrote to the president.

PROBLEM: Other kids had some pretty good suggestions, too ... like build more baseball fields and make parents go to school, not kids....

Most parents who heard this copy read on the air may not have shared the writer's view of how good an idea that last one really is.

Editorials

Avoid editorial statements.

PROBLEM: On a more positive note about firefighters, expect to see more women than ever dousing fires here in Columbus.

PROBLEM: When will those big-time musicians stop selling out? That latest rock band to sing ditties for Pepsi....

The writer in the first example got into trouble by trying to force a transition from one firefighter story to another. Unfortunately, what went on the air was a position statement. The second example is just silly commentary. Even if you think most people agree with you or that your view is right and just, skip the editorial.

Clichés

Don't use clichés – ever. Listen to the collective audience groan after the umpteenth *and only time will tell* or *that remains to be seen*. Clichés have absolutely no redeeming qualities.

KGO-TV reporter Wayne Freedman also hates reporters who make themselves the story and tell people how to feel and what to think and use hackneyed phrases like, "something went terribly wrong."

Freedman has his own list of pet peeves: "Reporters saying, 'meet so and so.' Makes me crazy," says Freedman.

Other clichés we can do without:

A parent's [or other group's] worst nightmare ...

The edge of anyone's seat ...

Never seen before (until now) . . .

Whole new ball game . . .

All and sundry . . .

Both feet on the ground . . .

Foregone conclusion . . .

Been there, done that . . .

Rests on his/her laurels . . .

Turn over a new leaf . . .

Roll with the punches . . .

Writing's on the wall . . .

See the light . . .

Picture of health . . .

[Anything] as big as all outdoors . . .

Marriage made in heaven . . .

Time is ripe . . .

At long last . . .

Consider that just a partial list of phrases that should never come out of your computer – or mouth.

Of all those tired and overused clichés, the worst these days is probably "a _____'s worst nightmare." The phrase has become so overused that it no longer has any meaning at all. Worst, perhaps, is that it's now being used in clearly non-nightmare contexts. A traffic tie-up, for instance, is not a "commuter's worst nightmare." Getting in a fatal car accident, for instance, is considerably worse. And being stuck on a school bus or getting head lice are also not a parent's worst nightmare. Not even close.

I'm changing the name of the city in this next example to protect the guilty:

THOUGHTLESS: For a lot of people, getting a parking ticket in downtown Cityville is an absolute nightmare – but now the city is looking at an alternative way for you to take care of this ticket through charity.

No, it's not an "absolute nightmare." It's an annoyance – and a self-induced one at that. Stop the writing nightmare.

Sexism

Avoid sexism. Don't use *he* when the reference is really to men *or* women. But also work to avoid *he or she* because it's so cumbersome.

It's almost always possible to write around the problem, frequently by using the plural.

Sexist: If your child goes to Big Walnut, Logan Elm or Teays Valley ... keep him home tomorrow. School has been canceled.

Better: If your children go to Big Walnut, Logan Elm or Teays Valley ... keep them home tomorrow.

And avoid male gender job descriptions when neutral ones are available:

■ Use *councilors* or *council members* – not *councilmen*
■ Use senators and representatives or members of Congress – not congressmen or congresswomen
■ Use *police officers* and *firefighters* – not *policemen* and *firemen* (You don't usually say *policewomen*, and you would never say *firewomen*.)

Don't take the sexist liberties one reporter did with this story:

A former school teacher took a shotgun this afternoon, killed his wife and then killed himself.
Jeanne Smith was found in the front yard of her Clinton home. She apparently was running from her husband Lafe Smith ... a retired math teacher.
Smith had been depressed about his declining health. Jeanne must have known this kind of thing could happen.

Dealing with a story involving husband and wife with the same last name may be a bit more difficult than most. But you can't call him *Smith* and her by the too-familiar-sounding first name any more than you can do it the other way around. Either use first and last names for both or use *Mr. and Mrs. Smith*.

Personalization

Personalizing news copy is common in our business. Properly used, there's nothing wrong with it. If you (as announcer or reporter) and the audience will be paying a new, higher sales tax, there's nothing wrong with saying:

Yes: We'll be paying more money ...

But don't separate yourself from the audience as one major market all-news station did:

No: `You'll be paying higher prices for gas than other`
`parts of the country.`

The implication here is that somehow the announcer is above all that.

Certain highly charged issues should always be handled with great care and never lend themselves well to personalization:

Problem: `If you believe in polls, then most of us do not`
`want things like Uzi machine guns sold over the`
`counter.`

`A Newsweek poll released today showed 72 percent`
`of us favor a ban on the sale of semi-automatic`
`weapons. An L-A Times poll showed 80 percent of us`
`favor such a ban.`

This story, which aired on a large market television station, is nothing but trouble. The line *if you believe in polls* is, at best, gratuitous. People will believe it or not as they wish; never say it. Uzi machine guns are not sold over the counter; that's just plain wrong. The issue here involves semiautomatic weapons. Machine guns are automatic, and different laws apply to their sale. In addition, a story like this begs to be misheard. Drop the personalization (*of us*) on stories about gun control, abortion and other highly charged issues.

Better: `A new poll says most Americans want to ban the`
`sale of semi-automatic weapons ...`

●●●●●

Last Note

As with words, phrases must be precise and telling. Write as if you had to defend every phrase you use. Sometimes, you will.

●●●●●

Summary

Inaccuracy and creating confusion are the two worst writing sins you must avoid. Use active voice, and try to stay with present or future tense in stories, especially leads. Be clear and concise, and use positive phrasing. Watch out for pronouns and time and space problems created by words. In broadcast, titles and identifiers go before the name. Avoid state of mind statements, generally don't quote and minimize the use of numbers. Be careful with race identification, and avoid sexism and clichés.

●●●●●
Key Words and Phrases

active voice . . . passive voice . . . present, future and present perfect tense . . . problems with pronouns . . . time and space problems . . . titles and identifiers . . . attribution . . . state of mind statements . . . race and diversity . . . editorial meanings . . . sexism . . . clichés

●●●●●
Exercises

A. Put an "A" next to the sentences which are active . . . and a "P" next to passive ones:

1_____The airplane was landed during the storm.

2_____The lawyer wrote an angry letter to the judge.

3_____The man will be arrested by a deputy.

4_____The bell is rung at noon.

5_____A stranger helped police chase a man down the alley.

6_____The spotlight had been focused on downtown.

7_____The man was going to town.

8_____The car was driven by an escaped convict.

9_____The doctor sent an enormous bill to the patient.

10_____The woman will be rescued by a firefighter.

11_____The alarm has been sounded.

12_____An investor wrote a nasty letter to the company.

13_____The athlete is upset with himself.

14_____The lawyer drove the car straight into a ditch by the side of the road.

15_____The jet was brought down on the wrong runway.

16_____The student is two credits shy of graduation.

17_____The reporter has been shut out of the meeting.

18_____The boy was told to get ready fast.

19_____The delivery service spent two days trying to find the address.

20_____The train was stopped at the station.

21_____Police have been unable to find the robber.

22_____Forty protestors were arrested at the barricade.

23_____The man was pinned between the guardrail and the car.

24_____Passengers fled the scene as quickly as possible.

25_____Soldiers lined up for their shots.

B. Convert the passive sentences above into active voice.

C. The following sentences have errors and/or words, phrases, or means of expression not acceptable in writing for broadcast. Make them acceptable.

1. Police announced that only a few people bothered to demonstrate this morning at the Iranian Embassy located in downtown.

2. The number of fire code violations supposedly more than doubled it's number last year, according to the head of the fire department.

3. The unemployment rate plummeted 0.1% last month, according to the Labor Department.

4. The governor spoke with the author of the school bill, but the former said later that his impression of the latter was that he would not do anything to change it.

5. Luckily, only 2 of the 27 men and women taken hostage have become deceased so far.

6. The cops finally caught the man suspected of burglarizing 3 persons over the weekend.

7. Red light cameras located in Springfield intersections have identified twelve drivers who wrongly drove through the intersections after the lights turned red, but officials say that tickets will not go out to the offending drivers until tomorrow.

8. American auto makers, in response to attacks by Democratic senatorial candidate Mike Smith, have asserted today that they are not lagging behind in quality control to foreign car companies.

9. The presidents of IBEW, the Teamsters, the Amalgamated Clothing and Textile Workers of America and the United Mine Workers Union have all agreed to sit down with the Secretary of Labor to discuss what can be done to maintain the beneficially low level of inflation that the country is now enjoying.

10. The tortile remains of the 2008 Ford Explorer were used by police in front of Central High School as a reminder to the students at Central who were to be celebrating their prom tonight.

D. This assignment is about attribution (and good writing). Reread pages 103–106 on attribution . . . and the crime and legal section of Chapter 21 before you start.

The following information comes from the Springfield police. Re-write it, using correct broadcast style, good writing, logical story development, proper attribution, and a reasonable slug.

A former truck driver named John A. Jones has been charged with the robbery yesterday at the Smith Trucking Company. $5,000 was taken in the robbery. Most of the money was found in his home. John Jones, the former driver, was fired by the president of the Smith Trucking Company 2 weeks ago. Jones went into the trucking company office with two handguns yesterday and left with a paper bag stuffed with $20 bills. The office manager called police, saying she recognized Jones. Jones was arrested at his home, which is located at 1324 Highland Avenue in South Springfield early this afternoon.

9

Sentences

Ultimately, words and phrases are fashioned into sentences – which, of course, are fashioned into stories. The rules are different if you're writing online for the eye (see Chapters 17 and 18 on social media and online). If you're writing for the ear, you need to keep broadcast sentences short, simple and straightforward. The most common grammatical sentence structure in English is subject-verb-object. That's what we're used to; that's the way we generally speak; and that's going to be the easiest sentence structure for the broadcast audience to understand. Use it often.

Keep It Short

Broadcast writers are frequently told to keep sentences short. There are two overriding principles.

First, there's only so much information that the audience can absorb into the brain through the ear at one time. That's not a reflection of the intelligence of the audience but a reflection of our ability to assimilate information that we only get to hear. There is nothing so lengthy or complicated that it cannot be understood orally. What's involved is breaking down the material into small, absorbable bits. Use more, short sentences rather than fewer, longer ones.

Second, an announcer can read only so many words without gasping for air. And no one reads well, using proper life and emphasis, with lungs starved for oxygen. Generally, announcers can read well no more than about two dozen syllables at a stretch.

One Important Idea

As a general rule, a broadcast sentence should contain no more than one important thought or idea. All sentences contain many bits of information, but they still should contain no more than one important thought or idea.

TYPICAL

BROADCAST

SENTENCE: `Robbers shot a man this morning during a holdup`
`at the First National Bank.`

IMPORTANT

   IDEA: `man shot`

SMALLER

   IDEAS: `robbers did the shooting`
`this morning`
`during a holdup`
`at the First National Bank`

This type of lead also logically takes us to video of the bank, which will, most often, start with the next line.

Put People First

Had a man not been shot, the sentence would be restructured to make the holdup the important idea. Remember that, ultimately, people are more important than things.

TYPICAL

BROADCAST

SENTENCE: `Two people are dead and three hospitalized after`
`a house fire on the west side today.`

IMPORTANT

IDEA: `two dead and three hospitalized`

Note the use of *are dead* rather than *died*. It happened recently, it's technically accurate, and we frequently use this phrasing in broadcast because it's more current-sounding. However, some prefer the present perfect *have died*, finding that construction more conversational. Note also that it's not *and three others hospitalized*. That would be wordy and unnecessary.

SMALLER

   IDEAS: `house fire`
`on the west side`
`today`

Generally, put people ahead of things, dead before injured or sick. Information on the fire itself will come in line two – having been set up in line one. Again, that's also most likely to match available video. Even if no one had been killed or injured in the fire, the lead would not be *There was a house fire on the west side today.* So what? Lead with people and/or what the story means to people. If appropriate:

POSSIBLE
BROADCAST
LEAD
SENTENCES: `Firefighters spent most of the afternoon ...`
`or`
`Fire investigators are sifting through ...`

Keep It Simple: Subject-Verb-Object

Keep the flow of ideas simple in construction – not simplistic but simple, as in understandable.

COMPLEX: `The family of a two-year-old local girl killed`
`by a pit bull last year will have to wait to hear`
`from the State Supreme Court before the case can be`
`resolved....`

The contorted sentence construction of this already complicated story makes it impossible to follow. The most common grammatical sentence in English goes subject-verb-object. Not all your sentences have to be constructed that way, but if you deviate too much or too often from that basic form, your copy will be harder to follow. Keep the construction simple, short and straightforward.

SIMPLER: `Contradictory rulings in the case of a pit bull`
`that killed a two-year-old local girl. Last`
`year....`

Note that the lead includes new information, resisting the mistaken temptation to start the complicated story with old news. Always think about what's *new* in a story. **History and background may be interesting and important, but they're not why the story is going to air today. Never lead a story with history or background. Never.**

Use Some Variety for Interest

The risk in writing short and simple is that the story sounds choppy and tedious. You avoid that by varying sentence length and structure just enough to ride that line between easy to understand and interesting to hear. Note the sentence variety in the following:

`About 24-thousand people here will find themselves`
`homeless – for at least a while – this year. That's`
`two thousand more than last year ... which was`
`two thousand more than the year before. Next year,`
`it'll be worse, still.`

```
(nat sound bridge)
    The wind chill is 15 degrees, but it feels even
colder when it comes off the river. It's a tough
place to call home.
    This is not the economic fringe of society. This
is beyond it.
```

The basic form is simple, and most sentences are short, but the variety of phrasing and sentence length helps keep the story moving and gives the audience a feel for the subject.

See Chapter 11 on the use of conjunctions to smooth out writing and improve story flow.

Split Up Complex Sentences

Simplify complex sentences and information by dividing the material into more short sentences.

COMPLEX: Two local men, John Doe and David Glass, charged
    in a series of crimes ranging from armed robbery and
    drug dealing to extortion, today were sentenced to
    20 years to life by Judge Jane Smith of the City
    Municipal Court.

SIMPLER: Two local men will spend 20 years to life in
    the state prison. John Doe and David Glass were
    sentenced today after their convictions in a series
    of crimes including armed robbery and drug dealing.

● ● ● ● ●

Make It Clean, Clear and Concise

Make all your statements clean, clear and concise.

WEAK/WORDY: Adverse weather conditions have caused quite a
    bit of school closings ...

That's what thousands of people heard a top station in a top 10 market say a while ago. Make it tighter and more direct:

BETTER: Bad weather has closed lots of area schools ...
UNCLEAR: People who woke up this morning. . . saw the
    ice ... heard all the school closings ... and
    wished you were back in school with the day off.

That sentence, which actually went on the air on a large-market TV station, must have left the audience wondering – wondering about the people who didn't wake up this morning . . . and wondering exactly who wished to be back in school (which wasn't being held) with the day off.

What the reporter wanted to say was something like this:

BETTER: The crystal landscape from last night's
storm ... reminded me of carefree days as a kid
when we were lucky enough to have school canceled.

But you're still better off resisting the temptation to romanticize a bad weather day. Parents who suddenly have to cope with kids at home probably don't see much positive in either the weather or what they have to do to cope with its consequences.

Make Every Sentence Count

A sentence that doesn't contain critical information about the story is a waste of words and the listener's or viewer's time. Change it or drop it.

Robbers shot a man this morning during a holdup at
the First National Bank. The First National Bank is
located at the intersection of Main and Green
Streets.

The lead is okay, but the second sentence has no meat to it. Even if the specific location of the bank is needed, that's not the way to do it. Not only does it interrupt the logical flow of the story, but it contains no critical information. Work the general location (e.g., the part of town) or cross streets (if that much detail is needed) into a sentence that contains other, more important material.

BETTER: Robbers shot a man this morning during a holdup
at the First National Bank. It's the third robbery
this month at First National's branch at Main and
Green.

Avoid Repetition

Construct sentences so you don't have to immediately repeat the same names or information.

REPETITIVE: Both Hudson's and the United Auto Workers Union
are declaring victory ... after a weekend of U-A-W
pickets at Hudson's Department Stores.

Tighter: Both sides are declaring victory after a weekend of picketing by the United Auto Workers Union at Hudson's Department Stores.

Stay Positive

Don't introduce material in a negative way. The issue isn't good news versus bad news. Positive statements are always simpler, shorter and easier to understand.

Negative: The governor today denied charges that he has no effective drug program. The criticism came from a special legislative panel that released its findings this morning.

The problem in this kind of story is that you want to lead with the newest information (the governor's denial), but it just won't work unless the audience is aware of what is being denied. That's seldom the case, and in broadcast, denials cannot precede audience awareness of what the denial is about. It's simply too hard to follow and digest the information that way.

Better: The governor is defending his drug program today ...

That makes the statement positive, and the writer can then go on to explain why the governor is defending the program.

Make Sense

Make sure you make sense. The audience can judge only what it hears, not what you know or meant to say.

Puzzling: Accidents all over the city as the storm slams into Columbus. If you haven't been outside yet, don't bother looking. The weather has turned Columbus into one big mess.

Don't bother looking? A line like that not only sounds foolish – it's absolutely guaranteed to send people away from their television sets and straight to the window.

Puzzling: Well, we've got a warning here for you that you may not like. Breathing Ohio air may be hazardous to your health.

Why would the writer suppose that the audience *might* not like that? Who do we suppose *would* like it? And how many *good news* warnings do we give?

Provide the audience with information they can understand and use – unlike this:

Unclear: Right now, Steubenville residents are paying two
    dollars more per one thousand gallons [of water] ...

But how much is that? Sometimes being correct isn't enough. No one knows how often they use a thousand gallons of water, so they won't have any idea how much extra this is – in terms of dollars and cents. As with tax stories, you have to convert this number into something that people can understand – like the average extra amount a typical family might have to pay per month.

The next example is from 2016, but it's such a useful mess that I can't resist using it.

Puzzling: Meanwhile, Democrat Bernie Sanders is gaining
    ground on Clinton in California. A Los Angeles
    Times/U-S-C poll out tonight shows Sanders in the
    lead right now. . . by one point. Sanders is
    gaining ground thanks to young voters. Still, Clinton
    is leading by 10 points among "likely" voters.

So, is Sanders ahead by one or behind by 10? Is the distinction based on overall adults versus likely voters? The audience will never know (nor do I, so I can't help sort it out – although Clinton did win that primary by 12.5).

This next example went on the air as the last line of a story about a defendant who pleaded not guilty by reason of insanity:

Puzzling: Smith claimed he was on a mission from God.
    Apparently the jury agreed.

The jury may well have agreed that the defendant was insane, but it's unlikely they agreed that the defendant was on a mission from God.

End Strong

End sentences strongly. There's a natural break at the end of every sentence, and that means the audience gets a moment to digest what has just been said. Use the end of the sentence to bring home an important point. Wherever possible, avoid ending sentences with weak words or phrases. Watch out, especially, for weak prepositional phrases at the end of sentences.

Weak: Several homes and businesses had to be evacuated this afternoon when a natural gas line was ruptured by a construction worker.
Stronger: Several homes and businesses had to be evacuated this afternoon when a construction worker ruptured a natural gas line.

In this example, restructuring to end on *gas line* creates a stronger ending, as well as making that part of the sentence active rather than passive.

• • • • •
Last Note

Make your point directly in every sentence. Don't dance around ideas, spilling words around a page. Just as you should be able to defend every word you use, you should be able to defend every sentence those words form. If you can't defend it, rework it or drop it.

• • • • •
Summary

Keep sentences short. The audience can only take in so much information at a time, and an announcer can only read so much material between breaths. No more than one important idea per sentence, but make every sentence count. Remember the audience is people, so structure sentences to put people (or what interests them) first. Most sentences should be subject-verb-object, but use some variety (and conjunctions) for interest. Avoid repetition, stay positive and end strongly.

• • • • •
Key Words and Phrases

keep sentences short . . . one important idea . . . put people first . . . subject-verb-object . . . make every sentence count . . . end strong

• • • • •
Exercises

A. The following stories and paragraphs have errors and/or words, phrases, sentences or means of expression not acceptable in writing for broadcast. Make them acceptable. Do not assume that the sentences are in a logical sequence. Note that for the purposes of this assignment, you are in Springfield.

1. People living in neighborhoods that are tired of living right near to homes in foreclosure or which are abandoned or unsafe and are overrun by animals and insects will have something to celebrate on Wednesday when the city opens bids for the demolition of more than 30 of those properties in the Carnival-Hill area, many of which have been featured on the website of the local organization, CleanUpOurNeighborhood.org.

   A variety of animals will be displaced in the clean-up. Sam Smith said that there's a groundhog den beneath the decaying, rundown house at 2000 East Grant St. A black cat wandered around the dilapidated front porch of 1000 West Carnival Ave. Jane Jones said the dilapidated house at 1500 West Hill St. was a den for opossums.

2. It has been 25 years that have gone by since a string of home break-ins and sexual assaults had people who lived here in Springfield on edge in the summer and early autumn of 1995. Back then, the arrest of John Paul Smith, then 21 years old, after he made the mistake of trying to break in and rob a city police officer's home not long before Thanksgiving, seemed to bring the crime spree to an end.

   After a jury in May 1996 found Smith guilty – but mentally ill – of criminal deviate conduct, Judge Hank Jones imposed a maximum 50-year prison term. That 50-year prison term passed considerably faster than some might have expected because even though Smith, due to violating parole in an earlier case, didn't officially begin serving the 50-year sentence until 1997, state Department of Correction officials confirmed he had recently been released from prison on parole and is currently residing at a relative's house here in Springfield.

3. Springfield Metal Works President John Smith informed metal workers this morning the company will lay off 130 designers and engineers because work on the next generation of R-2000 engines will be moving from the design and engineering phase to the full production phase.

   In a letter that was distributed to all the metal workers today, Smith wrote that while there was going to be a drop in the size of the design staff at the plant, that there was also a corresponding ramping up in the work force that has taken place on the production side of the business where more than 200 jobs have been added over the past year as work to construct the new, state-of-the-art engines has been intensified, Smith wrote. Smith wrote that the 130 announced layoffs will become effective in 3 weeks.

4. People who live in northwest Springfield will have to wait three weeks before finding out more information about a possible settlement

proposal that has been offered to the city to stop various litigation over a City Planning Board decision not to grant a variety of permits for a cell phone tower to be built in the Springfield Valley neighborhood. Following the Planning Board's September 28, decision not to grant a conditional use permit for the company's proposed 85-foot bi-pole cell phone tower that the company wanted to construct at 100 Gearly St., the applicant, Capitol Cell Phone Tower III, LLC, filed a lawsuit on October 22, in U.S. District Court for the Southern District, and which has set a court date in February.

Thursday, the proposed settlement offer, including camouflaging the tower as a pine tree, was one of four items the members of the City Council would be considering to discuss at the next public hearing at the next City Council meeting scheduled to take place in three weeks, before city council members would decide on placing them on the agenda in order to vote on the matter at the special town meeting scheduled to be held three weeks after that.

5. After extensive discussion of several proposed changes to a proposed property maintenance ordinance Wednesday, the Springfield City Council decided to schedule another workshop on the subject for next week, when members of the city council will again continue examining and combing through the document.

Some members of the city council expressed their frustration that the draft ordinance of the property maintenance ordinance did not more clearly reflect their intent for the whole plan, which was to force properties along the Main Street corridor to become more welcoming to travelers to the region. The proposed ordinance called for the city to be able to fine property owners whose tourist zone properties fall into disrepair, including a list of standards including prohibition of broken glass, peeling or missing paint, unkempt yards or weeds, garbage left outside, and unsightly porches or foundations.

10

•••••

Leads and Endings

The broadcast lead must capture the interest and attention of the audience. It may announce important developments; it may summarize complicated data; it may scream in joy, cry in pain or wonder in astonishment. But whatever it does and – within reason – however it does it, the lead must grab hold of the audience. That's the only real function of the lead.

Newspaper's traditional inverted pyramid lead attempts to answer, in abbreviated form, most of the basic journalistic questions of a story: the who, what, where and when (and sometimes even why and how). That kind of lead works when you're writing for the eye online.

But the inverted pyramid style has no place in broadcast journalism, and the broadcast lead has no real relationship to the print lead. **The broadcast lead most closely parallels the newspaper *headline*, boldly demanding the audience's attention. Think of the broadcast lead as the headline for the story.**

If geometry helps in understanding structure, then while many newspaper stories and online stories may be inverted pyramids, the broadcast story is a circle. The lead is the most important part of the story, and the last sentence of a broadcast story is the second most important. That doesn't mean the last sentence contains the second most important bit of information in the story. It does mean that, structurally, the ending closes and completes the story, bringing it full circle.

Because newspapers' inverted pyramid story form puts the most important information at the beginning and less important material at the end, it works well for both editors and readers. Editors can cut for length simply by chopping off the bottom of stories, and readers can stop reading a story at any point, knowing or sensing that what they haven't read is less important than what they have. Most of the newspaper audience never reaches the end of a story. However, the newspaper model doesn't work in broadcast. If our audience tires of a story, they can't simply move on to the next one, as they can in the newspaper or online. We can't afford to fade out; either our audience is with us for the whole story or they tune us out.

● ● ● ● ●

Types of Leads

There isn't a single best kind of lead. What the story is about, how it fits into the newscast, who's going to read it and what precedes it – all help determine each particular story's best lead in a given newscast. And there are plenty of different kinds of leads to choose from. In most cases the reason the audience should care about the story is the story's innate importance. In that case – in the majority of cases – start with a main point lead.

Hard Main Point Lead

Main point leads include four variations.

Hard main point leads tell what the story is about in an absolutely straightforward manner:

HARD

LEAD: `The state legislature voted overwhelmingly today to`
`cut back school funding by 20 percent.`

This lead tells exactly what the story is. There's no subtlety here, but it's not designed for that. No lead gets you into the meat of the story as directly and quickly. A fairly simple story that's on the air because of its importance to the audience will usually work best with this kind of lead.

HARD

LEAD: `A chemical spill on the west side drove hundreds`
`of people from their homes this afternoon.`

Soft Main Point Lead

Contrast that directness with the *soft main point* lead, which starts with what the story is generally about or the *general* impact of the story. Converted from a hard to a soft lead, the first lead above might look like this:

SOFT

LEAD: `School systems throughout the state may have a`
`tough time getting by. The state legislature today`
`voted....`

This kind of lead delays the real content of the story by one line, substituting, at the top, a bottom-line sense of what it means. Notice that line two will almost always be a variation of the hard main point lead.

So why slow down the details of the story? First, depending on available video, it might make more sense to start with the anchor on camera giving a sense of the story for a line before going to voiceover video with details in line two. Visually, that's how most stories on TV start.

Video	Audio
Anchor CU	((Anchor))
	Two of the crack houses city police raided last night are owned by city police officers.
VO ENG	This one, on Main Street ...

Second, the soft main point lead is an excellent way to start a complicated story. By stating the sense of the story, you make it easier for the audience to follow the twists and turns that may be involved in getting there.

SOFT
LEAD: Another setback today in efforts to end the
    sanitation workers' walkout.

Throwaway Lead

Throwaway leads just introduce a subject using a short sentence or, more commonly, a sentence fragment. The throwaway lead version of that first lead might look like this:

THROWAWAY
LEAD: Trouble for state school systems. The state
    legislature today voted....

A throwaway lead can give a general sense of the story, as the above example does, or it can create a general feeling or mood or just grab the audience's attention:

THROWAWAY
LEAD: An ominous warning tonight from police.

Throwaway leads can be especially good for varying the pacing of a newscast – especially to speed it up – and provide a short bridge between related stories:

THROWAWAY
LEAD: And another drive-by shooting tonight.

Umbrella Lead

Umbrella leads are among the most under-utilized techniques to help add coherence to a newscast. Where some group, government body, business, or individual has taken several significant actions, the umbrella lead can set up the audience for different aspects of a single story:

UMBRELLA

LEAD: The state legislature today passed bills that will raise taxes, lower some salaries and change school funding.

This approach tells the audience that you're about to give them, in this example, three related stories. Note that when you write the rest of the story, tell each part start to finish; don't try to weave in and out of the different parts.

When an event will be covered from several angles, the umbrella lead can set up the audience for a series of reports:

UMBRELLA

LEAD: The vice president made a whirlwind tour of the city today ... looking for support for the administration's new tax plan ... stumping for a local politician ... and raising money for the Republican party. We have a series of reports, starting with Jane Smith at the airport.

Or the umbrella lead can connect different stories that have a common thread:

UMBRELLA

LEAD: Three unrelated strikes have 50-thousand workers in the state walking picket lines. In Smithville....

Delayed or Suspense Lead

The *delayed* or *suspense* lead works completely differently from any of the others. Typically, the entire story, including the lead, is told chronologically. For most stories, we relate information chronologically (if there is a chronology) after the lead. Here, the whole story is told chronologically, with the punch line or point of the story coming at the end:

DELAYED

LEAD: John Smith drove to his job at Jones Trucking today – just as he has every other day. He stopped at the nearby Brown Donut Shop – as he has every

```
morning.  But today, just as he went in, he noticed
another customer choking.  Smith rushed over,
administered the Heimlich maneuver - pushing in on
the man's ribcage - and saved the man's life. Smith
said he learned the technique during a short
training session at lunch - yesterday.
```

Normally, we never use a name that is not widely known in a lead. The delayed or suspense lead is the exception. The audience should feel that there's a reason they're hearing this story, even if the exact reason isn't made clear until the end. If the writing is tight, the story short, and the punch line worthwhile, the technique works. It won't work for most stories, and it should be used sparingly for greatest effect.

Question Lead

The *question* lead is just what it says:

QUESTION
LEAD: `Why would you look for an elephant in a church?`

For a question lead to work, it either has to be sufficiently intriguing that the audience really wants the answer or a question that the audience will want to answer in the affirmative:

QUESTION
LEAD: `Do you want to make a lot more money?`

A question lead like the last one may get people's attention, but if the story doesn't support and answer the question logically, the audience will simply become annoyed.

Use question leads once every blue moon – perhaps less often. Most question leads exist because writers were too lazy to come up with anything else. Questions contain no information; you're supposed to be answering questions, not asking them; and question leads sound more like commercials than news. Save the questions for teases and promos (see Chapter 15).

● ● ● ● ●

Figuring Out the Lead

The kind of lead that works best depends on the story. Hard leads tend to work best with hard, breaking stories. Others are more variable. The best newscasts mix different leads. Too many hard leads can make a newscast sound choppy and staccato. Too many soft leads will slow the pacing down and diminish some urgency in stories that should have it. Vary your leads.

What's the Story About?

The most important parts of the writing process are the thinking and planning that take place before your fingers start dancing on the keyboard. Start by thinking, "What is the story about? Why is this story going on the air?" Ask yourself, "Who cares?" and "So what?" The answers to those questions should not only tell you how to write the story, but also answer the critical question of how to start it. The lead should usually be that brief headline you'd use if you were telling a friend about the information – although not quite as informally stated. When we tell a story to a friend, we frequently start with something like, "Did you hear about X?" Maybe X is Dan's accident or Lindsay's storm damage. Figuring out the lead is a similar concept.

Good

LEAD: Sunscreen ... the stuff that's supposed to protect you from cancer ... may actually cause the disease.

The lead tells us what the story is about . . . in a way that gets our attention.

Good

LEAD: The mayor went to jail today ... not as a prisoner but as an observer ... to see for himself how serious a problem jail overcrowding has become.

This last example looks like a long, complex sentence, but broken up the way it is – and read properly – it's really a series of short fragments following a short, catchy sentence.

Say Something Meaningful

The lead must contribute to the telling of the story, including why the audience should care. With rare exceptions, meetings aren't news. Don't start the lead with them.

AWFUL: At its monthly meeting tonight, the city council....

It might be news if the council *didn't* meet, but sheer existence is rarely news. The lead should say something the council (or school board, organization, etc.) did that made the meeting sufficiently significant to justify air time.

Better: Good news for city workers. The city council tonight approved a five percent pay raise....

In this case a soft main point lead tells us the essence of the story. The city council isn't even mentioned in the lead; it's in line two.

Weak: If you think you are paying a lot for utilities – News X has learned that some Ohio Valley residents may have to pay even more.

The first phrase of this lead (which did, indeed, go on the air) is completely meaningless and just delays telling people what the news is. First, everyone thinks they're paying a lot for utilities. Second, the story isn't about utilities in general, it's about water rates, so the copy is too vague. Third, even if you don't think you're paying a lot for utilities, your water rates may go up. Keep it tighter and more direct.

Better: News X has learned that some Ohio Valley residents may have to pay more money for water.

Keep It Simple

Although all broadcast stories must answer the basic questions of *who, what, where, when, why* and *how*, don't try to answer them all in the lead. You can't have more than one important thought or idea per sentence, and the lead should be one of the shortest and simplest sentences in the story. Remove noncritical information that can wait until later; otherwise, you have the all-too-common overloaded lead. Break up the information.

Overloaded: Five people are being treated for smoke inhalation today after a two-alarm fire blamed on faulty wiring at a small office building on the south side.
Better: Five people are being treated for smoke inhalation today after a two-alarm fire on the south side. Officials say faulty wiring at a small office building....

Notice that we've used a hard main point lead to get right into the story. We've told the audience *what* happened, and, critically, we've made clear in the lead that it happened *here*. Other aspects are dealt with only in skeletal form.

Overloaded: Thousands of Detroit students and school teachers are waiting in limbo on the outcome of negotiations between building engineers and school officials.

Remember: Keep leads short, and save the detail for later. Not only does the sentence above (which went on the air) try to give way too much information in the lead, it also understates numbers and improperly shifts the focus of the story from the larger group of students and teachers to the much smaller group of school officials and engineers.

Better: Tens of thousands of Detroit students and teachers are waiting to see whether there's school tomorrow.

Again, we've used a hard main point lead. The story is on the air because it's significant to a large number of people in the audience, so a straightforward – but tight – statement of fact is all you need.

Start With New News

The saying goes, "Three-quarters of news is new." Keep that in mind as you work on the lead. **No story is on the air because of background and history. It's on the air *now* because of something that just happened. That's what you need to tell the audience in the lead.** Background and history – if used at all – come later. There is a natural tendency to want to start with background and history. Resist that. That's not why the story is on the air *now*.

Old news: A district court judge found a local man guilty of murder two weeks ago. Today, John Smith was sentenced to ...
New news: A local man was sentenced to ... [then you can talk about the trial and the crime]
Old news: The Coast Guard rescued two men from the freezing waters off Point Falcon last night.
New news: Two men are hospitalized in good condition today – after the Coast Guard pulled the pair from the freezing waters off Point Falcon last night.

Don't reminisce. Don't start a story with a phrase like *You may remember,* followed inevitably by a recap of the earlier story. Some of the audience will remember, but most probably will not – either because it didn't make that much of an impression or because they didn't see it at all. Regardless, you still have to recap, so why start the story with a weak lead that simply asks the audience to try to remember old news? Instead, work harder to come up with a strong lead for today's story and then note that it's a follow-up with a phrase like *We first told you about.* If all else fails and you can't come up with a strong, fresh lead, then fall back on

So-so lead: A follow-up tonight to a story we first told you about ...

At least this lead says at the top that the audience is going to learn something new, and the audience likes follow-up stories.

Focus on People

Our audience is made up of people, and, generally, what they care most about are themselves and other people.

Weak: Business is booming for the people who market cell phones, but they're running into some problems.
    Smith's cellular business has doubled in the last year, and the company is looking for places to build new transmission towers.
    This is an example of what they need. It's 285-feet tall.
    Smith is trying to put up a 200-foot version on this land on the north side. Today they bulldozed the area to get ready to build. But there's a hitch. The people who live around here don't want a big tower in the backyard and are fighting it.

Notice that this story's lead (a real story that went on the air) focuses on people who sell cell phones and ends with homeowners concerned about property values. You can choose to focus on cell phones and the narrow issue of the few people who market them – as the writer of this copy did – or the wider issue of property values that could affect much of the audience.

Better: Some north side residents say a local business [or high technology or a cell phone company] is threatening to destroy the value of their property.

In addition to getting to the point of the bigger and more important story faster, this second version also properly shifts the focus of the story from technology to people – and allows us to start video of the story in line two with either people (first choice) or a new tower (second choice).

Focus on Local

Your audience cares most about news that's closest to them. Unless you're writing for a network, that means local – local people, local issues, local events. If you're writing a story with both local and national implications, generally, focus on local first.

No – NATIONAL
LEAD: Unemployment rose sharply, nationwide, last month.
YES – LOCAL
LEAD: Unemployment rose sharply here last month.

Both stories would likely contain the same information; the issue is what goes first. Understandably, the local audience cares a lot more about what's going on in their own community and with their friends and neighbors than about a faceless mass elsewhere. Start a mixed local/national story with the local part first.

Put Location in the Lead

Always make clear in the lead where a story is from.

No: Three people have died in a nightclub fire earlier
     this evening.
No: A gunman entered an elementary school and started
     firing today.

Where did those things happen? The audience is likely to assume that they're local stories. If that's the case, make that clear in the lead so there's no confusion.

YES: Three people have died in a downtown nightclub fire
     this evening.
     or
     Three people have died in a nightclub fire here this
     evening.
YES: Officials at Smith Elementary School in Cityville say
     it was a miracle no one was hurt. A gunman . . .

In all those examples the audience knows right away that they're hearing about a local story. If the stories are not local and you didn't make that clear in the lead, you're likely to have an audience that rightly feels angry and betrayed. If the story is not local, tell people that.

YES: Three people have died in a nightclub fire in
     Rochester tonight.

YES: A gunman entered an elementary school in San Diego
and started firing today.

In both of those cases you have no one in the audience panicking,
thinking that it might be a local story (assuming, of course, that the audience isn't in Rochester in the first example and San Diego in the second).

Keep in mind that there are lots of ways to include that mandatory locator in the lead. For stories in your area, the choices include not only the name of the city, community or neighborhood, but also words like *downtown, here, locally, nearby* and so on.

Be Direct and to the Point

Don't back into a story. Give the audience a reason to care right from the beginning.

BACKING IN: An interesting thing happened at the city
council meeting last night.

The only thing being said in the line above is that the audience will learn something meaningful in the future. We can't afford to waste that much time or be that boring.

BETTER: The city council last night voted to close all
city recreation areas.
or
All city recreation areas will be closing down.
The city council last night voted ...
or
The city plans to close all its recreation
areas ...

Envision a busy audience taking time out of their day to find out what happened. Just tell them.

BACKING IN: A homemade single engine plane crashed nose-first
into some Delaware farmland today. It exploded into
flames, and the pilot, James Smith of Columbus, and
his passenger, Tom Jones of Powell, were killed.

Although there are advantages to telling a story in chronological order, this story (real except for the names) takes the idea too far. Buried at the end of the long, second sentence is the real news: Two people died. The plane crash is *how* that news happened, but the real news involves the two local men who died, not the crash itself.

Better: Two local men are dead after the homemade plane
they were flying crashed into a Delaware farm and
exploded.

Notice, again, the use of a hard main point lead to get across the main point of the story. It tells the audience what happened and how. Again, the lead makes clear that the story is local. It also doesn't use the names of the men in the lead but sets up the use of the names in line two. If one or both of the men were well known in the area, the lead might include that information.

Save the Name for Later

Unless the person the story is about is extremely well known (such as the president, the local mayor, or a popular celebrity) or you're using a delayed lead, don't include the name in the lead. The answer to the question *who?* must be in the lead, but that doesn't necessarily mean that we need the name. Generally, it's better to use a brief description (e.g., *a union leader, two office workers, a local woman*) in the lead to set up the actual name(s) for early in line two:

Set up

names for

line two: Police have arrested an unemployed truck driver
for yesterday's robbery at the Jones Trucking
Company. Police say John Smith went in to see
his former employer armed with ...

Set up

names for

line two: A man charged with robbing, raping and then
murdering a local teenager went on trial today.
David Jones sat silently ...

In both the previous examples the lead described the subject of the story, but the actual name – the detail of the name – didn't appear until line two. This helps keep the lead shorter and tighter.

Save the Day and Date for Later

Don't start the lead with the day or date unless it's the critical part of the story. Always have the date somewhere in the story, usually in the lead sentence, but remember that almost all stories we report happened *today* – that's not news.

No: This morning, dozens of police officers called in
    sick in what's believed to be the latest attack of
    the "blue flu."
Yes: Dozens of police officers called in sick this
    morning, in what's believed to be the latest attack
    of the "blue flu."

Sometimes, especially in the morning news, at noon and in the late news, we want to emphasize the time of day to demonstrate how timely the story is. "This morning" might work at the top of a story or two in the morning or noon news, and "tonight" might work at the beginning of a story on the late news. But if story after story starts that way, then the impact is lost.

Update Leads

Update leads whenever possible. Frequently, the future effect of an earlier action makes a lead sound more timely and interesting.

OLDER: The city council last night voted to increase
    property tax rates.
UPDATED: Property tax bills will be going up.
OLDER: The fire that began at an industrial complex
    yesterday continues to burn.
UPDATED: The smell and smoke from tons of burning plastic
    continue to blanket the south side.

Responsibility

If you're unsure whether to use a clever lead, a delayed lead or anything other than a main point lead – don't. A lot of tasteless journalism has been on the air because someone picked the wrong time to try to be clever or cute. You'll never go wrong with a well-written main point lead. You may have missed an opportunity to do something a little different, but you won't embarrass yourself or your news organization. If the lead doesn't demand something a little different, proceed with caution.

NEVER: The two sides are practically killing each other
    over whether a woman has a right to an abortion.

You can get the attention of the audience by either shouting or whispering. Shouting is easier, but it isn't nearly as riveting.

Above All . . . Get It Right

How you express information makes little difference if you screw up the facts.

WRONG: `A yearly survey on global terrorism ... shows`
`Iraq is a main sponsor.`

That sentence, which went on the air on a top 50 market TV station is tight and straightforward. The only real problem is that it's wrong. The survey said that *Iran* is the main sponsor – not *Iraq*. There's just no excuse.

●●●●●

Types of Endings

Not only do broadcast stories need to start strong, they need to end that way, too. We bring them full circle; we wrap them up. **We are, in the end, telling the audience stories, and a good story always has a beginning, a middle and an end.** Think about how you're going to wrap up the story at the same time you think about how you're going to start. In television, where stand-up bridges in recorded packages are recorded at the scene, reporters really need to figure out, at least generally, how they're going to structure the whole story even as they're covering it.

Future Ramification Close

Probably the best ending – and one of the most common – is the *future ramification* close:

> `Smith says they'll appeal the decision to the`
> `state Supreme Court.`

This kind of ending tells us where the story goes from here. If the facts you're dealing with include that kind of information, this will almost always be the strongest ending.

> `Jones says no matter what the council decides,`
> `he'll never give in.`

Part of what makes the future ramification close so strong is that there's almost never any doubt that you've wrapped up and ended the story.

Summary Point Close

The *summary point* ending restates, in different words, what the story is all about:

> `What it all means is that food prices are likely`
> `to stay just about where they are.`

This kind of ending is particularly useful in a complicated story in which at least some of the audience might have gotten lost in the data. Frequently, a story started with a soft main point lead because of its complexity will work best with a summary point ending. Just make sure, in restating the sense of the lead, that you change the exact wording.

```
    All the legislators we talked to said schools
    should expect lean times and layoffs for the
    foreseeable future.
```

Information Close

Some endings close the story with a new, related bit of *information*:

```
    The airline carries more than a million passengers
    a month.
```

The information ending tends to add some general perspective to the story. But be careful in an information ending that you don't raise new questions instead of closing the story.

```
PROBLEM: This is another in a series of problems the
    airline has had all year.
```

Ending a story like that will drive the audience crazy, wondering about what those other problems have been. Bring the story to a clear conclusion; don't raise new issues.

Opposition Point of View Close

The *opposition point of view* may end a story:

```
    But opponents argue that the new law won't work
    and will only make things worse.
```

Be careful with this kind of close, too. Because you're leaving the audience with a different point of view than you focused on for the story, you may elevate a minor point to undeserved prominence. If the story is long enough, it's generally better to raise opposition points inside the story. Above all, be fair, and don't use this kind of ending as a means of furthering your own point of view.

Punch Line

The last type of ending is the *punch line*. A story that uses a *delayed* or *suspense* lead always ends with a punch line. The punch line – the last line – is typically the unexpected twist in the story that puts every-thing into perspective. See the delayed lead and ending earlier in this chapter on pages 129–130.

●●●●●

Summary

The broadcast lead is like the newspaper headline; above all else, it must capture the attention and interest of the audience. There are four main point leads: hard, soft, throwaway and umbrella. The two other types of leads are delayed or suspense and the question lead. To figure out the lead, figure out what the story is really about, what's new and focus on people and local. Put some form of locator in the lead. Don't use names of people who aren't well known in the lead. Because all broadcast stories must come to a close, the ending is the second most important line in the story. The five types of endings are future ramification close, summary point, information, opposition point of view and the punch line.

●●●●●

Key Words and Phrases

main point lead . . . hard lead . . . soft lead . . . throwaway . . . umbrella lead . . . delayed or suspense lead . . . question lead . . . start with new news . . . focus on people . . . focus on local . . . put location in the lead . . . save the name for later . . . future ramification close . . . summary point . . . information close . . . opposition point of view close . . . punch line.

●●●●●

Exercises

A. The following lead sentences have errors and/or words, phrases or means of expression not acceptable for broadcast writing. Make them into acceptable broadcast leads. Again, for the sake of this assignment, you're in Springfield.

1. Janice R. Hennessy, Associate State Commissioner of the State Liquor Commission, has called for a new crackdown on underage drinking.

2. The mayor said that, "I think it is counterproductive to have the state take away funding from urban renewal programs here when it is clear that the benefits of the program, in producing new tax revenue from buildings formerly costing the city money in upkeep and now generating dollars by being in private hands, clearly outweighs the cost."

3. An extremely serious car accident last night resulted in 6 injured and 2 dead.

4. A low interest loan by Samuel J. Clarke to a member of the County Commission that for the past 3 weeks has been considering his request for a zoning variance appeared today – when information about the loan was first released – to raise questions of propriety and ethical behavior and jeopardize his already-questionable zoning variance request in more uncertainty.

5. The Fire Department's arson squad head says the severity of last Tuesday's fire at the Smith General Store, Incorporated, in which 3 customers were hurt and 1 fireman died, has been traced to a broken sprinkler system in the building.

6. Last evening, not long following the unsuccessful negotiations with the city council broke off, local city workers voted then to begin striking against the city this morning.

7. FBI agent Mary Smith said this morning that the Union Bank and Trust, Incorporated, of 200 West University Ave., lost $2500 to burglars some time around 4 a.m. in the morning.

8. In it's regular weekly session this afternoon, the Long Beach City Council discussed in a heated manner what would become of the Westminster Nursing Home project.

9. There was a lot of activity last night if you were a Springfield fireman. A house fire on the east side left two families homeless tonight in a fire that took firemen 2 hours to control, while near downtown, three families lost their homes and a fireman collapsed and was taken to the hospital.

10. Three innocent bystanders and a member of the U.S. House of Representatives were shot by an unidentified man with a gun at a campaign rally for the Congress person this morning in front of the entrance to the Colorado State Park. The bystanders all died, and the Congress member, Eve Gallagher, is in critical condition. Police say they have the shooter in custody.

11

●●●●●

Stories

No one said writing is easy. At least, no one should have said that. "People think, 'You're good at this, it must be fun to you,'" says CBS' Steve Hartman. "It's not . . . it's work." **Hartman knows the secret to writing success that all good reporters learn sooner or later: It's not about the writing . . . it's all about the rewriting.**

The first time I write something down, it's never any good, says Hartman. "Sometimes it might take you five times, and sometimes it might take you 25 times. Don't ever think you're going to be a great writer on the first pass. That's not how it works."

There has always been a debate about whether good writers are born that way or whether they've learned to be good writers. Is it an art or a craft? Hartman comes down firmly on one side of that. "It's not a gift you're born with," says Hartman. "It's a craft, and like any craft you get better at it the more you practice it. If you do it repeatedly, as I have, you're going to find that eventually you get better and better." There's no question that he's right, but I've seen some of Steve's earliest work . . . and some people clearly have an easier path to climb.

●●●●●

Stories Are Like Music

Charles Osgood, former host of CBS *Sunday Morning*, says we should think of broadcast writing in terms of music. "Good writing has to be musical, with a sense of balance, a sense of beauty, melodic, a sense of phrasing." As with music, sentences should be constructed in a "graceful way." As with music, "the beginning should sound like the beginning and the end should sound like the end."

The point is, we call them stories, and we do best telling them that way. It doesn't apply to every item in the news. There are timely events that simply require a straightforward recitation of significant information – well written and constructed. But they're still stories.

There is no one right way to tell a story. Regrettably, there are considerably more wrong ways than right ones, and **most stories that don't work**

start out badly and never recover. That's why the lead is so important. The keys are thinking and planning. If you figure out both how you're going to start the story and how you're going to end it *before you start writing,* you're most of the way home.

Stories also frequently fail because they're illogical in telling the information. Call the concept *story logic.* The phrase is easier said than explained, but it starts with understanding the story itself.

●●●●●

Plan and Focus

Why Run the Story?

Why should this story go on the air? If you can't answer that question, the rest is probably hopeless. There are lots of plausible answers.

The story is of sufficient importance to the audience that it needs to be in the news:

- A chemical spill that endangers people
- A major plant closing
- The results of the day's election

The story is useful to the audience for day-to-day living or long-range survival, sometimes called "news you can use":

- Consumer stories
- How to make your way through new highway construction
- Surviving unemployment

The story is particularly interesting or particularly unusual:

- Senior citizen beauty contestants
- The wranglings over whether someone can keep his pet alligator at home
- The dramatic rescue of a young child (not in your area)

The story involves important and/or well-known people:

- Almost anything the president does
- A big-name celebrity visits your town
- The high-profile leaders and leading characters every community has

Other reasons are possible. Other factors such as timeliness or proximity certainly enter into the decision. Think about why the story should be on the air, and think about what's *new* in the story because **the lead must address the issue not only of why the audience should care but also why they should care *now*.** There's an old saying that "three-quarters of news is new." Stories are not on the air *now* because of something that happened in the past.

Former network correspondent Deborah Potter says there are two steps to follow *before* you actually start writing. The first is to answer the question, "What is this story really about?"

It's not enough to say what happened, she says. It's what happened, and what are we supposed to make of that? What does that mean? Come up with a focus statement that's short and tight. Potter says that if describing that focus takes more than one sentence, you're not yet ready to write the story.

Former NBC correspondent Don Larson says you should be able to determine the focus because, "It will make you smile, it will make you shake your head in disgust, it will make you sense a shared truth. It might make you think of your own neighborhood, your own childhood, your own family."

In a story about a kid in juvenile detention, Potter says the focus statement might be, "Ernie survives jail." Or maybe, "Jail breaks Ernie." Once you figure out the narrow focus, get rid of everything that doesn't fit. That includes bites you collected along the way. Even good bites, if they're not right on point, have to go. Remember Larson's phrase, "kill the babies." (see Chapter 5). Finding that story focus not only tells you what to concentrate on . . . but also what to leave out. And in a reporter's busy schedule, the faster you can find the focus, the more time you'll have to work on crafting the story and taking care of the social media you're also expected to do.

Do You Understand?

Do you understand all the aspects of the story? Nothing *you* don't understand will ever get clearer on its way to the audience. **If you don't fully understand what's happening in the story and the answers to all of those basic *who, what, when, where, why* and *how* questions, then you're not ready to start writing anything.** If there's something in the story you don't understand, you have three choices: get the issue(s) cleared up, drop the part you don't fully understand or drop the story. If you don't understand something, it's inconceivable that the audience will.

The following story, word for word, went on the air on a top station in a top 15 market:

```
Incinerators in the metro area may get their plugs
pulled. The Air Control Commission will review a
```

letter today that would shut down incinerators that
pose potential health and environmental hazards at
hundreds of schools.

According to Department of Natural Resources
records, there are 733 burners on school and college
campuses in the area. Some may not be running. If
the letter is approved, it will be sent to every
school district. Today's meeting could be the last
for the commission; it will close down in January as
part of the governor's reorganization of the
department.

Even leaving aside some serious writing problems, it's clear that the writer had no idea what this story was really all about. Neither did any of the people who heard it. In most of this book, I provide corrected versions of bad stories and bad phrasing. I can't do it here, however, because I'm really not sure what the story was supposed to be about either.

And this story must have left its Midwestern (but nowhere near Chicago) audience a bit puzzled:

Fog blanketed Chicago's O'Hare Airport today.
Ninety-eight percent of the flights out of the windy
city were canceled before noon.

That pea soup covered all of northern Illinois.
The F-A-A is blaming the fog for the cancellation of
all landings at O'Hare today as well.

That story is at least understandable; it just suffers from inadequate thought in the telling. Why split up the takeoffs and landings? And because this story was broadcast outside of Chicago, the far greater *local* effect would be on flights going in to Chicago from the city where this broadcast took place. That's the primary local story, along with the secondary effect of planes from Chicago that don't get to land in your local city. Either start with the local story:

BETTER: Make sure you call ahead before heading out to
the airport today. We're feeling the effects of
a fog-inflicted shut-down at Chicago's O'Hare
Airport ...

or at least combine the Chicago information:

BETTER: Dense fog has virtually shut down Chicago's busy
O'Hare Airport ...

The problem in the original O'Hare story is nothing compared to the following story, which went on the air, exactly as written, on a top 50 market TV station:

```
    Thinking of investing in the stock market? Well,
now's the time to do it. The consumer price index
is down ... the inflation rate is, too ... and that
makes the market ripe for the picking. And you don't
need a lot of money. Analysts say if you do it
right, you can be successful with as little as six
thousand dollars. The trick is to diversify. Put
a little in a short-term option. And, above all,
be honest with yourself about how much you want
to risk ...
```

Having a news anchor offer advice like this is frightening. Among other things, the market is never *ripe for the picking;* most people think of six thousand dollars as a lot of money; and short-term options are among the riskiest investments someone can make. This story went well beyond both the reporter's area of knowledge and the proper role of a journalist. Don't write what you don't know.

What's the Story About?

Think what the story is about. Remember, we're still talking about all the things you need to do in your head – or on paper if it's complicated – *before* you actually start writing. While you're writing is no time to be thinking about where you're headed; you need to know that beforehand.

That's a lot harder than it sounds. It's easy to get overwhelmed by facts and try to deal with information in the sequence in which you collected it rather than digesting the whole thing and figuring out the story. Unfortunately, there are no shortcuts. Collect all the information, figure out what the story is really all about and then figure out how you're going to tell the story – the whole story.

THE FACTS: A young girl gets out of a defective child restraint, wanders from her yard and falls into a river. She is pulled out by her father, revived by mouth-to-mouth resuscitation by a neighbor and taken to a local hospital by paramedics.

The facts are simple enough, but should this be a story of safety, survival or rescue? Since you can't say everything in a lead, what's most likely to capture the attention of the audience? The issue isn't as simple as choosing the right path versus the wrong one. It's picking a single, simple story to concentrate on.

THE FACTS: A small fire breaks out in a service room, filling apartment building corridors with smoke, upsetting residents of the senior citizens' complex, who must leave their apartments and wait outside in the cold while the fire department deals with what turns out to be a minor fire resulting in little damage.

Is there a story here at all? If so, what part of it would get anyone's interest and attention in a lead?

What's the Lead?

Find the lead. A story that's broadcast because of its importance, news-worthiness or usefulness will most often demand a fairly straightforward lead. If you've selected the story properly, that kind of information should capture the attention of the audience. A story that's broadcast because of whom it's about should obviously include the *who* in the lead. A story that's broadcast because it's unusual or interesting frequently allows more leeway in how you get into it. But don't confuse leeway with sloppiness. This kind of story is harder to write because the facts of the story won't write themselves. You've got to sell them. See Chapter 10 for more on leads and endings.

In What Order Do You Tell the Story?

In broadcast, we tell stories to one another in a manner in which we think the other person will best understand. If we do that face to face, we have the advantage of visual and perhaps oral feedback. We can usually tell whether the person we're speaking to understands and cares, and we can adjust accordingly. We don't have that feedback in this business. We have to think about the story from the standpoint of the audience the whole time we work on it. Generally, after an appropriate lead, telling stories chronologically will be easiest on the audience. That means that we first get the audience's attention with a strong lead. We then tell the story from beginning to end, in the same sequence in which it actually happened.

GOOD

LEAD AND

BEGINNING: Two men teamed up for a dramatic rescue of a
   young girl today. Six-year-old Sally Jones ...
   [starting at the beginning and going to the end of that sequence of information from earlier in this chapter]

GOOD

LEAD AND

BEGINNING: Clouds of smoke drove elderly residents from
   their apartments today. It all started ... [again, from
   the beginning to the end of the information given earlier in
   this chapter]

GOOD

LEAD AND

CHRONOLOGICAL

STORY

DEVELOPMENT: Police have arrested an unemployed truck
driver for yesterday's robbery at the Jones Trucking
Company. Police say John Smith went in to see his
former employer armed with a sawed-off shotgun.

An employee at the firm said the robber demanded
all the money kept in the company safe – and that
he threatened to shoot anyone who moved. Police say
Smith made off with two-thousand dollars, which
police say they recovered in Smith's south side
apartment this afternoon.

Note that after the lead – which is a simple statement of what took
place – all the information is relayed in the same sequence as it happened.
Note also all the attributions in the story. It feels a little cumbersome, but
each one is necessary to avoid *your* accusing Smith of a crime. (See "Attribution" section in Chapter 8 and "Crime and Legal" section in Chapter 21.)

The robbery story above is a clean, clear, straightforward development that will be easy for the audience to follow and understand.

This story is a little old, but it's a good example of a story that takes an
unfortunate turn out of sequence:

ILLOGICAL

SEQUENCE: Meantime, Democratic presidential hopeful Hillary
Clinton is planning a stop in Nevada on her way to
the Democratic National Convention next week.

The convention begins a week from Monday in
Philadelphia, and Clinton's schedule calls for her
to be in Las Vegas this coming Tuesday.

Campaign officials say she'll talk about the need
for investing in our infrastructure at the
international convention of the American Federation
of State, County and Municipal Employees.

The lead is acceptable, but, after that, the writer lost track of what
story she was telling. The story is supposed to be about Clinton's trip
to Nevada, but after the lead, the writer tells us about the convention
instead. That's better handled in an information ending.

BETTER

SEQUENCE: Meantime, Democratic presidential hopeful
Hillary Clinton plans a stop in Nevada on her way
to the Democratic convention next week.

Clinton is scheduled to appear in las Vegas on Tuesday ... where she's expected to talk to a meeting of municipal workers about investing in the country's ailing infrastructure.

The Democratic convention begins a week from Monday in Philadelphia.

●●●●●

Story Logic

Handling the Basics

As reporters, every statement we hear leads us, or should lead us, to the next logical question. We want answers to all of the *who, what, when, where, why* and *how* questions, but we don't ask those questions at random. Each one has its place. The same is true when we're writing the story for the audience. As we go along, logical questions come up in the minds of the audience. If each succeeding line in our story answers the next logical question in the minds of the audience, we have achieved story logic.

Florida officials sprayed an 80-acre marijuana field with the controversial weed killer, paraquat. It's the first time the chemical has been used on pot in the U-S. Opponents fear some of the treated drug might get on the market where its use might damage smokers' lungs. But officials say the spraying saves time and labor getting rid of the stuff – and that the field will remain under 24-hour guard until all the plants are destroyed.

The story starts with a hard lead: what happened. The second sentence really functions as part of the lead, splitting up material that would overload the sentence if written all together. The lead says the weed killer is controversial. Sentence three must explain why. Having said that officials did this controversial thing and what the potential hazards are, the next logical question is why, then, did officials spray? The last sentence answers that and brings the story to a logical information/future ramification close.

The story is tight and straightforward, but it's certainly not the only way to deal with the information. Alternative leads include:

Florida officials are trying a new way to get rid of marijuana.
or
A marijuana field in Florida is under 24-hour guard right now.

The first alternative will require that line two explains what the new method is. The second example will require that line two explains why. The point is that every line you use in a story takes the listener or viewer deeper into the information, and each line should lead logically into the next. Where that logical flow doesn't exist, there's a problem.

```
Students who skip school may really get hit where
it hurts.
The Ohio Senate passed a bill that would take away
the drivers' licenses of kids under age 18 who drop
out of school.
Officials in West Virginia say a similar law there
has cut the drop-out rate by one-third.
The Ohio version is expected to be approved by the
House and signed by the governor some time next
week.
```

This clean, clear story starts with a soft main point lead. Line two gives the specifics of what's taking place, followed by what could be an answer to the question, *Can this work?* The story ends logically with a future ramification close. Nice, straightforward story.

Will It Stand on Its Own?

Every story should be able to stand on its own, as if it were the first time the audience ever heard about the subject. Although we should not underestimate the audience's intelligence, we cannot overestimate the audience's knowledge and background on a story. News people talk to themselves too much; most people don't follow the news with the kind of interest and intensity that reporters do. Many people receive only bits and pieces of news for days at a time – or longer. People frequently miss the news completely.

With a few exceptions for major, ongoing stories, think of each story as taking the audience from a clean slate to some measure of understanding. The lead line takes the audience from point A (nothing) to point B (some new information). Point B should include, depending on the kind of story it is, something of the significance of the item – why it's on the air and why it's on the air now. Having written the lead, stop. Think about where you've taken the audience. The choices for line two are limited. You've raised certain questions in the lead; you've given partial explanations in the lead. What's the next logical question? The answer to that is line two. Now that you've taken the audience from A to B to C, stop again. Where will you go next? Use this process all the way through the story. If your *answers* to logical questions come when the *questions* do, you've achieved story logic.

WHAT

HAPPENED: The city council today voted to raise property taxes by 20 percent.

WHAT IT

MEANS: If signed into law, the cost to a homeowner with an average 150-thousand dollar house – an extra 220 dollars a year.

WHY—

AND ONE

SIDE: Council chairman John Smith proposed the tax hike – saying it was the only way the council could balance the city budget.

WHY NOT—

THE OTHER

SIDE: Council member Jennifer Jones was the lone dissenter in the five to one vote. She warned that the tax hike will drive businesses out of the city.

WHAT WILL

HAPPEN

NEXT: The mayor did not attend the meeting – and has not said whether she'll sign the measure.

Answer the Logical Questions

Never leave logical questions unanswered. Some people will always want more detailed information about a given story. That's not the issue. The issue involves logical questions that a good portion of your audience is likely to wonder about. It might be the possible effects of something; what someone thought about the event; why the person did that anyway. Sometimes you don't know the answer to a logical question, as in the example on the mayor's position. Then say so. But don't ignore it. If it's not in the story, there's no telling what the audience will assume, but there's no guarantee they'll assume you would have told them if you knew. In the last story, leaving out the last line would leave a logical question unanswered. Even though the mayor's position is unknown, the last line of the script means the audience knows that it has all the relevant answers the reporter has. Remember that the audience looks to you for answers. That's your job.

After inaccuracies and confusion, leaving logical questions unanswered is the next greatest sin in news writing. Look at the problem created in the following story, which ran on a large-market television station:

> Last night, police found themselves in a tense
> situation after busting a crack house.
> Narcotics and SWAT officers charged into the house
> on Main Street and came face to face with four kids
> armed with semi-automatic weapons.
> Detectives found about six-thousand dollars worth
> of crack inside the place, and they also confiscated
> a tech-nine and a 45-caliber semi-automatic. The
> teenagers ... 16 and 17 years old ... are charged
> with drug trafficking.

But what happened to the *tense situation*? What happened when the officers found themselves *face to face with four kids armed with semi-automatic weapons?* That's likely to be exactly what the audience was thinking about as the rest of the story slid by unnoticed. The writer needed just one more line to take the audience, logically, from the *tense situation* to the aftermath.

●●●●●
Story Structure

Make the Writing Structure Interesting

Vary sentence length and structure. There are only so many words that can be read well together, but if sentence after sentence is structured the same way grammatically and close to the same length, the story will sound choppy and boring. Be careful with sentence structure variations, though. You still need to keep sentences short and simple, or they'll be confusing. Go back to the city council story on page 152. It's a short, simple story, but notice the variation in sentence length and structure even in a quick story like that.

> There was another chemical leak in Delaware
> County. It was the second chemical leak this week.
> A couple of officers with the state highway patrol
> noticed some sort of fluid leaking from this tanker
> this morning.
> They stopped the driver. The fluid turned out to
> be hydrochloric acid. The driver himself fixed the
> leak. The officers charged him with carrying an
> insecure load.

The story is reasonably clear and told in the right sequence, but it's boring and badly in need of some writing variation and connector words to smooth it out:

```
    Another chemical leak in Delaware County - the
second one this week.
    Highway patrol officers pulled over this tanker
this morning when they spotted some fluid leaking.
    The fluid turned out to be hydrochloric acid - a
dangerous chemical, although it caused no problem
here. The driver himself fixed the leak, but the
officers charged him with carrying an insecure load.
```

What made the second version better? The second version took the first two identically structured, passive sentences and combined them into two short sentence fragments without the weak *to be* verbs. The resulting lead is one-third shorter than the original two sentences – and a lot punchier. The next sentence of the new version again combines two sentences of the original version while tightening up the writing. In fact, the new version trims the wording of the middle of the story by almost half. The new version and the original start the next sentence exactly the same, but the new version adds new information – that hydrochloric acid is a dangerous chemical – and answers a logical question that was unanswered in the original: Did the chemical cause a problem? The revised version then combined the last two sentences of the original using a conjunction (*but*) to smooth out the copy. The second version of the story actually contains more information, reads better and is still a little shorter than the original. In this business, shorter is almost always better.

● ● ● ● ●

Transitions

Use transitions to smooth out the writing.

Transitions Within Stories

Within stories, transitions help the audience understand the story better by drawing connections and improving the flow. Transitions express:

cause and effect: *because, so, that's why*

comparison and contrast: *but, on the other hand, however*

groupings: *and, with, along with, also, in addition*

size or quality: *more or most important, even (bigger or older or whatever)*

spatial relationships: *nearby, just down the street, on the other side of town*

time relationships: *in the meantime, at the same time, just as, meanwhile, now, then, so far, when, while, yet, soon*

Look at how the use of transitions helps to smooth out this copy and draw connections and contrasts:

```
    Three years' worth of city reports have called
for programs aimed at going beyond homeless
shelters ... and helping people restart their lives.
But three years later, almost none of it exists.
According to city officials, there hasn't been a new
low-cost or subsidized housing project built here in
more than five years. And none is planned.
```

The story uses three conjunctions. The first one serves more to provide a breathing point than anything else. The next two – one *but* and one *and* – serve to smooth out the copy by drawing a contrast between two facts in one case and adding additional information in the other.

Make sure you use conjunctions correctly. The following examples, which were actually used on the air, were more likely to puzzle the audience.

PROBLEM: THE project will be built over the next
10 years, and won't start for several months.

Given that these two bits of information are really *contrasting*, the conjunction should be *but*, not *and*.

BETTER: The project will be built over the next
10 years ... but won't start for several months.

The correct conjunction helps the audience understand what's taking place.

PROBLEM: They arrested one man, but another man in the
house tried to run out the back door but was met by
SWAT officers.

The second *but* does its job well – contrasting situations. But because the second man was arrested, too, the first *but* really doesn't make any sense. In fact, the audience is likely to be confused because the word sets up the idea that the guy got away. Better to drop that first *but* completely:

BETTER: They arrested one man. Another man in the house
tried to run out the back door but was met by SWAT
officers.

This version will be far easier for the audience to follow.

PROBLEM: No charges have been filed against the 16, but
officials say most were in their late teens and early
twenties.

Don't force transitions and connections where they don't exist. Since there's really no known relationship between the filing of charges and the ages of those arrested, the *but* connecting the otherwise unrelated parts of the story simply confuses the audience. Drop it.

BETTER: No charges have been filed against the 16.
Officials say most are in their late teens and early
twenties.

In this case, the copy is clearer with no transition.

PROBLEM: Applications from foreign students for the
upcoming semester are down 30 percent over last year.

The idea that something can be "down . . . over" just doesn't sound right. Better to tighten the copy and change the preposition.

BETTER: Applications from foreign students are down 30
percent from last year.

Conjunctions help the flow of the story, but only if they're used correctly. Make sure you've used the right transition word to describe what's happening in the story.

Transitions Between Stories

In broadcast, we don't run stories individually in a vacuum; we run them within newscasts. Because of that, we also use transitions *between stories* in an attempt to have one story flow into the next.

Too often, we forget that a newscast is really only organized chaos. The stories we call news are related only by the decision that a given collection of material should go on the air, rather than the many other choices available. Taken from that standpoint, anything we can do to make the journey through the newscast a little easier can only help the listener and viewer.

Transition lines can help light the path of the newscast and make it easier to follow. Only two things legitimately connect news stories. One is *geography*; the other is *subject*. Stories that are connected by either of these common bonds should flow one from the other more logically than stories that have nothing in common. But don't force the transition as this large-market writer did in the last line of a story on a single-engine plane crash:

PROBLEM: Tonight, the F-A-A is trying to figure out why
the plane crashed and killed the two men.
    Thousands of people on the East Coast are <u>not</u>
worried about air safety in lieu of the Smith
Airlines strike. . .

In other words, there is no connection between the content of the two stories. A forced and inappropriate transition just sounds stupid – like this bizarre "transition" in the last line of a story on wrong information from IRS personnel:

PROBLEM: Anyway, they say they won't hold you to blame for
wrong answers if you can document the name of the
person you talked to, the question you asked, and
the date of the call.
    You won't find much wrong with Ohio's wineries.
It's becoming very big business ...

Charitably, these are forced transitions. The first example is really irresponsible. The Smith Airlines story (I'm protecting the name of the innocent airline) that night had absolutely nothing to do with safety. The writer raised the issue in the lead line, in the negative, only for the purpose of contriving a transition. But given that both stories related to aviation, the writer really didn't need a transition at all. The second example is just plain dumb.

Related stories should be easy to handle, like the opening line of a story about people who work on Labor Day, after a story about the holiday itself:

But Labor Day was just that for many people ...

A line like that means a virtually seamless transition from one story to the next.

Even a single word and short phrase can help the flow:

Also in federal court today, a Newark doctor
pleaded guilty ...

Individual reporters and anchors may handle each story beautifully, but if someone isn't looking at how they fit together, the newscast just won't flow. That's the job of the producer.

Transitions can smooth the flow from one story to the next, but those transitions have to be logical. If they're not, just move on to the next item in the newscast. See more on this and newscasts in general in Chapter 15.

● ● ● ● ●

Before You're Done

Does the Story Support the Lead?

The lead of a story is like a headline: It catches our interest and attention. If the rest of the story doesn't support it, you've butchered either the lead or the rest of the story.

Will the Audience Understand?

Remember that as reporter, writer or producer, you're close to the story. Even if you do understand the information, there's no guarantee the audience will. Too often, what we know about a story never fully makes it onto the written page. Especially in complicated stories, as we read over what we've written, we may internally supplement what we actually write with information that only we know. Unfortunately, the audience can't do that. Always go back and make sure you've answered all the logical questions and that what you know and mean to say really got down on paper in the manner you intended.

```
Democrat officials say the very survival of the
party in Ohio may hinge on the outcome of the
elections. They say if Republicans are allowed to
dominate the state appointment board for the third
straight time, the Democrats could be pushed out of
business in Ohio.
```

Other than party officials or students of government, it's inconceivable that members of the audience could have understood what this story was about – although it did go on the air. This is a much-too-shortened story on the complicated controversy of reapportionment. The writer may well have understood the issue, filling in the many gaps in written information with the background and knowledge *within* the reporter. The audience would have had no idea what this story meant.

Another common, related problem is providing accurate information that has no discernible meaning. Take this real story as an example:

```
The river is at its highest level since 1982.
The Louvre is relocating priceless pieces of
art ... in rooms ... that could be flooded out.
```

```
The Seine burst its banks yesterday and is
expected to crest at 21 feet. The flooding in Europe
has claimed 12 lives.
    It could take two weeks before the river returns
to normal levels.
```

This is a pretty typical example of your basic flood story, but – as with many if not most flood stories – it doesn't provide useful information. A river cresting at 21 feet means that that's the highest level of water (or wave in the case of an ocean), but that measure doesn't tell you anything about flooding unless you add that information. Without knowing the flood stage – where the water runs over what is normally dry land – the crest number has no meaning. What would be more useful in this story is to know either how much higher the water is than the flood stage or how much area has been (or will be) flooded.

By the way, officials are certainly *not* "relocating priceless pieces of art . . . in rooms . . . that could be flooded out." They're undoubtedly relocating the art *from* rooms that could be flooded. Watch your prepositions, too.

Contrast that with this nicely handled version of a fairly complex story:

```
There is a glimmer of hope tonight that Smith
Airlines and its disgruntled mechanics may be able
to avert a strike, set for midnight tomorrow.
    The airline says there's a new proposal on the
table ... the two sides are talking ... but they
have a long way to go.
    Smith is demanding 150 million dollars in wage
concessions from the mechanics. The mechanics say
the best they can do is accept a wage freeze for
one year.
    Smith claims it's losing a million dollars a day
and can't afford that.
    Pilots and attendants today said they will honor
any picket lines ... and won't fly in planes which
haven't been serviced.
    Other airlines, though, say they're not sure
they'll honor Smith tickets if there is a strike.
    We'll keep you posted.
```

Note the use of short, clear sentences and the back-and-forth approach to the issues: one side and then the other side. Nice, clear summary of a complicated story without any sense of whether the writer is more sympathetic toward one side or the other.

Use Humor Sparingly

If you're really good at humor, you should probably be a comedian. Few news people are nearly as funny as they seem to think they are. Use humor sparingly and only when it's clearly appropriate.

PROBLEM: Those of you who work at Smith Instrumentation and its neighbor, Jones Company, might want to call the boss before work tomorrow. Both places are pretty well gutted tonight....

PROBLEM: A knock-down, drag-out fight between two women ended in gunfire tonight on the west side. Witnesses tell us a woman named "Vicki" lost the fight in the first round at the Green Apartment complex. And then won the second round ... not with her fists ... but with a gun.

Other than changing the names, both of these stories went on the air as written. They shouldn't have. People who have been thrown out of work and those who have lost everything they've worked for in the first story will find little that is cute or amusing about the situation. And getting shot is seldom funny. Misplaced humor is offensive.

Read the Story Aloud

Always read your story aloud before it goes on the air. That's the only way to tell:

■ Real length. Numbers, especially, can easily make a computer's automatic timing highly inaccurate. To most computers, it takes the same amount of time to read *the* as it does to read *999*.

■ Whether the lines can really be read comfortably and with proper emphasis.

■ Whether you have words that are difficult to pronounce without sounding awkward (try *desks* out loud for example).

■ Whether in writing a bit too quickly you have omitted words that you meant to write.

■ Whether you've misspelled any words – assuming your errors were oversights rather than ignorance. Misspellings commonly turn into mispronunciations and muddled reading.

● ● ● ● ●

Summary

Most stories that don't work either start out with bad leads and never recover or try to convey information in an illogical sequence. To figure out how to tell a story, think about why you're running the story, what's new that the audience didn't know about, what's the lead, and what's a logical sequence. The three biggest problems in storytelling are inaccuracy, confusion and not answering logical questions. Make the writing more interesting by at least some variation in sentence length and structure and use transitions to smooth out the writing.

●●●●●
Key Words and Phrases

Why run the story?...What's new to the audience?...Do you understand all the facts? ... What's the story really about? ... What's the lead? ... What's the best sequence to tell the story? ... story logic ... answer the logical questions ... story structure ... transition – within story and between stories

●●●●●
Exercises

A. Convert the following random bits of information, for five separate stories, into coherent 30–40 second broadcast stories. For this assignment, imagine that you're a reporter in Springfield.

Story 1

a) Yesterday, the Fourth National Bank of Springfield was robbed.

b) Police arrested James Smith and Harry Jones in connection with the robbery.

c) Police are looking for a third suspect in connection with the bank robbery. No name has been released.

d) The robbers made off with an undisclosed amount of money.

e) A bank customer was shot and seriously injured during the robbery. His name has still not been released.

f) Springfield General Hospital says the injured man is in serious but stable condition.

g) Sally Hannon, a bank customer, said the robbers made everyone lie down on the floor and hand over valuables and money.

h) The robbery took place at 4:45 p.m., just before closing time yesterday.

i) The bank branch that was robbed is located at Main St. and 14th Ave. It's the bank's biggest branch outside of the main office downtown.

j) Chief Detective Samuel Greene said that police apprehended the two male suspects at 11 a.m. this morning . . . and that police are confident that they will make a third arrest today.

k) Police said they have not recovered any of the missing money yet.

Story 2

a) General Engine and Aeronautics employed 2,500 workers at its plant in Springfield.

b) That's one of 3 plants in the U.S. The other two are in Bakersfield, CA and Mobile, AL.

c) GEA also has a plant in Brazil and another in Mexico.

d) The company makes airplane and heavy truck engines.

e) GEA just announced that it will lay off 2,000 workers in Springfield in 60 days.

f) The company will stop making engines in Springfield, and the smaller workforce will just make engine parts.

g) The layoffs are part of a general restructuring of the company.

h) The Bakersfield plant will shut down completely, and the Mobile plant will remain the same. There are 1,500 and 1,800 workers, respectively, in Bakersfield and Mobile.

i) Production – and hiring – in Mexico will increase.

j) No workers will be offered relocation, according to George Hansen, the local company spokesperson.

k) The company said that it had to lower labor costs in order to compete on a global basis, according to Hansen.

l) Theodore Ripson, the head of the local Teamsters union, which represents most of the soon-to-be-laid-off workers, says he is shocked by the announcement, and that the Teamsters will fight the layoffs.

m) Ripson said GEA did comply with state labor laws in giving the workers 60 days notice.

n) GEA is one of Springfield's largest employers and the largest manufacturing plant in town.

Story 3

a) The state's general fund revenue comes mostly from sales, income and corporate taxes.

b) Newly elected Governor Mary Smith is seeking an 8 to 10 percent cut in pay for state workers who aren't covered by union-negotiated contracts. Smith says that would save the state about $300 million.

c) Smith said that voters must approve a continuation of the state sales tax and vehicle license fees. Those fees will then go to local governments to help pay for the shifting of some expenses from the state to local governments.

d) Smith said her recommendations would close a 12-month budget gap estimated at $18.5 billion, and that everyone in the state must sacrifice at least some in order to bring the state back from the brink of insolvency.

e) Smith's office said the only area of state spending that would not be cut would be K-12 education. That's because that area had already been cut last year. Even so, spending in that area would be frozen for at least 2 years.

f) Smith called for $10 billion in spending reductions, including cuts in social services, welfare, health care and the statewide university education systems.

g) Smith also acknowledged that the restructuring of state government to shift many responsibilities from the state to counties and cities will be complicated and controversial.

h) Smith is proposing a $70.5 billion general fund budget, slightly less than last year's $73.2 billion budget.

i) Smith's new proposed budget would cut funding to most areas of state government and maintain a group of tax increases for five years to close the state's enormous budget deficit.

j) Smith's proposal to extend taxes will require support from both parties in the state legislature, many of whom have vowed to oppose all taxes.

Story 4

a) An out-of-state development group from Montana completed the purchase of approximately three acres of land along East Main Street in Springfield on Wednesday.

b) The soon-to-be-formed Springfield Hotel Group, incorporated plans to build a new hotel on East Main Street between the Marriott Hotel and the Hampton Inn.

c) Developer Henry Jones said several people that he has met in Springfield have questioned how there can be enough business for so many new hotels.

d) Jones said he is optimistic about the hotel's long-term success because of the steady growth in the area.

e) Jones said he has already purchased the land, and he expects construction to begin within the next three months. He said it will take 18 months to complete the construction.

f) Construction of a new hotel near downtown is expected to begin within 90 days, according to an announcement by the developer earlier today.

g) The land purchased is a portion of a larger tract of land owned by former Springfield Mayor Marvin Summers.

h) The developers say the total investment for the 160-room hotel will be approximately $30.9 million. When complete, it will be the third new hotel constructed in Springfield since 2017.

i) The construction phase is expected to mean about 200 new jobs. When the hotel opens, it will mean about 85 full time and part time jobs.

Story 5

a) Land-based pollution is handled by the state, but pollution in the water is handled by the U.S. Environmental Protection Agency. The EPA started Springfield River PCB dredging last spring.

b) New studies will estimate how much PCB and other pollution is present in East Springfield ... along with how much it could cost to clean it up

c) A lawsuit by the residents in the area and the town against General Wire and Metalworks for damages is pending.

d) New state grants will pay for studies to spell out cleanup and revitalization plans for two polluted sections of East Springfield. Those areas make up over 300 acres and include 6 "brownfield sites."

e) Money for the studies will come from a $400,000 grant from the state, announced this morning, under a program meant to clean up so-called industrial brownfields. Those areas sit nearby the old GWM plant that released PCBs and other chemicals into both the river and the land decades ago.

f) Residents nearby have complained for years that the contamination makes their homes almost impossible to sell or even refinance.

g) In that area of East Springfield, GWM has installed basement ventilation systems in some homes, to exhaust tainted air left from underground industrial pollution.

h) East Springfield Mayor Janet Burroughs said the state will cover 90 percent of the study costs, but the town will have to cover 10 percent – which is likely to come in services rather than actual cash.

i) Burroughs said East Springfield has been struggling for decades to recover from its history of pollution ... and has trouble attracting new development because of the perception of widespread contamination.

j) A state-mandated cleanup of a nearby storage area by GWM began in 2016 where as much as 100,000 pounds of PCBs were believed to be buried.

B. Now, convert those random bits of information (above) into coherent 20 second broadcast stories.

12

•••••

Working With Bites,
Actualities and Natural Sound

The most important concept to understand when writing into or out of bites, actualities and natural sound is that those elements are as much a part of the story as the script itself. Since you can't rewrite what someone says, you must frame your writing to blend in the bites and sound so that everything flows smoothly and logically and becomes one cohesive story.

•••••

The Feel of Natural Sound

In both radio and TV, we collect natural sound to help give the audience a feel for "being there." We run the natural sound *under* the voice track of the reporter. In radio a report from a city council meeting will commonly have the natural sound of the meeting under the voice of the reporter. In television the reporter track is recorded and blended with the natural sound under whatever we're seeing in the video. The natural sound under the voice track gives the audience a sense of what the event was really like and puts an audio presence under the reporter's voice.

We also use natural sound full. In both radio and TV, that's when we bring up that natural sound – the meeting, the kids playing, the crowd cheering and so forth – so that it's full volume in the story. It's a short pause in the story, usually no more than a few seconds, when we let the story breathe and give the audience a real feel for what the location, meeting or event was like.

What exactly is the difference between natural sound full and an actuality or bite? Frankly, there's no universal standard, but it's easiest to distinguish between the two on the basis of function. Natural sound full is used simply as a pacing device or sound bridge in the story, and the *content* of the sound does not really contribute to the information. When the sound contains real substance and needs to be understood to contribute to the content, then we usually consider it a bite or actuality.

Natural Sound as Pacing and Punctuation

"Sometimes you can use actuality and sound as punctuation," says CBS and WCBS reporter Mike Sugarman, like a period between thoughts.

In radio, Sugarman says that once he's found that "center" – the focus of the story – he needs to find the sound that best represents it. If it's something about homelessness, it might be a car door slamming when they're living in a car or the sound of the soup line. "It's whatever strikes your ear as trying to get that point across," says Sugarman.

"You want just enough natural sound to keep you in a sense of environment or moment," KGO-TV reporter Wayne Freedman says. Not so much, he says, that it breaks the flow of the story but enough to maintain the rhythm that you set.

Former NBC correspondent Bob Dotson says he used natural sound to help people go beyond seeing or hearing about the story so that they're actually experiencing it. That's exactly the point.

● ● ● ● ●

Key Rules

When you write stories, you always have to keep the information flowing. The two most common errors in working with bites and actualities are (1) stopping the story flow dead in its tracks, and (2) repeating in the lead-in what the bite or actuality is about to say.

Don't Stop the Story

Here are some examples of the most common ways to kill the flow of a story:

TERRIBLE: `The mayor had this to say on the proposal.`
          `(BITE)`
TERRIBLE: `The mayor explains what she thought of the`
   `proposal.`
          `(BITE)`
TERRIBLE: `I asked the mayor how he felt about the proposal.`
          `(BITE)`

None of the above lead-ins has any redeeming qualities. In all of those cases the lead-in brings the story to a dead stop because the audience learns no information from the sentence. Those are just empty words whose only function is to tell the audience that a bite is coming. We would never put a line into a story saying that, "the next sentence will contain information on what the mayor thinks," so never go into a bite using anything like the above examples.

Don't Repeat

The other common error is to repeat in the lead-in what the bite is going to say:

ALSO
TERRIBLE: The mayor says he's against the proposal.
   Mayor bite: "I'm against the proposal."

Doing this makes it sound as if you have no idea what's going on in the story. It's not that the lead-in is bad per se. The problem is the repetition of the material. Even having the lead-in repeat just a key word or phrase from the bite makes the whole thing sound repetitious.

PROBLEM
LEAD-IN: The mayor says the proposal is counter-productive.
   Mayor bite: "I just think that the plan is counter-productive."

Even though the bite only duplicates one word from the lead-in, it's going to sound repetitious because it repeats a key word from the lead-in.

Watch Out for Partial Lead-Ins

Generally, don't go into a bite that's being played live with a partial sentence lead-in:

RISKY
LEAD-IN: But the mayor says:
   Mayor bite: (bite)

If the bite doesn't come up – usually because of technical problems that seem to be reserved specifically for when you've violated this rule – you're left hanging there with you and the audience waiting, knowing something went wrong. Even in packages, in which all the material is prerecorded, you should be cautious about partial sentence lead-ins where a bite completes a sentence started by the reporter. The audience adjusts their listening each time there's a change in who's speaking. It doesn't take long, and a pause built into the end of one sentence and the beginning of the next will usually handle the adjustment. But when you switch speakers mid-sentence, the edit is tighter, the adjustment period is shorter, and it will be harder for the audience to follow what's being said. It's even riskier when the voice quality of the reporter or anchor is similar to the voice quality in the bite itself.

Making the Story Flow

All the words in your lead-in must contribute information to the story and keep the story moving. The story flow should not be interrupted just because you're using sound.

GOOD
LEAD-IN:　The mayor says he's against the proposal.
　　　　　Mayor bite: It's too expensive; it won't work; and
　　　　　I think there are better ways to approach the
　　　　　problem.

The transition from the lead-in to the mayor's bite flows as seamlessly as if the writer had scripted everything – including the bite. That's exactly the way it should sound. No wasted words. Easy to follow and understand.

Finding the Lead-In

The best place to look for material for a good lead-in is the first line of a good bite:

GOVERNOR: The issue is jobs. We've got thousands of
　　people who want work here but not enough industry to
　　support them all.

In this case, use as a lead-in the governor's opening line about jobs, and pick up the bite with line two:

LEAD-IN: The governor says the issue is jobs.
GOVERNOR'S
BITE: We've got thousands of people ...

This type of lead-in also won't make you look foolish in the event of technical problems. If you're running this story live and the bite doesn't come up, you simply have a slight pause. Depending on how well you or the anchors know the story, it's possible to ad lib a line summarizing the governor's view – or you can just keep going. Either way, the story will sound reasonably complete.

Occasionally, there isn't good information for the lead-in. In that case, minimize damage:

LEAD-IN: Mayor John Smith.
      (bite)

This type of lead-in isn't nearly as good as the other because it doesn't really keep the information flowing smoothly and seamlessly. But it's a decent second choice, since it's short and to the point. All it does is give the next speaker's name.

Television Lead-Ins

There's less of an issue leading into bites in television than radio because we seldom need to introduce anyone. Mostly, we just cut directly to a bite and super the name and position in the lower third of the screen. That helps to keep the flow of the television story going, and it prevents the painfully weak five or six seconds of video of someone *not* talking (but usually sitting at a desk) while that person is introduced. Introducing people on TV can work if you need to do so and have some interesting video of that person actually doing something. But if that isn't the case, skip the introduction, just go to the person and tell us who it is with a super.

Writing Out of Bites

Usually, we don't need to do anything special coming out of a bite or actuality. Normally, the bite is so short that we don't need to remind people who was speaking; we can just move on. In any case, writing out of a bite or actuality involves the same concept as writing in: Keep the information flowing. Never come out of a bite with something like this:

WEAK WRITE
OUT: That was Mayor John Smith.

If you need to repeat the name because the bite was long, include new material:

BETTER
WRITE OUT: Mayor Smith also said....

An Alternative to Traditional Bites

The use of sound can help tell a story, break up the monotony of a single speaker and prove to the audience that you were there covering the event. Even one-word responses or short phrases can work as bites if you write into them and out of them properly. Because they're so short, using them can be risky in a live newscast, but they'll work fine in a pre-recorded radio or television package.

Look at how KGO-TV reporter Wayne Freedman wove one and two word responses through a portion of his script on the clean-up following a San Francisco earthquake:

FREEDMAN SCRIPT: For people in the quake zone, this has been a day for finding and taking care of essentials.

MAN OUTSIDE HARDWARE STORE: Spackle.

ANOTHER MAN OUTSIDE: Metal straps to go around hot water heaters.

CLERK IN HARDWARE YELLS: Roofing nails.

FREEDMAN: They're the building blocks of recovery. By beginning with little things, the big ones will fall into place as well.

FREEDMAN TO WOMAN: So how's the house?

WOMAN: It's standing.

FREEDMAN TO WOMAN: And how's the car?

WOMAN: It's dirty.

That entire sequence, including reporter track and bites from four different people, took a total of 18 seconds.

● ● ● ● ●

Packages

Writing Into Packages

A TV package (or pack) is a prerecorded report, normally with reporter narration over video, a stand-up, and bites. Radio's equivalent is the wrap or wraparound, which includes the reporter narration, preferably over natural sound, and one or more actualities. In both cases these go on the air only after being introduced by the news anchor. As with writing into bites or actualities, always try to keep the information flowing. This common form of package lead-in is *not* how you should do it:

WEAK

LEAD-IN: Mayor John Smith has come out against a new highway plan for the city. Jane Jones has the details from city hall.

(package)

It's not a terrible lead-in, but it's weak because the last line serves only to introduce the reporter. Otherwise, it says nothing at all. We should be able to do better:

BETTER

LEAD-IN: Mayor John Smith has come out against a new highway plan for the city. Jane Jones at city hall says the mayor is ready to fight the issue in court.
(package)

That's better because, in this example, the same last sentence that introduces the reporter also says something about the story (that the mayor is ready to fight the issue in court). Make every word count.

PROBLEM

LEAD-IN: XXX's John Smith was in Clark Lake this morning when Virginia Jones got <u>the</u> word of her husband's release <u>and he has more in this report.</u>
(package)

Strengthen this network lead-in (that went on the air) by eliminating the extra words (underlined) that slow down the story:

BETTER

LEAD-IN: XXX's John Smith was in Clark Lake this morning when Virginia Jones got word of her husband's release.
(package)

This version is better because it's tighter and more to the point. Those seven extra words that were in the original story just slow it down and weaken the writing.

Introducing a Package That Starts With a Bite

How a package begins determines how the lead-in should be written. Most package lead-ins are designed for a package that starts with the reporter track or, preferably, natural sound full followed by the reporter track. In the above example the dual introduction of the reporter and Virginia Jones would actually allow the package to start either way. If you're going to start a package with a bite, make sure the package lead-in is written in such a way that you don't confuse the audience.

PROBLEM: Reporter John Smith is at City Hall and has the story about what's happening with the city budget.
(package that starts with a bite from a city council member)

This doesn't work because the lead-in clearly has the audience expecting to hear from reporter John Smith. If you're going to start with a bite, this would be poor form in TV and impossibly confusing in radio. In television, a super can reorient the viewer, but the confused radio listener may never catch up with the story.

BETTER: Reporter John Smith is at City Hall and spoke with
    Council Member Jane Doe about what's happening with
    the city budget.
        (package that starts with a bite from a city council member)

In this example the audience clearly knows that John Smith will report, but they're also expecting to hear from Jane Doe. No one will have any trouble following the beginning of the story.

Understand Where the Story Begins

Nothing improves lead-ins (and tags) to reporter packages as much as the reporter understanding that the story actually begins when the anchor lead-in starts and ends when the next story is about to begin. The reporter may think that the story begins and ends with the package itself, but the audience doesn't see (or hear) it that way, and why should they? The story begins with the anchor introduction.

Too often, reporters write the prerecorded portion of the package first. After that's all done, they go back and try to tack on an intro and sometimes a tag. The problem is they've said just about everything in the package, leaving nothing of consequence to say in a lead-in or tag. That results in weak, sometimes redundant lead-ins and meaningless tags. Reporters should start writing with the lead-in and end with the tag, before recording anything. Even when time is tight, the reporter must at least figure out what the lead-in and tag will say – before writing the package itself.

Package Tags

Generally, a reporter package is self-contained and requires no additional information coming out of it, but that's not always the case. Sometimes there's additional information that is most logically added to the end. Sometimes there's another aspect to the story that is better handled in a short tag. Sometimes TV stations insist on an anchor tag after reporter packages to improve the flow of the newscast and re-establish the anchors for the audience. The concept is good; the execution frequently is not. If the tag doesn't contain meaningful information, the effect is to grind the newscast to a virtual standstill at the end of every package.

TERRIBLE

ANCHOR

TAG: That was John Smith reporting.

NOT MUCH

BETTER: John Smith will be following the story as the petition drive progresses.

MUCH

BETTER: John Smith says the group hopes to deliver a thousand petitions to the mayor late next week.

A good tag can be a tough balancing act. It needs to contain meaningful information but must not sound as though the reporter forgot to tell us something in the package.

●●●●●

Summary

The key in using sound is maintaining the story flow while giving the audience the sense of "being there." The two most common errors writing into bites are stopping the flow of the story and repeating the same information that's in the bite. Generally, in TV, don't introduce people before bites; that's what supers are for.

●●●●●

Key Words and Phrases

don't stop the story flow . . . don't repeat the information . . . partial lead-ins

●●●●●

Exercises

A. For each of the following bites, write a lead-in and all of the words of the bite that you would use on the air at your Springfield television station. You may use all of the bite or just part of it.

1. Lab worker John Smith on the past experience of accused serial killer James Jones:

   "He did not seem to understand why all of this could be important and how deadly the chemicals could be for animals. He never really acknowledged our concerns. We were concerned about him not following the rules that the supervisor had clearly explained to him, and we told him not to return until he was willing to abide by the rules. That was the last we saw of him."

2. Springfield Mayor Marvin Summers on complaints about poor snow removal during the last storm:

    "We recognize that we did not do the job that Springfield residents rightly expect of us in the last storm. We were admittedly a little late getting started, and I think we really didn't follow through in all cases as aggressively as we needed to. We intend to make sure that does not happen again."

3. New Jersey Gov. John Smith on education:

    "I propose that we reward the best teachers, based on merit, at the individual teacher level. I demand that layoffs, when they occur, be based on a merit system and not merely on seniority. And perhaps the most important step is to give schools more power to remove underperforming teachers."

4. Mary Smith, head of Gun Control Advocates on the shooter of a US Representative:

    "The reason he was able to be tackled was he had to pause to reload. The problem is, he didn't have to pause to reload until he'd already expended 30 rounds. We need to go back to the slightly saner laws that we used to have where these high capacity clips were illegal. That's the way it used to be. If that were still the case, then maybe at least some of these innocent souls would still be alive today."

5. Deborah Parsons, head of Guns for Protection on the shooter of a US Representative:

    "The criminals are going to have guns, so why should we as law-abiding citizens be punished for what a criminal does? Maybe if more people attending the event had been armed, they could have done something before so many people were hurt. The judge who was killed knew how to shoot, but he'd just been to church, and he probably didn't have his gun."

6. East Springfield Chief of Police Evan Coulter:

    "A man was fatally stabbed in Springfield County on Monday evening in the 10th violent attack there in 10 days. We have stepped up efforts to curb the outbreak of deadly violence that has provoked concern and alarm in the suburban jurisdiction. In the most recent incident, the victim was stabbed during a fight in a supermarket parking lot in East Springfield."

7. Springfield Mayor Marvin Summers on the new convention construction in downtown:

    "Now we have a convention center and hotel set-up, airport and downtown that few cities in this nation can match. This will allow us to compete for some of the biggest and most important conventions in the country. And don't kid yourself, it's serious competition. Sure there's pressure. But all the pieces are in place here."

8. National weather service forecaster Carmen Hyde on the upcoming snow storm:

"At this point, right now in the Springfield area, there will be 4-6 inches of snow when it's all said and done. Wind will enter into the weather picture tonight, so blowing could become a problem by morning. Temps during the day will be in the 20s. The accumulation by rush hour this morning means commuters – as well as buses and parents taking their kids to school – will need to slow down. As we've seen, you don't need a lot of snow to create a lot of problems. Conditions are going to be deteriorating throughout the day. Take necessary precautions."

9. Gerald Jones on the fire which destroyed his home today:

"I left with my two dogs to run an errand, and when I returned home, my house was on fire. I think it started between 9 a.m. and 9:30 a.m., maybe near my wood stove. I left the house to go to the post office, and when I got back it was fully engulfed. My neighbors are helping all they can. I'm sure it hasn't hit me yet. If I'd have been home 20 minutes sooner, I maybe could have gotten enough water to it to put it out. But I couldn't even get into that room. There was too much smoke."

10. Springfield Mayor Marvin Summers on an ongoing dispute with a private water company on whether the company's assets are taxable:

"Hopefully we can work out a solution. We have a good relationship with the company, and there are going to be issues of discussion moving forward. We're not trying to pull a fast one here, we just have different interpretations of the law and we need to resolve that. A legal opinion provided by the state Municipal Association stated that the activity is taxable, and the town attorney concurred."

11. Springfield City Council Chair Helen MacDonald on a new proposal to clean up the town:

"I'm concerned that the plan would be making too many demands on businesses that are already having a hard time. I also think that some recommendations in the draft plan seem to be very personal, such as that specific driveways or yards be improved, might alarm people. A few business owners were alarmed. I explained that we wouldn't force anything on them and that the implementation committee, if so charged, would contact the owners and discuss possibilities of volunteer work or other options to help them spruce up their properties. We're not trying to be draconian; we just want to spruce up our image."

12. Jayne Darrow, head of the Business Development Office for Springfield:

"While downtown business comparisons turned negative for the first time since January 2016, we believe today's results simply reflect a minor bump along the road to a broader Springfield recovery. I know business conditions are difficult and painful, but recoveries take time. Our conversations with local retailers lead us to believe the next quarter of this year will see results largely exceeding expectations."

13. Sarah Devine, Springfield Police Chief:

"We found Springfield dancer Mary Flores's body in concrete 2 miles from her home. The coroner said she died from asphyxiation due to neck compression. Her death has been ruled a homicide. We have arrested Jason James, her ex-boyfriend, and have charged him with murder. It appears that this was a crime of passion that occurred in the heat of the moment after an argument."

14. Daniel Clemente, State Corrections Chief:

"State correctional officers can be given one unpaid furlough day per month without jeopardizing public safety. The last time we did this, we saw no increase in incidents in our prisons. Since those are the facts, and all other state workers are being forced into furloughs in order to save the state money, I simply cannot justify exempting correctional officers from the same pain that every other state worker is experiencing. Those furloughs will save the state $312,700 a month."

15. Alexander Mullins, professor of economics at Springfield State University:

"That's a big reason why much-ballyhooed loan modification and foreclosure mediation programs aren't saving people from losing their homes. There are issues because we have banks that not only hold their own mortgages, but they sold off mortgages. It's difficult for the homeowner to work with servicers and investors. Much of the time, it's hard to tell who even owns the mortgage – much less getting that company or those companies – to give the owner any kind of break."

16. Jermaine Hathaway, Assistant Chief of Police in Springfield:

"A 3-year-old boy was taken to Springfield General Hospital this afternoon after he was found at the bottom of a swimming pool on North 17th Street. The boy was unconscious. We do not know exactly how long he had been in the water, but we do not think it had been long. A neighbor spotted the child and pulled him out. At this point, the boy is in critical condition. We have no information that indicates this is anything other than a horrible accident."

B. Which one or ones would you change if you were running the bite on your Springfield commercial radio station? On your Springfield public radio station?
C. Which are the strongest five bites in A. Why do you think so?

13

TV: Story Forms

Story Forms

A television newscast is made up of a mix and match of five basic TV story forms.

■ The *reader*, in which the anchor appears on the screen reading the story, with or without graphics (GFX).

■ The *voiceover* (*VO*, pronounced V-O or VOH), which typically starts with the anchor on camera reading the first line or two of a story and then continues with the anchor reading live over video, with natural sound under.

■ The *VO/SOT* (sometimes spoken as letters, V-O-S-O-T, and sometimes pronounced as VOH-soht), which typically starts, as with the VO, with the anchor on camera reading the first line or two of a story and then continues with the anchor reading live over video, with natural sound under, and then goes to a bite (SOT: sound on tape). Variations can include going to VO again after the bite or starting with SOT, then going to voiceover and perhaps then going back to SOT.

■ The *package* (or pack), a prerecorded report normally with reporter narration over video, a stand-up and bites. If the package is introduced by the reporter live on location, the internal package stand-up may be omitted.

■ *Live*, in which a reporter or anchor broadcasts live directly from the scene of a story, often wrapping around a package or including voiceover video either shot earlier or live.

Readers

Readers are basically radio reports read on TV, and the writing style and approach are exactly the same – with one exception. If graphics accompany a reader, usually in the form of an over-the-shoulder box showing a picture or symbol, then the writer needs to structure the story in such a way that the words make clear what the audience can see in the graphic box. If the box includes a word or phrase, then that word or phrase should be included at the same general time the box appears. If the box appears with the anchor at the beginning of the story, then the lead should include that word or phrase. You can't make the graphic clear somewhere later in the story; it must go with the lead. For example, if you're using a picture of someone – or a picture and a name – on the screen with the anchor, you can't wait until well into the story to identify or talk about the individual. If the story starts with a graphic, then sentence one of the story must reference it in some way.

ANCHOR
WITHOUT
GFX: City officials are scrambling to meet a Monday
    deadline for a court-ordered plan to integrate a
    south side housing project.

ANCHOR
WITH GFX OF
MAYOR: Mayor Dan Smith and members of his administration
    are scrambling to meet a Monday deadline for a
    court-ordered plan to integrate a south side housing
    project.

ANCHOR
WITH GFX OF
HOUSING PROJECT: City officials are scrambling to meet a
    Monday deadline for a court-ordered plan to
    integrate this south side housing project.

Without graphics you write the story exactly as you would for radio. With graphics you must incorporate whatever the audience sees in the graphic into the writing.

Voiceovers

Most anchor *voiceovers*, or *VO* stories, are read live by the anchor, with the accompanying video started on cue. That means that the video (sometimes called b-roll) can easily start just a little early or a little late. Most voiceover copy should not be written so pointedly that it will not make sense if the timing isn't perfect with the visuals. The two best ways to avoid the problem are to have the anchor who will read the VO on the air time the copy before it's edited and to have anchors who can keep an eye on the monitor and know whether to speed up, slow down, or just ad lib a bit. Live voiceover narration that *points* to the picture works well if you have the anchors who can do it.

Anchor With Voiceover

Commonly, a voiceover starts with a sentence or two with the anchor on camera . . . then the anchor continues to read the script with the video full screen.

VIDEO	AUDIO
CU: Jean	((Jean))
BSS: drugs	Three more arrests in the latest drug roundup on the west side today.
VO—————	It's a follow-up to the two dozen arrested yesterday at the Village Apartment Complex.
CG: West Cityville	
IN: :02	
OUT: :06	

Note the *IN:* and *OUT:* after the super, giving the time during which a super can be run. Most computer systems today automatically run the super when the writer puts it in.

Phrases like *as you see here* and *watch the upper left of your screen* really help focus the audience attention on the story and get people to pay extra attention to the TV.

POINTING

NARRATION: An armed man charged into the store ... you can see him there, in the upper left of your screen ...

Phrasing like this works every time to bring the casual viewer back to the screen. But few things look worse on TV newscasts than having an anchor say . . . *as you see here* . . . and there's something else on the screen because the timing was off – or, as happened to a weekend network anchor a number of years ago, there was nothing there at all because the video didn't run.

VO/SOT

TV stories that are constructed for the anchor to read voiceover pictures leading into a bite (VO/SOT or VO/SOT/VO) must be written with particular care. The slightest error will result in either the anchor talking over the start of a bite or what will feel like an interminable pause between the anchor lead-in and the start of the bite. Two procedures help to minimize the chances of error. First, have the anchor time the voiceover copy carefully to calculate the amount of video to run before the bite starts. Second, the less voiceover copy before the start of a bite, the more likely that the anchor's timing will be correct. Conversely, the more copy to be read VO before the bite, the greater the chances that the anchor will read faster or slower than expected or stumble in the copy and run well behind the video.

The best way to hit the SOT cleanly in a VO/SOT or VO/SOT/VO is to have the bite separate from the video voiceover material that precedes it. That way, the video with the bite isn't run until the anchor is at that spot in the script, minimizing the chances for mistiming. That's how it's most often done today.

Anchor With VO/SOT

VIDEO	AUDIO
CU: Jean	((Jean))
BSS: drugs	Three more arrests in the latest drug roundup on the west side today.
VO———————	It's a follow-up to the two dozen
CG: West Cityville	arrested yesterday at the Village
IN: :01	Apartment Complex.
OUT: :05	Police Chief George Smith says it's all part of a new "get-tough" approach.
SOT———————	((———————SOT———————))
CG: Chief George Smith	"We're going to go in there and
Cityville Police	clean things up. The people of the city have a right to live
IN: :08	in peace, and we're going to keep up the pressure until
OUT: :13	we've gotten rid of every one of them."
VO———————	((Jean))
	Officers confiscated cocaine, marijuana, and L-S-D.

Packages

Packages, because they're prerecorded, allow maximum use of the medium. Because the material is prerecorded, lots of natural sound and many short bites can be used, and sound and picture can be layered on top of each other. The challenge is for the TV reporter to write and structure a story as it's being covered.

STAND-UPS. Stations expect a reporter to do an on-camera *stand-up* somewhere in the piece. Stand-up opens are now rare except in live reports, and most stations don't encourage stand-up closers either, although networks and some stations still use them. Most stand-ups are now internal bridges. Because the stand-up must be recorded at the scene of the story, the reporter needs to calculate in the field how the piece will work and how it will be put together. Some reporters record more than one bridge, allowing an option in case one doesn't work well, but that involves a time luxury that's not often available.

What a reporter needs to do is assess a story quickly and write in the mind. The stand-up section(s) should be scripted – mentally if not in writing. Some reporters are quick studies and memorize their stand-ups; most use or memorize notes and ad lib. A reporter who relies too heavily on notes on a pad, tablet or cellphone isn't making good eye contact with the audience. If you can't remember what you want to say in the stand-up, maybe you're trying to say too much. The only notes you should need to rely on at all for a stand-up are names or numbers. Generally, stand-ups work best within a package when:

■ available visuals are the weakest, particularly background material in a story;

■ the story requires a transition from one aspect to another; or

■ the reporter can actually demonstrate or point out part of the story.

Regardless, **the setting for the stand-up must be appropriate. A stand-up that could have been shot anywhere probably shouldn't have been shot at all.**

ANYWHERE
STAND-UP: The robber then ran from the store, firing shots at people walking by and passing cars, and then disappeared in nearby woods.

That's just a recitation of facts and could have been shot anywhere.

BETTER
STAND-UP: The robber then ran from the store, right by where I'm standing, firing shots at people walking by and passing cars, and then disappeared in those woods over there.

Now you're using the location to help tell the story, and you've built in some movement on the part of the reporter to help the audience understand what happened.

Live

Live reporting includes a number of different scenarios. It could just be a reporter on camera live on location. It could include the reporter, live, talking over edited video shot earlier or live pictures. Most often, it involves a live open and close with a prerecorded package in between.

● ● ● ● ●

Putting Packages Together

Because packages are prerecorded, they can be precise. Before writing anything, the reporter should see what visuals are available and think about how those pictures will tell the story. Pick out the natural sound bridges that should be interspersed throughout the story to give the audience a better feel for the characters and setting. Select the best bites and figure out whether they should be toward the beginning, middle or end. **Write the script based on what the pictures say, what they don't say, and the most logical sequence for telling the story – trying to spread out, throughout the story, bites from those interviewed and natural sound to be used full.**

Pacing

Pacing is critical, and long stretches of narration are boring. Generally, start your package with natural sound full or a strong, short bite. After that, keep the narration short before hitting the next bite or sound bridge. **Think in terms of 6 to 10 seconds at the most from the package start to the first bite or nat sound full. Shorter is better.** That means you need to resist the temptation to start stories with background and history. Those things may be important for the story, but:

- they're probably the least interesting part
- they're not why the story is on the air today
- it's far better to intersperse that material here and there throughout the package.

The package will be much more interesting if you keep it moving back and forth between natural sound full, reporter track and bites.

After recording a voice track, that track and the natural sound full and bites to be used are put together. The pictures used to cover the narration (with natural sound under) can then be edited precisely to coordinate with the script so that the audience sees what you're talking about. Generally, place edits at logical pauses in the script.

It probably surprises most people that Steve Hartman edits his own stories at CBS. He obviously doesn't have to; that's his choice. "So much of writing is about editing," says Hartman. "I lay the soundbites out on the timeline . . . and then once I have that skeleton, then sometimes I'll even start to lay in the video for different sequences that I want . . . and then I'll start to write." And rewrite. "I'll put down these shots, and I'll realize that for this sequence to work, this sentence needs to be a second shorter. So I'll rewrite it."

Don't Outdate Packages

Reporters must also be careful about putting potentially dated material in prerecorded packages. Think about what might change between the time the script is tracked (recorded) and when it will go on the air. In any kind of accident or disaster the number of dead and injured can easily wind up wrong by air time as more bodies are discovered, some of the injured die or numbers get corrected in the aftermath of a chaotic situation. People sought by police could be arrested; people lost can be found. **Before you record anything, think about what could easily and quickly change, and reserve that material for the live portion of a report or the anchor lead-in.**

If new information seriously outdates a package, the package shouldn't go on the air. A package that has to be corrected at the end should never have been broadcast. That's like lying to the audience. Given the difficulty of filling that much air time at the last minute, it's critical that the dilemma be avoided completely. Don't *ever* pre-record potentially dated information.

● ● ● ● ●

MMJ . . . Video Journalist . . . One-Man-Band

Different names for the same thing: the solo reporter without a photographer (local TV) or photographer, audio and other crew members (network TV). This is not a new phenomenon; smaller markets have used most or all one-man-bands from the earliest days of local television. What's relatively new is their spread to larger markets.

Today, most stations use at least some multimedia journalists (MMJs), and even some large markets use mostly MMJs. And there are times when you may have to be an MMJ even if your station doesn't use them. If news breaks out wherever you are, break out your cellphone, turn it horizontal, and start shooting.

Detailed instruction in how to be an MMJ are outside of the scope of this text, but a few quick content-related notes (thanks to CBS correspondent Adriana Diaz) are in order:

■ Shoot the stand-up twice – even if you think you nailed it the first time. There are always surprises in this business, and most of them are bad.

■ Get extra shots to prove you were there. After talking with someone up close, set the camera on a tripod to get a two-shot of you and the person you're interviewing, and ask a couple more questions.

■ For reverse/listening shots (for editing purposes), record different expressions of your listening so you can edit the appropriate cutaway considering what's being said.

• • • • •

Live Reporting

More and more reporting careers are made – and lost – on the basis of *live reporting*. The audience expects up-to-the-minute information, and they like the immediacy and feel of live reports. That's why there are so many of these, even if there is no longer much going on at the scene.

In live reporting, the typical structure involves some variation of an anchor lead-in to live reporter. Generally, the station starts on the anchor, then goes to a double box, where we see the anchor on one side of the screen and the reporter on the other side. Then the reporter starts talking, and we switch to the reporter full screen at the live location.

Depending on the situation, the reporter may present the whole story on camera (usually because the story just broke and the reporter and crew just got there) or will start and end on camera with video in the middle. That video could be live pictures, video shot earlier or an entire package recorded earlier. Frequently, live reports end with anchor-reporter question and answer (Q & A).

VIDEO	AUDIO
Mike (anchor) CU	((Mike)) The state Environmental Protection Agency has been out on the south side today, surveying a smoldering mountain of tires – the aftermath of yesterday's fire. :08
2-box with Mike left/Jane right	Reporter Jane Smith has been trudging through the debris with the inspectors. Jane, do they think there's any danger? :06
Jane full screen live super: Live Jane Smith Reporting South Side	((Jane)) No, Mike, they don't. Although water samples still need to be tested, officials tell me there's no evidence of any danger. But there is a very smelly mess out here. :08
take sot (package) full	((———————SOT———————)) Natural sound full of officials going through debris. :04 ((———————VO———————))

((Jane))
The fire department has been
standing by all day ... just
in case there are any more
flare-ups. :05
((——————SOT——————))
Natural sound full of firefighter
yelling to another firefighter. :02
((——————VO——————))
Firefighter Dan Jones says it's
been one of the longest nights –
and days – of his career. :05

super: Dan Jones
    City Firefighter

((——————SOT——————))
"The problems aren't just the
smoke and fire ... it's the
smell. It's almost impossible to
breathe out there. I can't tell
you how glad I'll be to get home,
whenever that is." :12
((——————VO——————))
((Jane))
Now that the fire is under
control, the city has to figure
out what to do with the estimated
50-thousand tires out here. :06
((——————SOT——————))
Natural sound full of bulldozer
moving tires. :03
((——————VO——————))
Tire Resale filed for bankruptcy
protection two months ago, so the
city will pick up the clean-up
tab ... at least for now. :06
((——————SOT——————))

super: Mary Cooper
    City Mayor

"What choice do we have?
The company isn't going to do
anything, so we have to. Taking
them to the landfill is the best
we can do." :09
((——————VO——————))
((Jane))
Not according to the state E-P-A.
Officials there say they've
already taken the city to court
to get the landfill shut down
because it's overloaded. :07

	((————————SOT————————))
super: Steven Small State EPA	"The city needs to come up with a plan. We'll try to work with the city, but I can't make any promises." :08
	((————————on camera————————))
Jane full screen live super: Live Jane Smith Reporting	((Jane))
	The E-P-A says it should have an answer for the city in about three days. If the E-P-A says no, the city will have to look at other landfills – at a much higher cost. Mike. :09
2-box – Mike left/ Jane right	((Mike))
	Jane, what kind of money are we talking about? :02
1-shot Jane	((Jane))
	If the city can use the local landfill, the cost is expected to be about a hundred thousand dollars. If the mess has to be shipped somewhere else, it could come to five times that much. :10
2-box – Mike left/ Jane right	((Mike))
	And what about the results of those water tests the E-P-A is running? :04
	((Jane))
	I'm told to expect those on Wednesday. But again, officials are not expecting any problems. :05

Note that the story starts *not* with the reporter live, but with the anchor lead-in, which should say that the reporter is live at the scene. Note also that the lead-in to the reporter contains meaningful information about the story, and the introduction goes right to the heart of the critical question: Is there any danger? Different stations may set varying time constraints on stories, but the above structure and times are reasonably representative.

The anchor lead-in runs 8 seconds before the double box and another 6 seconds afterward for a total of 14 seconds. The reporter then talks for 8 seconds before the video runs. That 8 seconds includes the scripted *very smelly mess out here* which is the cue for the director to start the prerecorded package. The total video time is 1:07. Note that within the package, the longest single continuous element is a bite that's 12 seconds long. The longest single stretch of the reporter track is only 7 seconds, but that hasn't stopped the reporter from including plenty of information on the story. There are three nat sound full bridges in the story – all of them in between sentences rather than splitting sentences apart. The reporter's live close is 9 seconds, followed by 21 seconds of Q & A – all worked out in advance. The entire story, from anchor lead-in to final answer, is 1:59.

Planning

The key to live reporting is planning. Some reporters are such quick studies that they can write out a script and memorize the material almost instantly. Most reporters are not quick enough studies to rely solely on memorization. Still, you can't leave the report to chance. Plan what you want to say. Make notes – one or two words if possible on the points you want to raise – in the order in which you want to report them. If a particularly good phrase occurs to you when you're sketching out your notes, write it down. Just the act of writing something will help you remember it.

Glancing down occasionally at a notebook or tablet or smartphone is fine, but simply reading won't work. And if you've got a phone in one hand and a mike in the other, gesturing is going to be pretty difficult.

As in the example above, recorded packages inside a live shot should start and end with natural sound full or a bite. Those front and back sound bridges mask the different sound of the reporter live in the field versus the reporter's voice track prerecorded at the scene or in a sound booth at the station.

Crosstalk

In live reporting, probably the greatest opportunity for foot-in-mouth disease comes in the live crosstalk between the anchors and the reporter after the story. Whenever possible, crosstalk should be scripted at least to the extent of what question(s) will be asked or subject(s) covered.

Everyone's credibility is on the line. Anchors who ask questions that have already been answered in the report look like they haven't been paying attention (probably because they haven't been paying attention). A reporter who can't answer an unexpected question looks inept. Producers should determine whether there's going to be Q & A after the report, and the reporter should go over with the anchor and producer what that Q & A should include and not include.

Perhaps some better planning would have prevented this bizarre – but real – example of *live* phrasing:

TERRIBLE: Now, Lou and Michelle, I'd be lying to you if
  I said there were absolutely no problems.

Lying? What kind of brain fade would have a reporter even suggesting that as a possible approach in reporting? Then there's the time that an anchor in a top 10 TV market asked the live reporter whether he agreed with a jury's verdict of guilty in a murder trial. Save that kind of editorial viewpoint for private discussion off the air. Fortunately, in that case the reporter had better sense than the anchor and managed to dance around the question.

Live reporting is both so important and so potentially hazardous that good reporters regularly study the recordings of their live reports to assess strengths and weaknesses – and improve.

Live Look

Stations also use what they sometimes call *live look* or *look live*. As the name implies, this isn't live at all. What's typically involved is a recorded open and close from the scene, introing a package and tagging it out. It looks live, but because it's prerecorded, there's no crosstalk. And the reporter should not be introduced as being "live."

●●●●●

Golden Rules

■ Reporters sound far more articulate when they're scripted than when they're off-the-cuff.

■ Reporters never sound as articulate off-the-cuff as they think they do.

●●●●●

Summary

TV newscasts are made up of five basic story forms: reader, voiceover, VO/SOT, package and live. Packages, because they're prerecorded, can be the most complex and sophisticated story form. Packages generally include reporter track, video (b-roll), bites, nat sound full (and under) and a reporter stand-up. Because live reporting plays to TV's strength of immediacy, packages are frequently introduced and ended with reporters live in the field. Generally, start packages with nat sound full, hit the first bite or nat sound full bridge within 8–12 seconds, don't start a package with history and don't outdate a package by prerecording changeable information. Pre-plan crosstalk so no one is embarrassed.

●●●●●

Key Words and Phrases

basic TV story forms . . . reader . . . voiceover or VO . . . VO/SOT . . . package . . . live . . . stand-up . . . bridge . . . crosstalk

●●●●●

Exercises

A. Watch a morning newscast (half an hour), a 6 p.m. newscast and a late (10 p.m. or 11 p.m.) newscast. Make a short list of each story covered and what form it took. How many packages were in each newscast? How many included a reporter live on location? Did any start with a reporter live in the newsroom or on the set? If so, why do you think it worked that way? What do you notice about the mix of story forms?

B. Record a local TV package and break it down by individual elements. Did it start live with the reporter on the scene? How long did that run? Could you tell what the roll cue was to start the prerecorded video? How did the package start, and how long did each element go: reporter track, bites, stand-up, nat sound full, etc. Note also what the reporter was trying to get across in each different element of the story. Do you think the story was effective? Why or why not? Were there elements of the story that you think the reporter could have left out? What and why? Were there things left out of the story that you think the reporter should have included? What and why?

C. Prepare a 20–30 second "live" intro to a prerecorded package, and deliver it – without notes – to the rest of the class. How did that go? How did the class think it went?

14

•••••

TV: Working With Pictures

•••••

The Power of the Visual Image

The most critical thing to understand in writing for TV is the power of the visual image. Long after the story ends, the impression in the viewer's mind is likely to be a strong picture – not the spoken word.

Working With Strong Pictures

Given the nature of the beast, TV tends to seek out the visual story, and to the extent that pictures tell a story, the writer or reporter is best advised to get out of the way.

VIDEO	AUDIO
Anchor CU	((Mike)) Today's high winds nearly turned deadly for some construction workers on the west side.
Take eng/nat sound full super: West Side	((————————SOT————————)) Natural sound full of wind swirling debris at site :03 ((————————VO————————)) ((Mike)) Just after noon, gusts of up to 40 miles an hour jolted this concrete wall ... sending heavy blocks tumbling down just a few feet from workers on their lunch break.

> The men told us that just
> minutes before, they had been
> up on what's left of this
> scaffolding ... and down below
> ... right in the path of the
> falling blocks.

Note that the story is written for the available video and clearly references what the viewer will see. In this story, the words help add detail and clarity beyond what the audience can plainly see.

Working Without Strong Pictures

On the other hand, many of the stories reporters cover use only weak visuals – pictures whose use would be mystifying if not for the words. Obviously, in that case, the pressure is on the script.

VIDEO	AUDIO
Anchor CU	((Sarah)) Testimony started today in federal court here in a trial that will determine the future of Smith Park.
Take eng/nat sound Full	((——————SOT——————)) Natural sound full :03 ((——————VO——————))
super: East Side	((Sarah)) Work at the park has been stopped after a lawsuit filed by the state contractors association. The group says too many contracts went to minority firms ... although the U-S Supreme Court struck down a law setting aside a minimum percentage of business to go to minority-owned companies. The city argues that it has removed minority requirements for the future ... but the contractors group wants the city to re-open bids on current work.

```
            The city wants the court to lift
        a restraining order so park con-
        struction can continue.
```

In a story like this, because federal courts will generally not allow cameras, the only possible meaningful visuals involve the construction site. That means the story has to be structured so that those pictures make sense right at the start of the story. Then, having made sense of the pictures from the park site, the script can move away to other parts of the story for which there aren't worthwhile pictures.

● ● ● ● ●

The TV Balancing Act

Television is a balancing act. Telling viewers what they can plainly see wastes their time and misuses the medium. But words that have no relationship to the pictures will surely confuse the audience – hence the balancing act.

Former NBC correspondent Don Larson says that once you've focused on what the story is really about, you need to *prove* your story with video and sound. If you're talking about how hard someone works, the audience needs to see that. "Allow your viewers to experience the same surprise, alarm, joy that you experienced when you first discovered your story," says Larson.

Use Pictures and Words for What They Do Best

Use pictures for what they can do better than words: convey feeling, emotion, action. Use the script to handle what the visuals don't: details, facts, background. As simple as this sounds, it's really the key to writing for television. It also means that if you're going to do this well, you need to know what your pictures are – and what story they can tell – before you start writing the script.

VIDEO	AUDIO
Anchor CU	((Steve)) Students at Smith Elementary School walked the picket line today – and school officials were glad they did.
Take eng/nat sound full	((————————SOT————————)) Natural sound full :03

```
((——————VO——————))
           ((Steve))
```

super: Smith
Elementary School
North Side

Armed with posters and banners
and led by the school's
drill team – about 500 kids took
to the streets around the school
to show the community they won't
give in to drugs.

They also urged others to stay
drug free ... and promoted
the school's anti-drug DARE
program.

```
((——————SOT——————))
```

"Give me a D-D, give me a A-A.
Give me an R-R. Give me an E-E.
What do you have? Dare." :09

```
((——————VO——————))
           ((Steve))
```

The idea for today's parade
actually came from Smith
Elementary's Parent Association.
Many of them marched, too.

```
((——————SOT——————))
```

super: Pat Green
Parent

"This is great. This is about
kids and families taking
responsibility for their own
actions and asking others to do
the same. It's about positive peer
pressure and having kids feel
better about themselves." :12

```
((——————VO——————))
           ((Steve))
```

Organizers say they'll all be
back out later this month ...
during the city-wide anti-drug
march slated for downtown.

Note that we started with natural sound full, setting the scene for the march. We start the voiceover script explaining what the audience can see: lots of kids with posters and a banner, led by a drill team. Then the script explains what may not be obvious from the pictures: *why* the kids are marching. Then we go back to natural sound and then to background. Notice that we're well into the story before we do that. Note also that this section of the script and the last section relate to the video but only indirectly. No one will be confused, however.

Use Natural Sound and SOT

Natural sound (*nat sound*) **can make or break a TV story. Natural sound is real life. It's what would have happened even if the cameras weren't there. Always look for it, and to the extent that you've got it, use it, write to it and let the story breathe.** Notice how it's used in almost every story in this and other chapters.

Always use natural sound under anchor and reporter voiceover. The far greater feel given to the story is incalculable. The same, by the way, is at least as true in radio packages. Hardly anything heightens the sense of "being there" as much as natural sound under. However, we generally do not run natural sound under a bite. Usually, the technical recording of the bite isn't strong enough to handle the competition of natural sound. Besides, the bite itself should provide its own ambient background.

For some reason, the use of nat sound seems to separate weaker, small-market news operations – that frequently don't use much nat sound – from larger-market stations that do. But nat sound is available to everyone. Use it.

Write TV Loosely

Write television loosely. That doesn't mean you can write sloppily, but you don't need to fill up every second with narration. In radio an absence of sound means an absence of news. In TV there's always the picture, and picture with natural sound can carry a story on its own. How long a story can go without narration depends on what's happening. A poignant picture may tell part of a story so well that voiceover narration would only detract from the moment.

VIDEO	AUDIO
Anchor CU	((Tina)) People on the city's south side say their neighborhood sounded like an airport runway this morning. Just listen to this:
Take eng/nat sound	((————————SOT————————))
Full	Natural sound full :03 ((————————VO————————)) ((Tina))
super: South Side	The roar was actually a high pressure gas line that the gas company started emptying at six A-M. The company is re-routing almost a half-mile of gas line near the intersection of Main and Oak because of development in the area.

```
                    The company says it decided on
                    the dawn reveille in order to get
                    the job done in one day with
                    minimal service interruption.
```

Here we point not to a picture but a sound. We'll also see what's making the noise, and so will the people tuned to the news, because this type of introduction is guaranteed to get people to pay attention. Having gotten their attention, we're going to tell them what it is. Then, as the pictures of the scene continue on, we move to the details and background of the story.

Co-ordinate Words and Pictures

You must not write copy that fights with the pictures. If there's a clash between what viewers see and what they hear, confusion becomes the only product. **The trick in TV is finding the middle ground where the words neither duplicate nor fight with the pictures.**

One technique that works well here is to co-ordinate the words and pictures at the beginning, then let the words move away to discuss related material while the pictures continue. That's exactly what we did in the earlier scripts. This way, visual scene changes make sense even as the script covers other, related ground. You can't move the script so far away that the words and pictures fight with each other. But if you start together and return periodically, you have plenty of freedom.

VIDEO	AUDIO
Anchor CU	((John)) The city said no at first, but it now looks like officials will come up with a pile of money to make up for what appears to be a wet mistake by the fire department.
Take eng/nat sound Full	((————————SOT————————)) (Water rushing along yards) :03 ((————————VO————————)) ((John))
Super: West Side	Officials suspect a fire department employee didn't follow regulations last night while flushing out some hydrants in the 14-hundred block of Smith Avenue.

Big mistake. The water backed up ... breaking underground lines ... and flooding yards and basements in 10 homes.

When neighbors were told they'd have to pick up the tab for repairs, they complained to the mayor and called the media. And that got just the response they wanted.

((————————SOT————————))

super: Kelly Watts
Homeowner

"It was outrageous. The city created this disaster, and then they wanted us to pay for it. Well, we got together and said we'd fight this for however long it'd take. And we said we'd sure remember this in the next election. That's when things turned around." :14

((————————VO————————))

((John))

Damage is expected to come to about 18 thousand dollars. As of an hour ago, fire and water officials were still wrangling over which would come up with exactly how much of the repair money.

Again, we start the story writing to the video, then move away to give related details of what took place.

Visualizing the Story

Obviously, TV's strength lies in visual stories. Because news refuses to limit itself to visual stories, the real challenge in the business involves imagining and creating video for a non-visual story. If a picture-poor story can be handled well in a reader, that may work the best. But a complicated – and therefore longer – story will need pictures. Think about what visuals are or might be available. Would a slightly different approach to the story make it more visual? Can you compare the issue to something that *is* visual and then move to the specifics of the story at hand? Could stills be used, inserting movement by the camera (zooming in or out or panning left or right) instead of the subject providing the action? Think about any graphics or animation that might make a story easier to understand or more visually interesting. There are some amazing data visualization programs out there that may help you demonstrate the story. See Chapter 18.

The writing in a non-visual story must be that much better to compensate for the visual weakness. The answer is never avoiding the story. A reporter's job is to make every story interesting – including the non-visual ones. After all, you probably don't need a reporter to tell a compelling visual story nearly as much as you need a good photographer.

"We're more like the Ford Company assembly line these days than we are storytellers," says retired NBC national correspondent Bob Dotson. "If the story itself is compelling, we're home free, but we spend tons of time trying to get the live truck up but not a whole lot of time during the day working to tell the story correctly."

Find time to do it right.

●●●●●
Picture Cautions

Use Meaningful Pictures

Although a TV story sometimes gets told in a certain way or sequence because of available pictures, there's no excuse for running video that detracts from or obscures the main point of the story. Video wallpaper – meaningless video for its own sake – adds nothing to a story. As obvious as that seems, look at how many times stations insist on running worthless video of the front door of a bank, for instance, that was held up some time earlier in the day. Nothing to see, and the doors look like any other bank, but the station took pictures of it, so it goes on the air. Why would a producer think the audience would rather see that than the highly paid, popular anchors?

Today's Pictures

It's understood that in the absence of a super to the contrary, video used on the air was shot for that particular story that day by that station. File footage that might in any way be misinterpreted should be noted on screen with a super, and any footage supplied from outside the station (or affiliated network) should also be identified.

Watch Your Supers

TV pictures allow some shortcuts in scriptwriting. Information like the geographic location, a name and title can be supered instead of written into the script. This can help move the story along, all but eliminating, for instance, the weak video of someone sitting at a desk while being introduced. But make sure all the appropriate identifiers are in the story, and don't keep the audience guessing. Late supers disorient and distract the audience.

●●●●●

Drones

More than half the country's TV news departments own and operate drones . . . with more planning to join them. Drones are tools – another camera that can offer a different perspective by revealing relationships between or among various different environments. It can reveal something in a story. It can safely shoot something that would otherwise endanger a photographer in order to capture. Drones can take us on journeys, following hikers or campers or re-enactors. It can show us perspectives that would be hard – maybe impossible – to get otherwise.

Be aware that operating a drone requires a license – which you get by learning the many rules of what you can and cannot do with a drone. The FAA's test for that drone license is $150, and most people take (at least) an online course in order to pass that test. Figure on another $200 to $300 for the online course. The point is, drones for TV news are not toys, and there are serious penalties for violating the rules, and the violation of those rules can endanger airlines, first responders and others. Be careful.

●●●●●

Strong Stories Have Central Characters and a Plot

"Television is at its best when it lets the viewer experience," says Dotson, and the easiest way to get the audience's attention is to start with someone affected by the issue – as opposed to just starting with the issue.

As an example, Dotson says reporters should spend less time at city hall talking to the usual officials and more time in the neighborhood.

"Find someone who's got the problem," says Dotson. "Put the information from city hall into a visual story that reflects the day to day lives of people who are watching TV."

"I call it a quest," says Larson. "What is the quest? Whose quest is it? Great stories begin and end with people, even when you think they're not there."

Freedman tries to hook people at the beginning by finding a main character and developing a little theme. "It's basic storytelling," says Freedman. "Beginning, middle, ending and a main character. And I've added the simple truth." That "simple truth" could be the moral of the story, or it could just be a human observation. Steve Hartman calls it a "life lesson."

● ● ● ● ●

Prove Your Story

This is another concept that's simple enough to explain but much harder to execute. **Once you have your focus, your story concept and main character, you need to use the detail and sound that you've collected to prove the point you're trying to make.** You do that not by telling the audience what to think or how to feel but by picking sound and bites that demonstrate the point and enable the audience to feel on their own.

"Attention to detail allows the audience to experience truths," says Larson.

> *You have to ask questions that go to the heart of the matter; you have to listen for poignant telling detail which will enlighten and move the audience, details which might illuminate or show the complexity or reveal the simplicity of a story. That's the craft of being a good reporter.*

Larson says reporters need to listen and pay attention for the right detail: the forgotten birthday, the patron saint, a nickname. "Keep sifting details until you find a way to care," says Larson, "and then allow your viewer the same opportunity."

A number of years ago, Freedman did a story about a woman named Pam who freeze-dried her newly departed dog, Beast, because she couldn't bear to be apart from her pet. Making fun of the woman would have been easy, but the story went beyond that. Freedman let you see the woman in the telling details he always finds. Beyond the large portrait of the dog on the wall, the general Beast decorating motif, Pam's computer opened with Beast's bark. She tended a garden of artificial plants arranged among artificial rocks. Near the end of the story, when Freedman notes that, "It's both amusing and sad," he's telling the viewer that it's okay to be confused. "If you don't understand you never will," the script reads, "and Pam wouldn't care anyway because sometimes, even in death, a pet provides comfort." That's the simple truth Freedman searches for in his stories. At the very end, we see Pam cradling the stuffed dog in her arms and petting it. Freedman asks, "Aren't you ever going to get another dog?" "There will never be another Beast," she says and pauses. "Besides, I already have a dog."

● ● ● ● ●

The Element of Surprise

Larson says that powerful stories must surprise the viewer. Not shock or stun, but "reveal something with power."

Larson says that surprise could be uncovering the truth in an investigative piece or the simple telling detail of how a mother misses a lost son. Most likely, it's what surprised you as reporter or writer when you first explored the story. It's what you learned that you didn't know, it's the surprise ending or a peculiar twist or turn along the way.

Dotson notes that if viewers can sense what's going to happen right from the beginning, then why should they watch? So he tries to add in something they didn't expect in every story he does.

Dotson once covered a "nothing tornado story" – no one hurt, limited damage. As they're shooting, they focus on an older man who keeps picking through debris.

Dotson edited the story in such a way that the audience knew he was looking for something, but he didn't find it until the last scene in the piece. Then the old man reaches down into a pile of rubble and pulls up a hunk of pink goo and puts it up right next to his face. He opens his toothless mouth and says, "Well, it got my teeth, but it didn't get me." "Now you have a piece that people are there for the last frame," says Dotson. "They notice it; they talk about it."

●●●●●

Connecting With Truths

"The simple truth is just whatever connects the viewer to the storyteller and the person in the story," says Freedman. It's the concept that you find a story about life in the news of the day. Something the viewer can relate to.

Larson speaks of universal themes, calling them echoes. "What it means to be alive," says Larson.

Sometimes we may miss the simple truth because it's so obvious. Freedman struggled with a follow-up story on some of the worst fires the San Francisco area had seen in years. Working on the story, watching emotionally drained people stare and sift through charred former possessions, Freedman thought that he couldn't write this story – didn't have the right to write this story – because he hadn't suffered as they had. "That struck me as being true," says Freedman, "and I wrote it down and used it in the story: 'No one can appreciate what these people are going through unless they have done so themselves,'" the script noted. A simple truth.

Freedman says he frequently puts the simple truth in the story in the same place where it occurred to him. **If you can find a story with a universal truth – or find a story's universal truth – the audience may remember it forever.**

"I think that fairness and unfairness are human variables," says Deborah Potter, "Whether it's affecting one person or thousands of people, these are stories that are just automatically going to connect."

Connecting is something that Larson says we really don't do well – or often. Think of the top 10 news stories of the year in your city or state, he suggests. An election, a major local crime, a scandal in government, perhaps. Then think about the 10 most important things in your own life.

Larson says that if we were really honest, our own list would be about the birth of a son or the fear for an aging parent or the concern about breast cancer or the insecurity about employment – critically important personal truths. And yet, so often, those aren't the stories we concentrate on in TV news.

"There was always a life lesson," Hartman says, referring to his "Everybody Has a Story" series on CBS.

> *Those life lessons often focused on faith and family . . . something that really matters to a lot of people but goes unreported for the most part on network or local newscasts . . . as opposed to the coverage of crime and murder and politics which is really irrelevant to our daily lives.*

If you want to be a better journalist, Larson says pay attention to the "personal truths, fears, loves, ambitions." That's what people care most about, share with each other, and most understand. And what journalism too seldom explores.

● ● ● ● ●

Care About the Story

Reporters generally do not get to choose every story they work on, and journalists must respond to events in the news. So you need to care about those events and the people involved, but you also need to find your own special stories to cultivate.

"You always have to have one story you're working on that you're passionate about," says Larson. If you are passionate, then sooner or later, you'll get to do it. And don't be afraid to take chances. It's hard to be really good without, occasionally, being really bad.

When you first start out, you're unsure of yourself, and you can't afford to fail. "But to be really good," says CBS and WCBS radio's Mike Sugarman, "you have to be bad sometimes, because you're experimenting, you're pushing the envelope, and you have to do that."

Larson says the first critical mission for every reporter is to find a way to care about the story. "If *you* don't care," Larson says, "no one else will."

It is as simple – and as difficult – as that. **If you don't care about your story or the people in it, you'll never make the audience care.** That caring starts with the job itself.

Part of great reporting is doing something special in every story – something that separates your effort from everyone else's. If you can't articulate what it is that made your story special . . . then it's probably not.

Dotson says the key to doing that is figuring out ways to reclaim the bits of wasted time everyone has through the day. That's how you find the time to make a good story great. He also notes, "Find hope. Report hope."

Larson says that too many reporters confuse the need to be objective with "a lack of empathy and a lack of passion." Reporters need to be more passionate and more empathetic, he says. "There should be stories on a regular basis where reporters finish writing them and start to cry because they care so much."

KGO-TV reporter Wayne Freedman tells people to look away from the action. "Your best story may not be the fire," he says. "Once you get the flames, look away." Look at the people watching those flames.

"The smallest, least powerful voice frequently holds the most powerful story," notes Larson. "Think big, but then search in the smallest of places."

"When I end a story," says CBS' Steve Hartman,

I want there to be some purpose for my telling it. I don't want it to just be some candy that people munched on and didn't get any nutritional value from it. I'd like people to be left feeling something . . . or better yet, having learned something . . . not necessarily about the world but, better yet, about themselves.

●●●●●

Summary

People tend to remember powerful pictures more than words, and if pictures tell a story, a good reporter should get out of the way. When video is more limited, you need to find relevant pictures, and structure the story around what's available. Use pictures for what they do best: convey feeling, emotion and action. Use the script to fill in what the pictures don't: details, facts and background. Natural sound is real life; use it throughout stories. Coordinate pictures and words. The real challenge in reporting is making the non-visual story interesting. Don't use video wallpaper. Good stories have a beginning, middle and end . . . and characters that we care about. The pictures and sound should prove your story. Stories will be more memorable – even everyday stories – if you can find the universal truth in them. The best reporters find a way to care about every story they do.

●●●●●

Key Words and Phrases

power of the visual image . . . what pictures do best . . . what words do best . . . natural sound . . . video wallpaper . . . caring . . . central characters and a plot . . . stories have a beginning, middle and end . . . story focus . . . story concept . . . prove your story . . . life lesson . . . connecting with truths

●●●●●

Exercises

A. Come up with three workable television story ideas. The first one should be a strong visual story for TV. The second should have a strong audio element (not bites but strong natural sound). The third should emphasize content but should specifically be a weak video story. Explain why each story is strong or weak visually or audibly and/or why it would be easy or hard to do on TV.

B. Do enough research on each story so that you can write out how the story might work on TV. You can actually interview people so you can write out exact quotes or you can envision what someone might say for the story. The goal here is to construct on paper how these stories *might* look and sound. How are you going to get out of the way of the strong pictures? How are you going to feature the strong audio element(s)? How are you going to visualize the story that isn't inherently visual?

C. Research, record and edit the stories for real. What worked out as you expected? What didn't?

D. Which stations in your area use one-man-bands, and how much do they use them? Note the categories of usage in the chapter, and make a list of the stations in your market area and where each falls in the list.

15

●●●●●

Producing News on TV

Producing is what brings order out of chaos. A television news program is, at its core, simply a collection of news stories along with specialized segments. **A well-produced show brings some measure of coherence and logic to what are otherwise unconnected bits of information.**

Viewers frequently remark that one station's news looks much like another. And on many days, they're right. Given a reasonably consistent definition of news, the more hard, breaking news events on any given day, the more likely that competing stations will look alike.

Most days, however, there are relatively few "must run" stories. So "slow" news days tend to highlight the different approaches that at least some stations take.

Many stations have an explicit news approach and philosophy. It might be an emphasis on consumer, investigative, crime, standing up for the underdog stories; it might be "live and late breaking"; it might be something else. What's typically at issue is a general approach to news and the kinds of stories that a station especially seeks out. Some stations take a harder edge, some put music behind stories, while others would never allow that. Some stations handle most significant stories with a live element; some stations frequently bring reporters on the set or live in the newsroom; some stations work at giving their video an edgier, gritty feel.

It's useful for everyone in the newsroom if the station articulates a news philosophy so that everyone understands what the station is trying to do and how it plans to accomplish that goal.

●●●●●

Overview

The typical local television station produces six hours of local news every weekday. Stations will commonly run two or three hours in the morning before the network morning news programs start at 7 a.m. That means starting local news at 4:30 or 5 a.m. Or earlier. Then there are local "cut-ins" during the network morning news shows. Many stations run news for a half hour at noon. Some run more. Then afternoon news starts at most stations by 4 or 5 p.m. (sometimes earlier) and commonly runs to 6:30 p.m. or 7 p.m. Depending on time zone, tradition and/or philosophy, the network news usually comes on for a half hour at 5:30 p.m. or at 6:30 p.m. Then stations commonly run 30–35 minutes of news at 11 p.m. in Eastern and Pacific time or 10 p.m. Central and Mountain time.

Those are typical times for stations that run news and are affiliated with ABC, CBS or NBC. Fox affiliates are most likely to run news an hour earlier than the late news: 10 p.m. in Eastern and Pacific and 9 p.m. in Central and Mountain. That newscast might run for either half an hour or an hour, depending on market, news tradition, competition or other factors. The number two news time for Fox affiliates is in the morning, followed by early evening.

Almost all (97%–99%) of the stations affiliated with ABC, CBS, Fox and NBC run local news. But more and more stations actually get their local news from another station. While more than 80% of ABC, CBS and NBC stations produce their own news, only 45% of Fox affiliates produce their own local news.

Considerably fewer CW or independent stations run local news, but if they do, they tend to follow a schedule similar to Fox affiliates.

Along with the 705 local stations that originate local news (and have their own newsrooms), another 393 stations – mostly Fox, CW and independents – also run local news that they get from one of those 705 stations. Over the last decade, the number of TV newsrooms has slowly but steadily decreased, and the number of stations getting news from another station has steadily gone up.

Currently, the biggest growth in local news is actually among Spanish-language stations, generally affiliates of Telemundo or Univision. Hispanic stations tend to run news early and late evening, but schedules and amount vary considerably.

Obviously, the cable news channels run news all day long. In addition to the national channels – CNN, Fox, FBN, MSNBC and CNBC – there are a few regional and local cable news channels running news 24 hours a day, and there are a few local, independent TV stations that run a huge amount of local news each day.

● ● ● ● ●

Audience

The audience available for each newscast varies by time of day; and how they watch the news varies as well.

The biggest growth area in TV news is in the morning. That's been true for several years, and the morning TV news audience has generally been stable or growing. Less clear is how the audience watches morning news. The presumption is that people turn on the news in the morning and go about their business – more listening than watching, much like radio news. The research isn't definitive yet, and audience behavior may also be changing.

The noon audience is primarily made up of three groups: retired, unemployed and housewives and stay-at-home parents. Overall, the audience tends to be older (because of the large number of retired people watching), and the audience tends to sit and watch the news rather than doing a mixture of other activities.

The blending of other activities and news tends to be the norm in the early part of the afternoon newscasts. The time before the 6 p.m. news tends to be busy in most households with kids returning from school or play, dinner preparations and so on. Newscasts in the afternoon tend to skew female. At 6 p.m., the news audience jumps as a lot more people return home, turn on the news and focus more on it, and the audience is more balanced by gender.

The late news audience is again balanced male-female (although some research suggests it skews male) and, at the end of the day, viewers tend to focus more on the newscast (rather than doing other things along with watching). For many stations, this is the most important newscast of the day. That's not because of content but because of money. Even though the 6 p.m. news usually has more people watching, the late news tends to have a younger audience that more advertisers want to reach, so the late news tends to have the most expensive local news advertising rates of the day and to bring in the most money (per minute) for the station. On the other hand, the late news audience has been steadily and, in some cases, drastically dropping.

Audience Flow

Never underestimate the power of inertia. Even with the remote control, the channel people have been watching has the advantage as people move from one half hour of viewing to the next. Lead-in is critical.

That also means that whatever channel people were watching when they went to bed is the one that comes on automatically in the morning, although that's not the case with some cable systems. People may well change the channel, but the late-night winner has a leg up in the morning.

A popular game show will bring a large base to the noon newscast (the *Price Is Right* is tough competition), and popular talk and judge shows in the afternoon provide a boost to the first afternoon newscast. The late news follows network prime time, so whichever network is particularly strong (or weak) in that last show before the news determines the potential base for the late news. Each network has particular strength on different nights, and different entertainment programs tend to deliver more or fewer men versus women, older audience versus younger. Generally, NFL football delivers the highest audience, which is why there's so much of it on TV on an increasing number of nights.

In any case, pre-show promos and headlines can make a huge difference in how much of the previous program's audience you can carry over into the newscast. You want them all, and the better material you have in the newscast and the better job you do telling people in advance about it, the more people you'll carry forward.

By the way, you'll need a strong second segment lead as well – along with a strong tease for segment two.

Why can't people just switch channels? They can, and they do. But whatever program people watch determines which news promos they see, so the news on that channel has an extra shot at convincing people to stay with the channel they're on. Then there's inertia.

What about people using a DVR (digital video recorder) to record and watch news when it's more convenient? The latest figures (Comscore 2019) show that 54% of US homes have a DVR, but the amount of TV viewing from DVR has changed little. And given the short shelf life of news, few people record and watch news through the DVR.

●●●●●

Newscast Structure

All newscasts contain news and weather, and that news includes a blend of stories and story types (see Chapters 3 and 13). Sports and special segments appear in select newscasts.

Early morning newscasts (before the morning network news) frequently skip sports unless there's something unusual, and special morning segments tend to be limited to large and major markets. Stations will run local, national and international news, and weather. Traffic, too, if it's a big enough city. The morning news is actually a series of mostly repeated newscasts. Depending on the station and market, the news cycle could be 20, 30 or even 60 minutes, largely repeating with some updates and minor changes after each interval. Since few TV stations have more than one or two reporters (at most) working in the early morning, much of the local news is actually from the night before.

Once the morning network news starts, the local station will simply supply local cut-ins: roughly three and a half minute newscasts each half hour with just local news and weather and maybe traffic.

In the afternoon, before 6 p.m. or the network evening newscast, local stations will generally run a mix of local, national and international news along with weather and, if applicable, traffic. Generally, there will be no sports, but expect to see health news, which tends to be especially popular with women.

The 6 p.m. news is commonly the local newscast of record. Expect to see local news, weather and sports. It would be unusual to have national or international news, since the network newscast is on right next to this newscast (usually just before).

The late-evening news summarizes, overall, the news of the day, so you'll see local, national and international news, weather and sports.

News, Weather and Sports

In a typical day, when there is not extraordinary local news, the audience is probably most interested in weather, then news, then, way back, sports. Generalizations are risky and not without exceptions, but that's the way it works.

So why don't stations start with weather? Well, sometimes they do. If the weather has been – or is expected to be – exceptional, stations will almost always start the newscast with weather. If the weather is ordinary, then stations start with news, as much to tell the audience that "this" (whatever the top story is) is the most important local news that it has. In some measure, it's a reassurance that the world is largely the way we left it when we last checked the news.

Note that the first commercial of the newscast doesn't usually come until at least eight or nine minutes after the start of the newscast. Note also that the weather almost always comes shortly after the quarter hour. Note, too, that sports almost always comes at the end of the newscast. Television is way too researched for accidents. This is programming for ratings.

Television station ratings are conducted primarily by the Nielsen Company and are tracked in 15-minute intervals, although people meters are changing that. If you take a look at a ratings report, you'll see that stations get a rating for 6 p.m., for instance, then 6:15 p.m. and then 6:30 p.m. and so on. In order for a station to get credit for 15 minutes of viewing, someone (or, technically, the household) must watch the station for at least 5 minutes of the 15-minute block of time. On a theoretical basis, that means the same person could show up as audience for three different stations. In practice, it doesn't work that way.

The reason a station runs its longest block of news at the top of the show is that a viewer is unlikely to change channels while the news itself is on. Once a station goes to a commercial, at least some people may hit the remote and check out the alternatives. Or turn off the TV. As long as that first commercial comes after at least 5 minutes, the station will get credit for the 15-minute viewing block.

Weather comes shortly after the quarter hour because stations know that it's another major draw for the audience. Stations run weather just after the quarter hour in order to get credit for another 15 minutes of viewing.

Sports comes at the end where it won't do much damage. Considerably fewer people follow sports, and a few stations have dropped sports as a defined unit in the newsroom, having regular reporters handle specific sports stories just as they handle other news. Part of the thinking behind dropping sports, or at least cutting it back, is that sports fans have so many other options for getting information, like ESPN and sports radio, that they no longer need the sports segment of the news. On the other hand, while the sports audience is relatively small (except in some markets), it tends to be rabid, so dropping sports completely could be a risky venture. My research on this [I ask the question periodically as part of the Radio-Television Digital News Association (RTDNA) Surveys] suggests that there's no mass movement to cut back on sports, but it's certainly not a growing area in local TV.

Special Segments, Franchises and Features

Along with the standard news, weather and sports, many stations run special segments. In a large city, traffic reports are common in the morning and afternoon newscasts. They might be delivered by the anchor, a reporter at a traffic center or a helicopter reporter.

Probably the most common beats that stations assign to reporters include health and consumer (and education, which doesn't usually translate into special segments). Many stations run health reports in the 4 p.m. and 5 p.m. newscasts. Some of those are done by the station itself; others are purchased from one of the several companies that supply health news either for a fee or in exchange for the station running ads that the company supplies or both.

A lot of stations run a consumer feature, although placement varies from one station to the next. Those segments are usually done locally with a particular reporter specializing in that area.

Some stations also produce regular features on child or pet adoption, food, gardening, entertainment reports and reviews, and a wide variety of specialty areas that stations have developed. Some of those run daily, some weekly, some in between.

Stations also purchase a variety of special interest segments that they use to fill out newscasts. "Mr. Food" is a common noontime feature. *Consumer Reports, Better Homes and Gardens* and some other publications and companies produce TV features. There are even companies that produce special series for use during sweeps (ratings periods).

Story Repetition

Chapter 3 notes that stories have a life cycle that ends within 24 hours unless there are new developments. But as stations run more and more news and add more and more newscasts, there's a growing tendency to "re-rack" stories from earlier newscasts. This is especially true on the weekend, where thin staffing leads stations into replaying complete packages one or even two days after their original broadcast. Networks aren't immune to this, either. Some networks have filled much or all of the second half of their weekend newscasts with stories lifted in their entirety from earlier news programs.

• • • • •

Building a Local Newscast

From a structural or form standpoint, the newscast producer has a mix and match of readers, voiceovers, VO/SOTs, packages and live shots (see Chapter 13). Chapter 3 discusses story types from an assignment perspective.

From a news standpoint, anything is possible. Keep in mind that, as noted earlier, certain newscasts only contain certain elements.

We have trained the audience to expect the top story at the top of the newscast. Barring staggering major national or international news, that's going to be a local story, regardless of the newscast. The strongest story should get the audience's attention; it sets the tone for the newscast; and it introduces the anchors. Many stations also start with what's called a "cold open." That means that the beginning of the newscast starts with natural sound or a bite from the top story, followed by the anchors talking about the story and, perhaps, introducing a live report. Then what?

First, let's back up.

As a producer, the first thing you look for is a lead story. What affects the most people or is the most affecting, and how can you make a real splash with that story?

Newscasts are broken up into blocks, separated by commercials. The exact number of blocks of news and other information tends to vary by both newscast and station – determined, ultimately, by the number and placement of commercials. Some stations number the blocks – typically four or five in a half hour – some use letters (A, B, C, etc.). The first block includes the top story, usually includes the most meaningful events of the day and is the longest block. Remember, it has to go eight or nine minutes to capture audience and ensure rating credit.

The second block, a much shorter one, also contains news, commonly contains station franchises (like health or consumer stories) and promotes the weather coming up. The second block also varies depending on events and the time of day. For instance, in the late evening news, the second block might well concentrate on national and international news.

The third block is primarily the weather. Weather is ultimately local, so a local events calendar or local arts or music events might go well there; or severe weather from elsewhere around the country; or a lighter local news story.

The fourth block is primarily sports. Because sports appeals to a relatively small part of the audience, it might be useful to add into that block some stories that might have a wider appeal, especially ones with strong and promotable pictures.

The fifth block may contain the kicker (a light story run at the end of the newscast) and a look ahead to the next newscast. The kicker should be a highly promotable story – preferably local and with video – that helps keep the non-sports audience through the sports. After the first three blocks, there's a bit more variety in approach from station to station.

So in putting together a newscast, it's not just an open pit into which stuff gets poured. There's a prescribed outline into which the day's events must fit, and good producers think about where each story might go when the assignments are set in the morning meeting (see Chapter 3).

There's been a trend away from starting the newscast with a traditional newscast open, promoting the anchors. More and more, stations start with the top story in order to grab the attention of the viewer. The old newscast open frequently runs later in the block. Also to attract interest, stations tend to try to start each block with a strong video story – rather than a simple reader.

Determining flow within each block depends on the events of the day. Are there stories that logically flow out of or somehow connect to the top story? If the top story is a strike at a major local business, do you have other local business/labor news to go afterward? You also need a strong lead for the second block, so think about what will go there. Promotion for blocks three and four concentrates on weather and sports, respectively.

As producer, you also need to pay attention to story form. Reporter packages tend to slow down the pace of a newscast because a package means a lot of time, relatively speaking, on one story. Readers and voiceovers tend to pick the pace up because they're usually shorter. So you need to spread out different story forms so that you don't run package after package after package and then reader after reader after reader. Some stations like to have what's called a "high story count." Doing that requires fewer and shorter packages. That means you should have given all of this some thought when stories were assigned earlier in the day.

The producer also determines which anchor will read which story. Generally, in a dual anchor situation, the producer will have each anchor read about the same number of stories, although many stations have a "lead" anchor who will typically read a little more and is more likely to lead the show and introduce the top story. Note that many producers don't have anchors simply alternate stories. That would create an annoying ping-pong effect in news delivery.

Just to give you an idea, here's what a newscast lineup might look like:

6 P.M. Newscast

00:00–00:08   intro
00:08–00:25   anchors lead in to reporter at the airport
00:25–02:25   reporter live at airport . . . leads into news package on an emergency landing . . . reporter live out of package . . . crosstalk with anchors
02:25–03:05   anchor VO/SOT follow-up to opening report

03:05–03:27	anchor VO (fatal accident)
03:27–04:43	anchor introduces reporter live from south side traffic tie-up . . . reporter package . . . reporter live tag
04:43–05:16	anchor VO (new state law on sex offenders)
05:16–05:30	anchors intro story and go to reporter on set
05:30–05:40	reporter on set intros story
05:40–08:10	package with voiceovers (child molestation)
08:10–08:34	reporter on set wraps up package
08:34–08:53	anchor intros story and goes to reporter in the newsroom
08:53–10:03	reporter intros story and does voiceover for video (teen-age bank robber)
10:03–10:14	tease: reporter promos upcoming story with stand-up
10:14–12:19	commercial break
12:19–12:36	anchors intro story and go to reporter
12:36–12:41	reporter intros story (development in neighboring county)
12:41–14:28	package with voiceover
14:28–14:33	reporter tags out
14:33–14:37	tease: weather
14:37–16:49	commercial break
16:49–19:27	weather
19:27–19:32	anchors toss to sports reporter
19:32–19:49	tease: reporter previews sports report
19:49–20:21	bumper: stock updates (visual, no voice)
20:21–22:38	commercial break
22:38–26:12	sports . . . including sports reporter live in the field
26:12–26:45	evening weather update
26:45–26:50	good-bye

11 P.M. Newscast

00:00–00:08	intro
00:08–00:29	anchors intro lead story (three dead in shooting) and toss to live reporter
00:29–02:58	reporter live intro into package . . . live tag and crosstalk with anchors
02:58–03:20	anchor VO on suspect at large
03:20–03:32	anchors intro story and toss to package
03:32–05:13	package (battered women shelter)
05:13–05:34	reporter tags out live from the newsroom
05:34–05:57	anchors VO follow-up (drunk driving)
05:57–06:22	anchor VO (radio fraud)

06:22–06:48   anchor VO (voting machines)
06:48–07:02   anchor VO (politician's father dies)
07:02–08:39   anchor VO (three quick national headlines)
08:39–09:10   anchor voiceover (health franchise)
09:10–09:44   tease: what's to come
09:44–12:00   commercial break
12:00–12:17   anchor intros story and tosses to reporter
12:17–13:46   package (new kind of Catholic prep school)
13:46–13:57   reporter tags story out from newsroom
13:57–14:40   anchor VO (air traffic control)
14:40–15:39   reporter VO (convenience store robbery)
15:39–15:54   tease weather
15:54–17:54   commercial break
17:54–18:12   anchors toss to weather
18:12–21:12   weather
21:12–21:29   anchor VO (former President Bush appearance)
21:29–21:45   tease: preview of upcoming sports
21:45–22:00   bumper: lotto numbers (visual, no voice)
22:00–24:32   commercial break
24:32–28:02   sports
28:02–28:05   tease: coming up later
28:05–31:07   commercial break
31:07–31:12   good-bye

The 6 p.m. newscast (pp. 213–214) runs a total of 26:50 (after subtracting commercials just before and just after the newscast). Of that, 12:56 is news, 3:34 is sports, 3:01 is weather, :45 goes to intro, teases, bumps and close, and 6:34 is commercial time.

The 11 p.m. newscast (pp. 214–215) runs a total of 31:12 (after subtracting commercials just before and just after the newscast). Of that, 13:16 is news, 3:30 is sports, 3:00 is weather, 1:36 includes intro, teases, bumps and close, and 9:50 is commercial time.

These two newscasts came from different stations, and you can see some differences in approach to commercials and teases.

Chapter 22 includes notes on standard newscast abbreviations and a typical format for newscast supers.

Determining the newscast lineup isn't the end of the job; it's really just the beginning. The stories in the lineup are there based on what you, as producer, think they're going to be. Stories change and that may affect their placement. Your lineup, determined hours (preferably three and a half to four hours) before the newscast, assumes that news won't break out between then and airtime. News has a pesky way of breaking out whenever, and a good producer has to be ready to completely change a newscast in order to respond to events of the day – even at the last minute.

Then there's the flow within the newscast. Reporters and writers should put together each story in the best way possible. In the end, those stories also have to flow one after the other as well as possible, and it's up to the producer to ensure that flow. That commonly means rewriting story lead-ins so that they *logically* flow from the previous story. *Logically* flow. If they don't or can't flow logically, just move on. A forced "transition" that basically says the next story has nothing to do with the previous one is a waste of time. See also "Transitions Between Stories" subsection in Chapter 11, pages 156–158.

Newscasts these days tend to be all about live reporting. Audiences have indicated that they like live reporting, and even while many people in the business feel that they too often go live for live's sake – from a site where nothing has happened for hours – the audience seems surprisingly forgiving where live is concerned.

Live reporting increases the producing challenge because it clearly offers an opportunity for problems and surprises. Technical issues could kill a live shot; events could make a live shot dangerous or inappropriate; a live camera is an idiot-magnet for spectators who have too little happening in their own lives, and there's no telling what someone may do in the background or to the reporter; and then there's simply controlling the total time spent in reporter talk and/or reporter-anchor crosstalk.

●●●●●

Teases and Promos

Teases are those things at the end of news blocks designed to convince the audience to stay through the commercials because what's coming up is worth waiting for. They're written much the same as *promos*, which are free-standing program elements – run like commercials within entertainment shows – intended to get people to watch or listen to the news. **Don't confuse either with journalism.** They're written in the same basic style as news, but they're not news, and, in fact, they usually fail if they have real news value to them.

Why cover them, even briefly, in a book about writing news? Two reasons: First, news people write almost all news teases, and news people are commonly called on to write or approve news promos. Second, the flagrant disregard for responsibility and the audience in teases and promos contributes heavily to the negative perception many people in the audience have about the broadcast news business. We'd be in a lot better shape if we wrote teases and promos better and more responsibly.

● ● ● ● ●

Promotion

Stations seem to view teases and promos as anything from among the most important products on the air – hiring people specifically to write them – to the least important – letting interns and production assistants handle the load. More often than not, the task falls to the newscast producer. At least some studies show that promos – especially in TV where some run in prime time – can make a big difference in the size of the audience. The more interesting the news program looks or sounds, the more likely people will watch. Teases can do the same thing. Later in the newscast, when people may be more likely to tune out – either because of the time or because they're not interested in sports – teases can make the difference whether the audience is still there.

● ● ● ● ●

Tease . . . Don't Tell

The most common mistake in teases and promos is telling the audience what the news is:

No TEASE: Coming up next, Mike tells us about the beautiful weather we have in store for our area.

No TEASE: Coming up next, two favorites of Cincinnati Bengals fans lose their jobs this Labor Day. John Smith and Jim Jones are among the latest players cut. We'll tell you why ... when we come back.

No TEASE: All the trouble on the University of Oklahoma football team has cost the job of their winningest coach. John has sports ... next.

There's really no reason for the audience to stay through the commercials to hear about any of those stories. The writers have already told the audience what the news is.

The key to successful teases is telling the audience just enough to get them interested – but not so much that they don't need to stay tuned. Take a look at how those three teases, which went on the air (with names changed), could have been improved to do what they're supposed to do:

BETTER

TEASE: You're going to like what's coming up next. Mike with the weather ... when we come back.

BETTER

TEASE: Coming up next, two favorites of Cincinnati Bengals fans lose their jobs this Labor Day. The latest list of who's been cut ... when we come back.

BETTER

TEASE: The winningest coach in college football loses his job. John has sports . . . next.

These revised versions give the audience a reason to keep watching or listening. In the first case it's fairly obvious that we're going to get a nice weather forecast, but the audience can't like what they don't hear. They'll be there. Both the second and third examples are designed to pique the curiosity of even the most marginal sports fan.

Note also that although these teases are designed to get people's attention, they also do nothing to irritate the audience by either promising something that can't be delivered or delaying information that might be considered critical to someone's safety and well-being.

• • • • •

Make Them Care

Another common problem in teases is that they're simply not compelling or not of wide enough interest. Too many teases are greeted with an indifferent "who cares?" attitude on the part of the audience:

WEAK

TEASE: The Logan Elm school district will have to cut its budget. We'll have a report.

WEAK

TEASE: A little extra sleep may help you. Dr. Jane Smith will explain on Health News.

The first tease will only work – if at all – with people in the Logan Elm school district. Even then, it's pretty dry. Worse, Logan Elm is a relatively small school district outside the core city, so its strongest appeal is to a tiny portion of the total audience.

Most people would grab a little extra sleep if they could, so the second example isn't much of a tease either. Neither gets the audience to care. Rewrite them to broaden the interest and raise a question the audience will want the answer to:

BETTER

TEASE: What happens to school districts when voters say no? We'll take a look at some of the tough cuts facing one system.

BETTER

TEASE: Is extra sleep good or bad? Dr. Jane Smith has the answer on Health News.

The first rewrite on the school system attempts to broaden the appeal to make the story a possible answer to problems that every school district might face – and to write the tease in a more compelling fashion. The second tease raises a question to which most people are likely to want the answer.

While questions in news stories are almost always inappropriate, questions in teases and promos make sense. In news stories we're supposed to be answering questions, not asking them. In teases and promos we're specifically *not* answering questions. We're commonly raising questions that require the audience to watch the news to learn the answers.

Here are some teases that went on the air that worked:

GOOD

TEASE: Just ahead, the naked truth about snowmen ... and the people who build them.

GOOD

TEASE: What's warm and fuzzy and now a part of the police force? We'll have the answer ... when we come back.

GOOD

TEASE: Up next ... a marriage where the groom got cold feet ... and cold hands ... and cold arms ... and we'll tell you about it ... right after this.

GOOD

TEASE: When we come back, a dying woman loses her money, her car, and her home. She says people she hired to take care of her ripped her off.

GOOD

TEASE: What do dogs and coffee have to do with our government? Coming up at five ... the strange studies being funded with our tax dollars.

These work because they're tightly written; they're cute, clever, intriguing or compelling; and they make you want to stay to find out exactly what they're talking about. Short and clever, the first example above makes a strong case for something worth seeing. The second and last use questions that are just peculiar enough to pique our curiosity. The third one sounds like a fun, oddball story. The fourth one says we're going to see a strong human story. All of them promise something that will get the audience's attention.

●●●●●

Going Too Far

Although some teases and promos don't work because they either tell us too much or don't get our attention, a bigger problem comes with telling people things we shouldn't.

■ Don't say *coming up next* if it isn't. At the least, if you use that phrase, make sure the story is in the next block – preferably, the first story up. If you're going to promote a story for the end of the newscast, tell the audience that it's *coming up later*, *still to come*, or something of the sort. We're in the news business; never lie to or mislead the audience.

■ Don't promise what you can't deliver. If you promote a story as *compelling*, make sure it's compelling. If it's not, do the story better, don't promote it or don't exaggerate in the promotion. People feel cheated if what they get isn't what you promised. Quite a few years ago, a large-market TV anchor told the audience that coming up, there were 10,000 dead in some small town not too far away. The dead turned out to be chickens. Think how amusing that story was for all the people who had friends and family in that town. Think about what station they *won't* turn to tomorrow. And If you're promising great pictures, make sure you can deliver. Again, don't lie or mislead.

■ Don't tease audience safety or well-being. If you really have a story that affects the safety and well-being of the audience, tell people what it is; don't blithely tease that you'll tell them the information later. If the story is that strong, tell people what it is, and tell them that you'll have more information coming up. If the story is real, they'll tune in. *Not* giving the audience information that's truly a matter of public safety makes clear that you care about the audience only as a commodity. You would never treat someone you cared about that way; don't do it to the audience.

• • • • •

Summary

In the end, the producer's primary job is to get on the air on time, get off the air on time and run all the commercials in between. Those are not optional. Everything else is potentially up for grabs and remains that way until the newscast is over.

For some, producing a newscast is seven hours (or so) of normal news work, a half hour of panic, and a half hour of chaos. The more productively those seven hours are spent, the less likely you'll face either panic or chaos.

Producing is what brings order out of chaos. The typical television station produces six hours of local news every weekday. Different newscasts appeal to different audiences and, therefore, contain different elements, although news and weather are in all newscasts. Newscasts generally start with the top story, and a newscast is divided into blocks, each of which contains certain material. The length and timing of the blocks are designed to achieve maximum ratings.

Teases run at the end of news blocks to convince the audience to stay through the commercials. Promos are free-standing program elements intended to get people to watch or listen to the news. Neither involves journalism. Good teases and promos get the audience interested without telling them exactly what's coming up. Don't tease real safety issues. If the public's safety is at stake, just give them the news.

• • • • •

Key Words and Phrases

producer . . . newscasts . . . ratings . . . blocks . . . franchises . . . audience flow . . . newscast structure . . . teases . . . promos

• • • • •

Exercises

A. Record a half hour of a morning TV newscast. Write down all the stories, elements, story forms and which anchor reads each story or lead-in in the newscast. Note when the station went to commercials (and for how long). What can you tell about the thinking that went into the producing of the newscast? Did the producer work to tie stories together? Did the producer mix up the different story forms?

B. Record another half hour newscast (5 p.m. or 6 p.m. or late news) and compare that one with the morning show. How are the shows different in terms of content? Can you see different approaches to the producing itself?

C. Take the material in one of the newscasts you recorded and see if you can rearrange the material in a way that improves the newscast. Why do you think it's better?

D. Using any edition of your local newspaper, assemble a half hour local newscast based on the material available in the paper. Explain why you did what you did.

16

•••••

Radio ... Audio ... Podcasts

Not so long ago, when we talked about audio, that meant radio. Today, radio is simply one aspect of the audio storytelling spectrum. Audio is now a standard part of information websites. Two-thirds of radio websites include audio – along with streaming audio. But it's not just radio websites. Many TV websites contain audio, including streaming audio. More and more newspaper websites include audio as well, and more and more slideshows are cut to audio.

Regardless of whether we're talking about websites or radio, the basic principles of working with sound remain the same.

••••••

Radio Story Forms

Television divides stories based on the technical aspects of the construction, but radio generally divides its stories based on a mixture of technical construction and the origin of sound:

■ The *reader*, as in TV, simply involves the newscaster/anchor/announcer reading a script with no outside sound.

■ *Actualities*, which are radio's version of TV bites, are the "actual" sounds of a news event or newsmaker. This can include chanting protestors or comments from the mayor.

■ *Nat, natural* or *ambient* sound (among other names) includes the "natural" or general sound of a meeting, traffic, playground – whatever the news event is about. Some consider the sound of chanting protestors (listed above as an actuality) to be nat sound, but it's probably better to distinguish the two on the basis of function. Actualities involve the use of words to be understood, and nat sound creates a feel for a part of a story, serves as a sound bridge between story elements or serves as an audio bed under the reporter in a wrap.

■ *Voicer* is a radio report that includes just the sound of a reporter reading a story, most often limited to 20–30 seconds in commercial radio and a little longer in public radio.

■ *Wrap* or *wraparound* is a voicer that includes one or more actualities. These are most often limited to 30–60 seconds in commercial radio but can be considerably longer in public radio, especially with the added use of nat sound.

■ *Live* or *ROSR* (radio on scene report) is a live report from the scene of a story.

● ● ● ● ●

Drawing Radio Pictures

The Words

In many respects, radio is the most visual of all the media. Television pictures are limited to the number of diagonal inches on the screen, but radio offers the opportunity for limitless images in the mind's eye. The price of that opportunity is the precision and storytelling ability necessary to evoke those images.

Unlike television, radio allows no shortcuts, no easy way out. Names and details cannot be supered on the screen. Other than online, charts and diagrams and animation cannot make clearer what the words do not. Poignant pictures can carry the television writer; radio writers must draw those pictures from scratch.

Using Nat Sound

There is some help available, although it's frequently not used. Natural sound can do for radio what pictures do for TV. Natural sound can give us the "feel" of being there. We may not be able to see the scene, but, properly done, we should be able to feel it and fill in the visual details coupling well-drawn words with listener imagination.

Nat sound is available for most stories. We don't get it for two reasons: (1) We don't think about it enough, and (2) We aren't there to get it. Radio's ability to gather news inexpensively via phone also contributes to its mediocrity. It's hard to gather nat sound over the phone. You can get actualities from anybody you can reach, but you can't get the sound – and feel – of being there. Cost factors will always limit the ability to get out and gather the news in person. It also means that you shouldn't miss local opportunities to collect nat sound.

Other than straight interviews, everything offers ambient sound. It's not just the obvious such as stories on racing and protest marches; even meetings have sound to them. Traffic, children at play or in school, factories, sporting events and lunch counters all have special sounds that can help give the audience the feel of going on location. One of the first things a radio reporter should do out on a story is to listen and record the natural sounds of the event. Frequently called a *wild track*, this sound is used either full (nat sound full) or as background under the track of a reporter's story or wrap. The effect makes all the difference between having the listener merely informed about an event and having the listener transported to it.

Weave the nat sound in and through every report you can. Natural sound bridges used full volume can also help change the mood or location of a story or presage new information not yet delivered. Critically, it continuously sets the scene and reinforces the credibility of the report. You cannot get that sound without being there.

"You have to have a passion," says Mike Sugarman, whose work at KCBS Radio in San Francisco and now at CBS and WCBS in New York earned him perhaps more local, state, regional and national awards than any other local commercial radio reporter in the country.

Sugarman says he gets really excited about good sound.

> *I remember coming home once doing some story where I was at a bowling alley, and my wife said, 'Some reporters go to Sarajevo and get really excited. You get to the back of a bowling alley, and that's what you get excited about.' Because it was great sound; I just loved it.*

Sugarman says he looks for that kernel, that little bit that he finds interesting or important or fascinating. "If *you* think it's dull," says Sugarman, "then it's going to be dull."

Listen to the Sound Quality

Be careful about the quality and clarity of both nat sound and actualities. First, remember where your audience is. A lot of radio listening takes place while people are doing other things – commonly getting ready for work or driving in the car. That means you're competing with the distractions of other things, including other people, road noise and the general obligations of paying attention to driving. It also means that actualities must be sharp and clear to be understood. A great actuality is worthless if the audience can't make it out. Don't depend on someone turning up the car radio and straining to hear. It won't happen.

Although you can run nat sound under a reporter track recorded cleanly in the studio, you normally can't run nat sound under actualities. Most aren't done under technical conditions good enough to handle the competition. Besides, the actualities should include their own ambient sound.

Putting It All Together

Watch the weaving of words and sound to create a feel for the story:

INTRO: About 24-thousand people here are expected to be without a home at some point in the next year. For most of us, that's pretty hard to imagine. But as reporter Bob Smith found out for this special series on homelessness, it's a harsh reality growing at an alarming rate. :15

MAN AT SHELTER CALLING OUT NAME: "Jones ... Jones ... is Sam Jones here?: 04 ... *fade nat sound under: man calling names*

SMITH: If you sign up early enough ... if you wait in line long enough ... you might get a bed. But even if you can't, usually there's still space. On a couch ... in a chair ... a patch of floor. :10

NAT FULL: people talking :03 ... *fade nat sound under*

SMITH: Just over half the area homeless will spend the night in a place like this ... one of eight emergency shelters in the city. :06

NAT FULL: street sounds/traffic full :03 ... *fade nat sound under*

SMITH: The rest? Well, some stay in cheap hotels ... a few with friends or family ... some will make camp under a bridge ... some will just be on the streets or in cars or shacks – like Shorty. :10

SHORTY: (*voice sounds old, shaky and with a hint of alcohol*) "I got no place to go. The only thing I got is gettin' cans. Copper and brass and stuff like that. That's all I got." (*fade voice under*) :08

SMITH: He's 46 years old ... but he looks and sounds twice that. He's bundled in layers of tattered cloth. Blood from a large cut on his forehead has dried where it flowed. :10

SHORTY: "When you're living by yourself like this, sometimes you need to get your mind off things." (*voice trails off ... under*) :06

SMITH: Shorty looks down at an empty bottle of vodka on the dirt floor of his shack ... a home of discarded wood and cardboard. :07

SHORTY: "Quite often I get depressed. But it's one of the things I have to overcome, you know? I'm the only one that can do it. I get depressed ... get lonely ... and lonesome. (*pause*) But I have my cat.

(*cat meows*) My cat keeps me company." (*cat meows*)
(*nat sound outside under*) :16

SMITH: Less than a week later, Shorty died. His real name
was L-D Beeler. The autopsy report says he died of
natural causes ... mostly alcohol. He's in the city
morgue now. :11

NAT FULL: sound of people in bar :03 ... *then under*

SMITH: A group of his friends at the West Broad Street
bar are trying to raise the money to bury Shorty.
:05 (*cross-fade nat sound under from bar to slight
wind outside*) If they can't ... and no one claims
him ... the city will have the body cremated.
Eventually, Shorty's remains will be buried with 60
others in a single grave. :09 (*start bringing music
up under*) Anonymous dust in a pile of ashes. :03 ...
total: :17

GROUP AT SHELTER SINGING: "Amazing Grace, how sweet the sound
that saved a wretch like me." (*sound under*) :14

SMITH: Back at the shelter, there's almost always a good
turnout for prayers and singing as supper time
approaches. :06

GROUP: prayer of thanks: :04 ... *and under*

SMITH: This is the story of the city's homeless ... and
the many different groups – and people – that
includes. Tomorrow ... day to day survival ... life
in the shelter. I'm Bob Smith. :10

At 2:28 tape time, this is a long radio story – more attuned to public radio than commercial radio, but there's no inherent difference in
technique. Notice the similarity in technical approach and pacing to a
television package. There's one 16-second actuality, but most are just a
few seconds longer than the many natural sound bridges that help to
give a feel for the story. Notice the physical description – the audience
needs to "see" Shorty. Notice also that the narration is broken up into
short bits, mostly 6 to 10 seconds. The only long one of 17 seconds has
two natural sound changes or bridges within it. Note also the use of a
strong central character to help tell a story. In this case, Shorty is a vehicle to tell a larger story of one segment of a city's homeless population.
We commonly attempt to humanize stories this way. It's easy for a story
about the homeless to seem distant and one-dimensional. A story tends
to have a lot more meaning when we bring it down to the level of a single
human being or family. It's about getting the audience to care. By the
way, the story – and names, other than the reporter – are real.

Former NBC correspondent Don Larson complains about all the
"empty people" in the news. He says there's no dimension to many of

the people we cover, and so there's no reason for the audience to care. "It's like there's been a vampire that runs through the news every day and sucks the blood out of every possible human being," says Larson.

That's part of why there's all that detail in the homeless story – like the description of the shack, the clothing, the bottle.

National Public Radio's Susan Stamberg believes details tell the story, and she works to draw strong visual images for her radio audience. That attention to detail is one of Stamberg's favorite parts of the writing. Listening and watching and making notes are critical, Stamberg says, "observing the bits and pieces that help tell the story and draw the images."

Sugarman calls it painting or cooking. "It's whatever you can use to make it tastier, make it interesting," says Sugarman. It could be a weird fact, a sound, part of an interview or an observation. It could be anything.

"The art of what we do," says former NBC correspondent Bob Dotson, "not just the craft – but the art – is being able to select the right stuff for the story. Not only so that the words and pictures don't fight each other, but more importantly, that they are compelling and create an experience."

"I want people to feel something," says CBS correspondent Steve Hartman. "Laughter and tears are pretty closely tied, and sometimes we think a story has to be either a funny story or a serious story. But really, when the story is both, that's when it's best."

●●●●●

Podcasts

The term podcast comes from combining part of the words iPod and broadcast. Technically, a podcast is a downloadable audio file that can be listened to whenever you want. In many cases, you can subscribe to a podcast, so future editions (files) will be sent to your computer, tablet or, most often, mobile device. Podcast hosting company, Libsyn, reports that about 85% of podcast listening is done on mobile devices.

Podcasts can be a onetime thing or a regular (or irregular) series. Some podcasts are available by paid subscription, but most are advertising supported. Edison Research reports that about a third of Americans aged 12+ have listened to at least one podcast at some point in their life. Podcast advertising revenue is projected to hit $680 million in 2019. That's a huge jump over 2018, and that revenue is projected to pass $1 billion in 2022. Still, it's a tiny fraction of the ad revenue in TV – or even radio. But big broadcasters are paying attention and establishing at least small units to dip into the field. That includes NBC, Fox, Scripps, Tegna, Graham Media and others.

Podcasts are like radio programs. In fact, virtually all NPR programs (outside the news) are available as podcasts, and podcast topics cover the full range of possibilities. But if there's a driving genre that powers podcasts, it's crime stories. Tegna's chief digital officer has been quoted saying that "about one-third" of the top 50 podcasts are in the "true crime" genre.

As this is written, the definition of a podcast is being challenged. More and more, "podcasts" are available via streaming – which isn't part of the original definition. The country's largest radio operator, iHeartMedia, is now running "podcasts" on many of its stations on Sunday nights, and "podcasts" are available via YouTube. Video versions are sometimes called video podcasts or vlogs.

A number of podcasts are extemporaneous, but when they're written – as they mostly are – the style is exactly the same as this text has outlined. You're writing for the ear, and all those rules apply.

One thing that might be holding podcasts back involves audience measurement. It's easy to quantify downloads, but it's not easy to quantify listening: when, how much or even whether listening takes place at all. So while ad spending for podcasts is increasing, the long term future remains unclear. On the other hand, there's a lot of growth potential. Scripps reports that just a third of the US listens to a podcast on a monthly basis and just 20% on a weekly basis.

● ● ● ● ●

Summary

The principles of audio storytelling remain the same, regardless of the medium. Radio divides its stories based on a mixture of technical construction and the origin of the sound. Those six story forms include reader, actualities, nat or natural sound, voicer, wrap or wraparound and live or ROSR. Many if not most commercial radio stations involve newscasts with an anchor reading a series of stories, possibly punctuated with some nat sound bridges. Non-commercial radio, especially National Public Radio and NPR-affiliated stations, tend to place more of an emphasis on reporting and the use of sound. Podcasts, downloadable audio programs, are gaining in popularity, and many of the big media companies are getting into the area.

● ● ● ● ●

Key Words and Phrases

reader . . . actualities . . . nat or natural sound . . . voicer . . . wrap or wraparound . . . live or ROSR . . . NPR . . . podcasts

●●●●●

Exercises

A. Listen to the major radio stations in your area.
   1. How many of them run local news?
   2. How much news do they run and when?
   3. How long are the newscasts?
   4. Do those newscasts include any sound? Are there actualities and/or natural sound?
   5. Was all the sound gathered on the phone, or did the station send a reporter out to gather interviews and/or natural sound?
   6. How many radio stations in your area actually have reporters who go out to cover news?
   7. Are there any all-news stations in your area? If so, do they cover the news differently from other stations?
   8. Are there any news/talk stations in your area? To what extent are they news versus talk? How do they cover the news?
   9. Are there any public radio stations in your area? How do they cover the news?

B. Write and record two different radio newscasts for two different radio stations in your area. Explain why the newscasts were written and put together differently. Who do you think is the primary audience for each station? Back that up with concrete evidence.

C. Listen to *Morning Edition* or *All Things Considered* on National Public Radio. How are the stories on those programs different from the ones you hear on most of the local commercial radio stations? Working either individually or in pairs, report, write and record a local story in the same style as you hear on NPR.

D. Compare the audio stories on radio, TV and newspaper websites. What similarities and differences do you notice? What are the similarities and differences you notice between those audio stories on the web and the stories you hear on the radio?

17

Social Media and News

In its latest study (2018), Pew Media Research found that 20% of adult Americans "often" get news from social media. And if that's where the audience is, that's also where journalists need to be. Consequently, social media has had a profound effect on how reporters spend their time.

Reporters that I spoke with gave staggeringly large ranges for the amount of time they spend on social media each day. Many said that creating web versions of stories and posting to social media probably added one or even two hours to their day. Since most stations clamp down on overtime, that one to two hours comes out of time that used to be spent on just creating news for TV. Some solve that time problem by doing some of their social media postings from home before or after work. Other reporters say the extra time spent on social media comes to maybe 10 to 15 minutes a day. Clearly, it's going to vary by newsroom, by reporter and by inclination.

At the same time, a lot of story ideas come in via social media. The challenge is verifying the information, and that can be difficult and time-consuming.

Social Media, Branding and the Reporter Workday

It's also important to understand that part of what anchors and reporters are doing on social media is creating a brand for themselves. That's something that ambitious reporters and news people should start doing in college. Branding is about creating extra value for a news person, and that extra value makes a difference in getting and keeping a job; it makes a difference in job opportunities; and it makes a difference in salary. It's a different world than in used to be. . . . for better and worse.

Pretty much everything online is measured, and the results of those measurements are available instantly. Keep an eye on the metrics of social media and the website. If something you post engages your audience, expand on that. Add comments to responses to extend the reach/engagement. Follow-up with more. If something doesn't work . . . move on . . . and learn from that.

Commonly, reporters and especially anchors are required to post/promote stories on social media and interact/engage with the audience. Others in the newsroom are frequently encouraged to post as well. It's unclear whether the audience is more interested in the news in various postings or more personal glimpses into the anchors and reporters who are doing the posting. Some are more interested in behind-the-scenes glimpses into how things work at the station. A mix of postings seems to work best, but station personnel need to be careful about crossing the line between sharing some personal aspects of their lives (like having pets and adopting a rescue animal) versus what should probably be private information (whom someone is going out with or their children, for example).

● ● ● ● ●

Do Everything

Today's reporter *must* be multimedia savvy – whether he or she operates as a one-man-band or not. You need to be on Twitter – mostly gathering information, but some reporters use Twitter on an outgoing basis to report on meetings. That's a smart use because it gives nothing away while maintaining a presence on Twitter. Use Facebook for posting video and articles . . . and engaging the audience, talking with the audience, correcting misinformation, clarifying issues in the news. Facts – not opinion. If you cross that line from fact to opinion, you jeopardize your credibility. Never do that. Podcasts can be a great way to engage the audience with some area of personal expertise or interest that you have. Lighten the load and make the podcast more interesting by doing it with a friend or co-worker.

To give you an idea of what's involved with social media, here's a recent ad for a social media producer placed by Nexstar, the country's largest owner of TV stations:

Nexstar Ad for Social Media Producer

The social media producer leads the transition from broadcast focused newsrooms to multi-platform newsrooms through active daily example; providing training in social media methods, processes and tactics; as well as creating/editing original content beyond that which is produced for on-air and sharing to social media using a creative, modern approach.

Essential duties and responsibilities

- Develops and leads winning strategy for station content
- Expert understanding of Facebook, Twitter, Instagram and other social median platforms
- Reviews copy and will correct errors in content, grammar, and punctuation, following prescribed editorial style and formatting guidelines
- Use our social media and website to build and reinforce brand recognition and drive viewers to television
- Determines a story's emphasis, length, and format and organizes material accordingly
- Research and analyze background information related to news stories in order to be able to provide complete and accurate information
- Gathers information about events through research, interviews, experience or attendance at political, news, sports, artistic, social or other functions
- Checks reference materials such as books, news files or public records to obtain relevant facts
- Shoots and edits content for on-air and digital
- Produces reports for all platforms
- Ensures that all content meets company standards for journalistic integrity and production quality
- Builds and calendars digital campaigns to promote local shows and specials
- Writes stories for the web and other digital platforms
- Creates snackable videos, graphics, and other original content to encourage social media engagement
- Finds new ways to use social media and our website to engage with viewers
- Performs other duties as assigned

• • • • •

Be Everywhere . . . But Not Indiscriminately

There's evidence that Facebook use is plateauing while YouTube and Instagram use are growing. Facebook still leads the way, but stations and reporters also need to have a presence on YouTube, Instagram and WhatsApp (at a minimum).

There's also evidence in the Radio-Television Digital News Association (RTDNA) survey and elsewhere that Twitter has far more use as a news gathering source than as an audience engagement tool. Collect news and information from Twitter, but put it out on all the other software before you put it out on Twitter.

Anchor Amy Wood was one of the first in the country to jump into social media in a really big way. She's been live streaming for almost 10 years and was one of the beta testers for Facebook Live. Her iPhone says that in the most recent week, she spent 10 hours on Instagram, 10 hours text messaging, and 4 hours each on Twitter and Facebook. She says the number is so high on Instagram because that's newer on her list, and she's trying to build up her following. She has about 12,000 followers on Instagram and 140,000 on Facebook.

Wood co-anchors the 4 p.m., 6 p.m. and 7 p.m. newscasts on WSPA-TV/WYCW-TV in Greenville-Spartanburg-Asheville-Anderson, SC/NC – market 38. She describes herself as an interactive news anchor. "It's an access thing," she says. "I want to be accessible to people." She does that through streaming behind-the-scenes material and talking about the shows. She gets news tips that way as well. Streaming on her personal Facebook page (for work) will generate anywhere from 1,000 to 5,000 views. "It's about engaging with people as a human being." Don't just *like* something, she says, "You need to comment on things in order to connect with people."

Wood suggests that people can take a more relaxed approach on Facebook Live in terms of performance. "Don't worry about being perfect." But you have to keep on top of comments. Don't be afraid of negative comments, she says, but you can't let people be obnoxious and attack you or others. "It has to be a safe space," she says. Otherwise people won't go there.

Show the audience what you do and how you do it, she says. "Be open with the audience about how things evolve and change as we cover them."

Wood was talking with a new reporter at the station who said that people in the area really weren't getting to know her as a person. Wood's advice: Go on Facebook Live on the weekend. Make yourself a human being. Show people your dog; ask what places you should check out as someone new to the area; ask what stories people would like to see covered. "Give people a chance to see behind the scenes," suggests Wood.

Wood has also tried some "mini-newscasts" on Instagram. She says she likes Instagram more but gets a lot more reactions on Facebook. She says she finds Twitter especially useful to get news and information but doesn't find as much interaction or engagement. She uses ITTT (If This Then That – a free app) to auto-post station tweets on her own Twitter feed. Saves a lot of time, but it's not a substitute for posting your own stuff as well. She finds that a lot of people read the headlines on Twitter but don't click through to the story. She says some people feel like social media takes too much time, but she says it can save time, too. If you've been posting to Twitter, for instance, you have written notes you can review when you go to put together the story later.

Wood thinks that social media allows people to check on things whenever they see them – like car accidents and small crime stories. That means that by the time the TV news goes on, people know about that stuff and really don't care anymore. Unfortunately, that's what too many stations tend to focus on in newscasts. So when the station started a new 4 p.m. newscast, she argued for more "news you can use" – consumer, development, issues around suicide, kids, health. Carolina's Family at 4 is doing quite well with more positive content.

She sometimes uses an app called SwitcherStudio with Facebook Live to produce multiple-source live reports. At this writing, it's just for iPhones and iPads. Wood is also thinking about TikTok, but she says she's not sure yet how she'd use it.

All the work with social media has been hard on some of the veterans in the business, but younger people don't have that problem. "Constant change is normal for them," she says. "That's all they know."

● ● ● ● ●

Use Each Social Medium for What It Does Best

Day in, day out, Facebook brings more users to the station website than any other social media. That alone makes it, by far, the most important.

Station KSNV-TV in Las Vegas has found that breaking news does best on Facebook. By far. Political does well – especially because of the potential engagement of users going back and forth with comments and responses. Anything contentious does well. Big development projects, education and anything related to taxes. In contrast, the station has found that unless there's something big or special about it, crime stories don't get much reaction. The station boosts engagement by posing questions to users asking how they feel about the issues being raised. Digital Executive Producer Rebecca Lewis says Facebook does best with 18- to 49-year-olds.

She says Twitter doesn't provide a lot of traffic to the website, but "weather stuff" does well – along with celebrity stuff (remember, this is Las Vegas), and off-beat topics. It does best with middle-age people.

The station says that Instagram also doesn't bring a lot of traffic to the website. Instagram does best with pictures, good images. It targets a younger audience.

The station uses YouTube for some longer-lived video, but says it also brings little traffic to the website.

The station doesn't really use SnapChat.

KSNV's social media usage is right in line with what I see in the RTDNA Annual Survey. Facebook is universal. Instagram and Twitter are just a few points shy of universal. YouTube and Snapchat are down in single digits of usage.

● ● ● ● ●

Facebook

Facebook is, by far, the most important social media outlet for broadcast stations, and every single TV station that produces local news has a Facebook page. Many have more than one. In contrast, 93% of radio stations have at least one Facebook page. The concept is simple enough: If that's where people are spending a lot of their time, then that's where stations need to be. Still, what stations are doing there – and whether it's accomplishing anything – varies a great deal.

Station Facebook pages follow a fairly consistent pattern. The station logo is in a circle in the upper left of the home page with a navigation menu below. The upper right is a large banner with either a still picture or video. There's a large middle column under the banner and a smaller column on the right which contains, among other things, information on the station. The middle column tends to be a mixture of text and pictures/video that the station posts. The postings are time-stamped, so you can easily see how active a station is in updating Facebook.

The navigation menu on the left offers a variety of options depending on the station. The basics include About, Photos, Videos, Events, Posts and Community. A bit less common headings include Groups, Apps, Today's Headlines, Jobs, YouTube, Facebook Live, Weather and a lot more that individual stations can customize. Most of these are self-explanatory, but Groups includes fan groups of the news, various programs on the air or interest groups like cancer survivors or pet adopters. Some home pages have links to Facebook Live.

Sometimes video posted on Facebook is actually embedded in Facebook and sometimes the video is actually on the station's web pages.

Note that on a mobile device, the two or three columns that appear on a computer become one column on a phone. The material simply couldn't be read well otherwise.

At least part of the success of a Facebook page (or pages) is how active it is. Stations that keep posting interesting things are likely to have more user engagement.

Typically, stations post photos of talent and events, upload videos of recent stories, promote upcoming stories, newscasts and events, run discussions and so on. That's much the same material that stations also put on their websites, and in that sense, the Facebook page is frequently another extension of the web.

KSNV-TV in Las Vegas requires its digital staff to post two stories per hour on Facebook plus breaking news. Livestreams are posted once an hour.

For many stations, Facebook is more helpful at locating people for news stories than providing a lot of other tangible benefits.

Facebook Live has resulted in significant changes in how stations use social media, with more and more converting what has been a largely promotional effort into a Facebook page that looks a lot more like the station website. Or maybe even a station.

● ● ● ● ●

Facebook Live

There has been a huge push in recent years for stations to get into the streaming business. It's a natural move, given that stations are used to going live from the scene of news.

Stations would love to have their audience simply follow the station online and watch video on the station's video streams. Stations make money on their website – not so much on social media. But, for a variety of technical reasons, it's hard to engage with the audience via streaming on OTT. That's a part of why stations use Facebook Live, where it's much easier to engage the audience in real time.

It's easy enough to go on Facebook Live from a mobile phone, but today's bonded cellular live cameras and battery packs are also designed to send video back to the station or direct streaming either from a station's website or Facebook Live or both or all three.

Bonded cellular is the number one way that TV stations go live today. It operates by pulling together enough cell bandwidth to put out a high-quality signal back to the station or streaming directly. Note that there are areas where reception problems interfere with adequate transmission. LiveU, TVU Networks and AVIWEST are among the best-known companies producing this equipment, but there are others as well.

So what do reporters, anchors, photographers and others put on Facebook Live? Everything. Anchors will do quick promotions for upcoming newscasts and even some behind-the-scenes looks at what's going on during a newscast. Reporters and photographers may run ongoing commentary on breaking news or just regular newsgathering. Stations will use Facebook Live for breaking news that's interesting but not worth interrupting normal TV programming for. Stations will even operate Facebook Live as a TV channel, and it's frequently used to cover local sports or even play-by-play coverage of (usually high school) games.

●●●●●

Twitter

Twitter is actually a social network service and microblogging tool. Users send tweets – or messages. Originally, the maximum length was 140 characters, but the limit was doubled to 280 characters in 2017.

If you haven't been on Twitter, start by following people who are involved in interesting things, especially news-related. See who they follow and follow them. Retweet interesting things. In other words, when you're getting started, start by following others before you start tweeting yourself. And, generally, follow the real people who follow you.

Newspapers tend to be much bigger on tweeting than TV stations. Personally, I think Twitter is more meaningful for collecting information than for its dissemination. Tweet out information on well-known events and meetings. Use links – especially ones that can take followers back to the station website.

For the last three years, the RTDNA Survey has shown a decided pull back on station use of Twitter. It's not so much that people stopped using Twitter as much as they're using it less. Since the last edition of this book, the "constant" use of Twitter has dropped 20 points; daily use has dropped by 12.

Station use varies widely, however. KSNV-TV in Las Vegas mandates that its digital staff send out a tweet every 15 minutes.

Probably most critical for stations, Twitter allows a station to monitor what's going on in the community to be able to respond quickly to potential news stories. The assignment desk and reporters (and others) should be monitoring the various community news, tipsters and columns that you can find almost everywhere these days.

Twitter is a great way to communicate with a segment of your audience. But no one likes constant chatter; be selective. Not everything is breaking news. Always include links to stories. You're better off posting news to the web first, and then linking to it in Twitter – rather than tweeting the information first.

Although stations tend to use Twitter more for distribution (sending material, promos, information and links) out, it's also a great news search tool and aggregation tool.

●●●●●

Instagram

Owned by Facebook, Instagram is a video and photo-sharing networking platform. Stations are using Instagram primarily to engage the audience and let them peek into the newsroom. Stations use Instagram to show community involvement, behind-the-scenes video, pictures (weather, pets, sunsets, fireworks, features).

Instagram has soared in popularity with TV stations in the last couple years. Part of that is because stations have gotten better about pulling back the curtain and letting the audience see how coverage decisions and the news itself are made. Instagram is about pictures – keep the text to a minimum, but don't post anything without some explanatory text.

• • • • •

Beyond Facebook, Twitter and Instagram

Facebook, Twitter and Instagram are the most-used social media tools in TV, but there are others. Well back we find Snapchat and then YouTube and LinkedIn.

Given enormous general usage, YouTube probably should be much more utilized by stations than it is now.

LinkedIn isn't just a way for you to get noticed and maybe some job leads, it's a good way to locate people you want to talk to and don't know how to reach. You'll need the (paid) premium version to do this right.

Beyond those, it's really sporadic use and experimentation with other software.

• • • • •

Crowdsourcing

Crowdsourcing is like Wikipedia for news. You're asking others to help with answers to a question or information on what's going on at a particular location or at a gathering of people. Keep in mind that just because someone sends you information doesn't make that information true. People mislead or simply don't understand. Crowdsourcing can provide some terrific leads, but it doesn't substitute for the real reporting you'll need to do after you've used it.

• • • • •

Blogging

Blogging can be a good way to develop a following . . . if you do it right. Most of what you blog about should provide value/interest to the community. The more you provide something of value to the people who follow your blog, the more people you'll have following it. Resist the temptation to make the blog mostly about you. Do that, and eventually you'll have a community of one.

Given the time involved in blogging on a regular basis – which is the only way it makes sense – you should consider partnering with someone to share the load. That can also make for a more lively and interesting blog.

• • • • •

MMJ, Backpack Journalists and One-Man-Bands

There are those who envision the new television landscape as one more and more populated with the super-journalist who can do it all: cover a story for television, post an expanded version on the website, send out tweets and handle a podcast or two. Call them one-man-bands (OMBs) (admittedly old school), multimedia (MMJ), VJs or backpack journalists – their use has been growing over the last decade. Until recently.

Certainly, we've seen the rise of the "backpack journalist" – equipped to do it all. Although some people are ready to pronounce this the era of the "backpack journalist," it's too early to be sure. One of the long-term effects of coronavirus social distancing could be an even greater use of MMJs – coupled with more and more reporters working solo from home. Generally, the use of MMJs has increased at the rate of about 2 to 3% per year. It leveled off and even dropped in 2018 and 2019 before heading up again in 2020. The biggest jump is actually in larger markets which have gone from no one-man-bands to some. Smaller stations always had reporters who operated as one-man-bands. Regardless of gender.

The tipping point for news reporter vs. MMJ is in markets 51 to 100. Bigger markets have more news reporters than MMJs, and markets smaller than that are overwhelmingly MMJs. In 51 to 100, the margin is 65 to 35 in favor of MMJs (Table 17.1).

Table 17.1 Percentage of TV newsrooms using one-man-bands – 2020

	Yes, Mostly Use OMB	Yes, Use Some OMB	Yes, But Not Much Use	No, Do Not Use
All TV	64%	21%	9%	6%
Market size:				
1–25	35	28	21	17
26–50	26	46	15	13
51–100	64	21	11	5
101–150	82	14	2	3
151+	88	6	6	0
Staff size:				
51+	20	50	19	11
31–50	71	20	6	3
21–30	88	9	4	0
11–20	92	4	4	0
1–10	75	5	5	15

There has always been a widespread expectation in the industry that new hires would know how to shoot and edit, especially if they wanted to be reporters. What's really new is a rapidly expanding expectation of web skills and, especially, social media skills.

● ● ● ● ●

Twenty Survival and Growth Tips

■ Always make sure you're right. Doublecheck facts and especially numbers. The trust of your co-workers and audience is at stake.

■ Read. Go back and reread what you wrote; you can evaluate it better after a day or two. Read what the best people in your shop are writing and figure out why it's as good as it is. Especially when you're new, identify the best people in the shop and learn from them. Read and analyze what they do and how they do it. And ask questions.

■ Stay on top of the news. Remember that most of your audience has lived in the area for years and probably follows the news more than you have. You need to catch up . . . or you'll just be trying to tell people what they already know.

■ Even if you're an expert in some area, don't show off. Your audience are all experts in some area or other, but few people will be expert in the specific story you're dealing with. Everyone needs to understand what you're talking about.

■ You'll develop a writing style of your own – over time. Don't try to force it and never copy someone else's.

■ Talk to real people – not just co-workers and other journalists. You always want a better handle on what people are thinking and talking about and story ideas. You'll get none of that from your co-workers.

■ Be curious. What's that new construction about? What's going on behind that fence or in that building with the strange name?

■ Learn to listen. People are always providing story ideas and critical information. Are you listening well enough to hear them?

■ Don't take criticism personally. Everybody will be a critic of you and the station or entity that you work for. That's just the way it is. And sometimes they're right, so consider what's being said.

■ Ask the tough questions that your audience wants the answers to. But it's usually best not to start interviews that way. In many cases, you're a surrogate for your audience. Ask the questions they'd want answers to and explain things in a way they can clearly understand.

■ Don't show off to other reporters when you're in a group situation. If you have a great question that no one has asked, why share the answer with everyone else? Try to outwait the other reporters and ask your questions when others aren't around.

■ Don't assume anything. It's natural to believe the people you're talking to and interviewing. But then verify.

■ Be human. Care about stories and the people in them. Don't worsen someone's suffering, and don't ask obviously insensitive questions.

- Be polite to people. Everybody. You'll be amazed at how that will pay off to you in ways that you never imagined. Besides, it's just common courtesy.

- Take chances. Not with the facts but with how you tell stories or how you put things together. You won't always be right, but you'll never hit it out of the park unless you swing big at least now and then. Be bold and brave . . . and work harder than anyone else. Especially starting out, when you will inevitably be catching up to everyone else.

- On every story you do, ask yourself what you did differently than everybody else covering that story. If you can't answer that, you didn't do it well enough.

- Make sure you keep getting better. Age and time don't necessarily make you better . . . just older. What are you doing today so that you'll be better tomorrow?

- If you make a mistake, own it. Don't explain it; don't try to deflect. Own up to it, apologize, and figure out yourself how you screwed up and what you'll do to make sure it doesn't happen again.

- No excuses. Journalism is hard. So are the jobs of many of the people who make up your audience. Their bosses didn't want to hear their excuses . . . and your audience doesn't want yours.

- Your first loyalty is really to your audience. Never betray that.

●●●●●

Taking Better Pictures

I'm not sure that this makes any more sense here than elsewhere, but getting involved with social media goes beyond including pictures in posts – it means you have to take them, too. And most often, that means you're doing it with your smartphone. So here are some tips for taking better pictures, generally, and especially with a smartphone:

- Turn the phone/camera horizontal. That's what a TV screen looks like, and that's what you should be shooting if you want the best pictures to be able to go on TV. Even for most digital-only shooting, horizontal is better.

- If you're going to record audio, make sure to put the phone in airplane mode. Otherwise, you could wind up with competing audio because of incoming calls or messages. And remember that audio quality on a phone isn't great. It'll work for ambient sound and for you if you talk into the phone. To record others, you'll need to get close.

■ Pay attention to light, and make sure that what you're shooting isn't being washed out because your subject is too heavily back-lit. It can be tricky because you want the primary source of light coming from behind you, but if it's too strong, people will squint and not look good.

■ Remember, you're taking the viewer somewhere. Show us where we are and what there is to see.

■ Hold the camera steady. Even with today's steady software, the steadier you hold the camera the more likely that the subject will be and will stay in focus. Try to lean against something to help keep you steady.

■ Get close. Closer. Shoot *60 Minutes* tight. Those pictures prove the story, but if we can't make it out, the pictures may not prove much of anything.

■ If there are a bunch of things going on, sure, get the wide shot, but then focus in on each of the parts of what's going on. We need to really see what's happening, clearly.

■ Show you (if you're the reporter) or whoever's the reporter on the scene and talking to people. Prove that you were there.

■ Remember that people see the whole frame, so think about what's in all the parts of the picture. Cut out irrelevant distractions and focus on the story.

■ The rule of 3s applies here. Divide both the horizontal and vertical screens into thirds. Those lines intersect in 4 places . . . and those 4 places are where the critical action should be when you're framing the pictures.

■ Shoot people doing things . . . it's a lot more interesting than static and posed shots.

■ The top of the head of someone you're shooting or interviewing should be at or near the top of the frame. In a super close-up, you can even cut off some of the top of the head. But never cut off the mouth or the eyes. That's where we express what we're thinking – it's all between the mouth and the eyes.

■ Shoot the reaction . . . then get the event (unless you're shooting serious breaking news with meaningful action). In most cases, what they're reacting to will still be there (if applicable), but the reaction won't be.

● ● ● ● ●

The Bottom Line

Facebook, Twitter, Instagram and the various other social networking tools all have potential value. But the best people in the business will tell you that the best way to get people to your station and website is to produce the best content . . . and then let people know in as many ways as you can. Try new things.

●●●●●

Summary

Stations' use of social media is steadily increasing. Most stations use Facebook, Twitter, and Instagram; TV much more so than radio. Station use of social media is changing, especially in TV, where more and more stations are using social media to conduct conversations with their audience and even as additional channels to the TV station. Radio tends to lag in this area, where most use remains promotional.

●●●●●

Key Words and Phrases

social media . . . social networking . . . Facebook . . . Facebook Live . . . Twitter . . . Instagram . . . crowdsourcing . . . YouTube . . . LinkedIn . . . Snapchat . . . TikToc . . . bonded cellular

●●●●●

Exercises

A. Compare the Facebook pages for your local newspaper with those of one of the major local television stations. How are they different, and how are they similar? Compare how each handles a major local news story that both are covering. Which does a better job on local, national and international news? What differences do you see in terms of philosophy or approach to social media? Support your views with concrete examples.

B. Compare the Facebook pages of the local television stations within your market. How are they different, and how are they similar? Compare how each handles a major local news story that both are covering. Which does a better job on local, national and international news? What differences do you see in terms of philosophy or approach to social media? Support your views with concrete examples. How are they different from the station websites?

C. Examine the various websites and Facebook pages for the stations in your market to determine what other social media the stations are using and how they're using them. Make a list for each station, note specific examples, and evaluate the effectiveness of what they're doing. Which station seems to be on top of the technology race. How does that compare to the ratings race and station viewership?

D. Examine the Twitter feeds from the local newspaper and the local TV stations. Compare the volume and content of the feeds and how they handle breaking local news. Back up your observations with examples.

• • • • •

The Radio-Television Digital News Association (RTDNA) Social Media and Blogging Guidelines*

In 2010, RTDNA's Ethics Committee and Al Tompkins, the Broadcasting and Online Group Leader for The Poynter Institute, developed the following guidelines for social media and blogging.

Social media and blogs are important elements of journalism. They narrow the distance between journalists and the public. They encourage lively, immediate and spirited discussion. They can be vital news-gathering and news-delivery tools. As a journalist you should uphold the same professional and ethical standards of fairness, accuracy, truthfulness, transparency and independence when using social media as you do on-air and on all digital news platforms.

Truth and Fairness

■ Social media comments and postings should meet the same standards of fairness, accuracy and attribution that you apply to your on-air or digital platforms.

■ Information gleaned online should be confirmed just as you must confirm scanner traffic or phone tips before reporting them. If you cannot independently confirm critical information, reveal your sources; tell the public how you know what you know and what you cannot confirm. Don't stop there. Keep seeking confirmation. This guideline is the same for covering breaking news on station websites as on the air. You should not leave the public "hanging." Lead the public to completeness and understanding.

■ Twitter's character limits and immediacy are not excuses for inaccuracy and unfairness.

■ Remember that social media postings live on as online archives. Correct and clarify mistakes, whether they are factual mistakes or mistakes of omission.

■ When using content from blogs or social media, ask critical questions such as:

– What is the source of the video or photograph? Who wrote the comment and what was the motivation for posting it?

– Does the source have the legal right to the material posted? Did that person take the photograph or capture the video?

- Has the photograph or video been manipulated? Have we checked to see if the metadata attached to the image reveals that it has been altered?

■ Social networks typically offer a "privacy" setting, so users can choose not to have their photographs or thoughts in front of the uninvited public. Capturing material from a public Facebook site is different from prying behind a password-protected wall posing as a friend. When considering whether to access "private" content, journalists should apply the same RTDNA guidelines recommended for undercover journalism. Ask:

- Does the poster have a "reasonable expectation" of privacy?
- Is this a story of great significance?
- Is there any other way to get the information?
- Are you willing to disclose your methods and reasoning?
- What are your journalistic motivations?

For Discussion in Your Newsroom

1. When an Army psychiatrist killed 13 people at Fort Hood, Twitter messages, supposedly from "inside the post" reported gunfire continued for a half hour and that there were multiple shooters. Journalists passed along the information naming Twitter writers as the sources. The information proved to be false and needed to be corrected. If one or multiple shooters had been at large, withholding that information could have caused some people to be in harm's way. The nature of live, breaking news frequently leads to reports of rumor, hearsay and other inaccurate information. Journalists must source information, correct mistakes quickly and prominently and remind the public that the information is fluid and could be unreliable.

Questions for the Newsroom

■ What protocols does your newsroom have to correct mistakes on social media sites such as Twitter and Facebook?

■ Does your newsroom have a process for copyediting and oversight of the content posted on social media sites? What decision-making process do you go through before you post?

■ What protocols do you have for checking the truthfulness of photographs or video that you find on Facebook, YouTube or photo-sharing sites? Have you contacted the photographer? Can you see the unedited video or raw photograph file? Does the image or video make sense when compared to the facts of the story?

■ Who in the newsroom is charged with confirming information gleaned from social media sites?

Accountability and Transparency

■ You should not write anonymously or use an avatar or username that cloaks your real identity on newsroom or personal websites. You are responsible for everything you say. Commenting or blogging anonymously compromises this core principle.

■ Be especially careful when you are writing, Tweeting or blogging about a topic that you or your newsroom covers. Editorializing about a topic or person can reveal your personal feelings. Biased comments could be used in a court of law to demonstrate a predisposition, or even malicious intent, in a libel action against the news organization, even for an unrelated story.

■ Just as you keep distance between your station's advertising and journalism divisions, you should not use social media to promote business or personal interests without disclosing that relationship to the public. Sponsored links should be clearly labeled, not cloaked as journalistic content.

For Discussion in Your Newsroom

1. Your consumer reporter at a major electronics show wants to give a glowing blog review of a new digital camera. When the company makes the splashy announcement, the reporter tweets the news. The message virals fast and wide. Your station will be running ads for the camera as part of the company's national advertising campaign. How will you tell the public that you have a business relationship with the camera company?

2. Your political reporter has been covering the challenger in the mayor's race. On his personal Facebook page, your reporter says, "I am covering another candidate who is dumber than dirt." The candidate's press secretary calls to demand that the political reporter be "taken off the campaign." Your reporter's defense: "What I say on my own time on my own website is my business. Plus I didn't name names."

How will you respond? What should you tell the public about the complaint and your decision?

Image and Reputation

■ Remember that what's posted online is open to the public (even if you consider it to be private). Personal and professional lives merge online. Newsroom employees should recognize that even though their comments may seem to be in their "private space," their words become direct extensions of their news organizations. Search engines and social mapping sites can locate their posts and link the writers' names to their employers.

■ There are journalistic reasons to connect with people online, even if you cover them, but consider whom you "friend" on sites like Facebook or "follow" on Twitter. You may believe that online "friends" are different from other friends in your life, but the public may not always see it that way. For example, be prepared to publicly explain why you show up as a "friend" on a politician's website. Inspect your "friends" list regularly to look for conflicts with those who become newsmakers.

■ Be especially careful when registering for social network sites. Pay attention to how the public may interpret Facebook information that describes your relationship status, age, sexual preference and political or religious views. These descriptors can hold loaded meanings and affect viewer perception.

■ Keep in mind that when you join an online group, the public may perceive that you support that group. Be prepared to justify your membership.

■ Avoid posting photos or any other content on any website, blog, social network or video/photo sharing website that might embarrass you or undermine your journalistic credibility. Keep this in mind, even if you are posting on what you believe to be a "private" or password-protected site. Consider this when allowing others to take pictures of you at social gatherings. When you work for a journalism organization, you represent that organization on and off the clock. The same standards apply for journalists who work on air or off air.

■ Bloggers and journalists who use social media often engage readers in a lively give-and-take of ideas. Never insult or disparage readers. Try to create a respectful, informed dialogue while avoiding personal attacks.

For Discussion in Your Newsroom

1. Edgy Facebook and Twitter postings create more traffic, so you urge your newsroom to get online and be provocative to get more attention. How will you respond when your anchor poses holding a half-empty martini glass on her Facebook site? How will you respond if your reporter's Facebook profile picture shows a bong in the background? What would your response be if a producer, who identifies herself as "conservative" on her Facebook page, tweets her opinions during a political rally?

2. A news manager "friends" a neighbor he meets at a block party. A year later the neighbor decides to run for mayor. The news manager gets an indignant call from the incumbent mayor's press secretary suggesting the station coverage will be biased, since your news manager supports the challenger. Does the news manager have to "unfriend" his neighbor to preserve the appearance of fairness? Could the manager make things right if he "friended" the mayor, too?

*RTDNA Social Media and Blogging Guidelines,
adopted in 2010. Reprinted with permission.

18
●●●●●

Online News

More and more, stations break news on the first, best available medium, and that's commonly mobile, social media and the station website.

In terms of station operation, it's critical to understand that stations make money on their website; they make little to no money on social media. So the point of social media is branding . . . and moving people to the website.

At KSNV-TV in Las Vegas, everything gets posted to the website first . . . then social media. That's the directive from station owner, Sinclair, the second-largest owner of TV stations in the country. Critical to the posting: video. The station says people are much more likely to click on a story with video; stories have a longer shelf-life with video; and they'll try to post video with every story.

Stations are also adding more and more web-only content and digital producers and multimedia journalists (MMJs) whose job it is to produce that content. The content includes shorter pieces, frequently without narration but with music and subtitles. It also includes much longer pieces or even series of stories that are designed to have a longer shelf life on the station's website. That's a critical distinction to keep in mind. News that gets broadcast runs once, maybe twice (or so) during the day. But the website also needs material that can live on the site for weeks or even months. Stations understand that the web isn't simply an extension of the on-air brand. It's a lot more than that.

And since the station's digital content is most often seen on a mobile device, the critical cosmetic question becomes, "What will it look like on mobile?" It's a small screen, and lots of print and lots of numbers in charts aren't going to work.

The audience is also spending increasing time with video. Work on creative ways to tell your stories visually and remember that what works best on TV is probably not the best way to visualize the story for the web.

Interestingly, the amount of user-produced content on station websites has only crept upwards. Almost everyone is a content-producer these days, and stations need to engage the audience more – including bringing the audience into content creation.

● ● ● ● ●

The Information Website

All television stations and almost all radio stations (97%) have websites. All television websites include local news (assuming the station runs local news), and 83% of radio websites run local news.

Among TV websites, virtually all include news video, still pictures and text. Most of the sites include live streaming of news and events, live newscasts and a calendar of events. Most also include mobile-related material, user-generated content and live cameras. Most have audio. In the optional extra category – we find streaming audio, recorded newscasts and blogs. Generally, the bigger the market, the more complex the station website is likely to be.

A majority of radio station websites include text, still pictures, streaming audio and audio. A lot have an event calendar. Podcasts, news video and recorded newscasts are less common.

The biggest push at station websites has involved more, better and/ or special content. That's included more news, more material exclusive to the web, more video, more weather, more investigative work, specialized reporting, polls and even mini-newscasts for the web or mobile. That group has topped the list of what stations are doing for the past few years. Right behind that is streaming. That's involved an increasing emphasis on streaming live events and breaking news and, to a lesser extent, sports.

Stations have also made big efforts with social media (see Chapter 17). And stations have worked at better coordination of their websites and their mobile apps; they've instituted more guidelines on who posts on their sites and how often that posting takes place; they've upgraded the content management system (CMS) and backbone of their websites; and more and more stations have hired people specifically to work on or coordinate efforts on the web and social media.

Stations would love to have their audience simply follow the station online and watch video on the station's video streams. Stations make money on their website – not so much on social media. But, for a variety of technical reasons, it's hard to engage with the audience via streaming on over the top (OTT). That's a part of why stations use Facebook Live (see Chapter 17), where it's much easier to engage the audience in real time.

Sinclair and some other broadcast owners try to boost online engagement with things like the "question of the day." Recent examples included, "Do you think the Senate will remain unbiased during the impeachment trial?" and "Are you better off financially today than you were a year ago?" KSNV-TV in Las Vegas says that the station will typically get 500 to 1,000 responses in the average day but can get to 1,500 if the question is particularly controversial. The questions come from Sinclair home office and are mandatory. Local stations can run local questions as well.

● ● ● ● ●

Content Management System

At its core, a content management system (CMS) is a computer program that allows digital content to be created and modified by multiple users who are operating on the same user interface. It's the backbone of how stations create and manage their website.

Just as consolidation has hit the media ownership business, it's also hit the CMS business. Lakana is one of the biggest media CMS systems. Lakana came about from the merging of several CMS companies by owner Nexstar Broadcasting. The system is now widely used by both broadcast and even some print companies. Sinclair Broadcasting expanded its station holdings by buying out a variety of broadcast companies, thereby inheriting a variety of CMS systems. Instead of consolidating down to one of the systems, Sinclair built its own, and all of its stations now use that proprietary system. WorldNow, which was one of the biggest broadcast CMS players, was bought out by digital messaging company, Frankly. A number of broadcasters defected, but WorldNow still handles a bunch of stations.

Some station groups, and almost all public broadcasters, use open source content management systems. Mostly that's an open source platform called Drupal with most of the rest using WordPress.

Does any of this matter to you? Sure. The system you use determines how you as a producer of news convey that news to people online, on social media and on a smartphone. While all the systems do the same general things, they all do them just a little differently. Just as with newsroom software, it's another bit of technology that must be learned for each place of employment.

Colleen Seitz remembers launching WEWS-TV's first website in 1998. She had been working as a producer at the ABC station in Cleveland but wanted to get into management, and this was the first step.

Now she's Digital Director at Nexstar's WFLA-TV in Tampa with a staff of 14 people who work almost exclusively on the station website and social media. The station also has digital reporters who gather original content to post as they determine which stories get the most attention. Other staff members post stories on both social media and online as well. Between smartphones and TVU video over cellular, reporters and photographers can post and/or go live from almost anywhere on either the station website or Facebook Live or both. "We encourage live reports throughout the day," says

Seitz, "whether it's a walk-and-talk update on the story, a news conference or showing off the most visual element of a story."

The digital work is different from regular producing, Seitz says. "You're producing in a different medium [in digital]. You need to think fast, look at a story differently, write better headlines than the competition and figure out the best placement for the story." Then you need to watch the analytics to see what's "moving the needle."

In fact, the newsroom morning meeting starts with digital. Based on the analytics, what are people in the audience connecting with? WFLA-TV uses Google Analytics, Chartbeat, CrowdTangle and Shareablee.

Seitz says the digital team handles the posting of most of the stories on the website/app and social media. Her digital producers find a mix of local and national news to post throughout the day, with breaking news and weather taking priority.

Reporters post their own stories with video – with the digital producers proofing the material and adding extra elements where needed or appropriate. Extra elements include more video – that's top priority – maybe a photo gallery, a poll, maybe infographics and maps. It depends on the story. They'll keep an eye on the analytics to see how the audience is reacting to what they post. That could raise or lower the website position of the story and result in additional material being added.

"The idea," Seitz says, "is to post info as soon as you get it, send in video or add from the field and update the story throughout the day."

At the same time, if the station's digital reporters are working on original content, the station doesn't have to post it at the end of the day like broadcast stories. "We can hold their stories until the next day," Seitz notes, "so it can post earlier in the day when they can build a bigger audience." The earlier a story is published, Seitz says, "the more likely it is to gain a bigger audience."

Reporters will also email in some updates to the digital team since they can get it posted quicker. Reporters are also responsible for regularly posting on their own social accounts and contributing to station pages through Facebook Live, live tweeting events and Instagram takeover days.

"We have a digital guidebook," says Seitz, "and we do a lot of training, guiding, discussions, best practices and social monitoring. There are always two sets of eyes on every digital and broadcast story."

"Instagram has been fun to grow," Seitz says. "We keep experimenting to find the right way to reach our audience. We get contributions from reporters and photographers who post to our page, and our Instagram stories have really taken off with 'swipe up' to get users to our stories online"

Seitz says that digital first means that reporters' deadlines are always,

> NOW, not the next newscast. There is no holding content or exclusives, because you will get beat. In breaking news, it's about getting to the scene and going live online and Facebook first. The station that gets up first usually wins the most viewers through the breaking event.

Live streaming for news is done on both the station website and Facebook Live. The station prefers that the audience goes to the station website because it makes money there, but Seitz says that Facebook Live is critical for branding – for letting people know that you're always live with breaking news and news event coverage.

The station has about six apps that the audience can use to get push alerts for breaking news, weather, sports, live streams, etc. On air, viewers will hear something like, "If you are signed up to get our app alerts, you would have learned first. . . ."

What the station does not do is use digital to tease the audience about news coming up on the next newscast. "News alerts contain real news – not just teases," says Seitz. And if they tell the broadcast audience that there's more online, that better be the case. "Our audience is smarter now," notes Seitz. "They EXPECT to find something more than just the package script online."

●●●●●

Constructing Web News

News on the Web

Start with how people use the web: They don't just read, they scan, surf, scroll, chat and click. It's activist sitting. When they're sitting. On the phone, it's everywhere, frequently just checking in or checking on something they heard about or wondered about or saw on TV. According to Comscore research, the average length of time a user spends with a news website is two minutes.

There are also divergent philosophies among information websites about what news to emphasize. Some are all about local. National and international news can be accessed on demand, but everything featured on the home page is local. Most TV information websites routinely include some of just about everything. Others vary, reacting to the day's (or hour's) events.

The metrics on websites and social media available to stations allow managers to know instantly what people are reading and responding to. Stations can then respond back by rearranging material on the web to raise visibility on stories that are trending and lower visibility on those that are not.

The most successful news websites are being updated constantly.

KSNV-TV in Las Vegas says its biggest online audience is "the lunch crowd," from 1 to 4 p.m. Then 6 to 9 p.m. The station says that 6 to 8 a.m. has a smaller audience, but they know that's not necessarily the case for other stations.

Web Design

We have arrived at a growing consensus on design and navigation. As you wander through station websites, notice the similarities. There's commonly a menu bar across the top or a menu icon in a top corner. Most station websites feature a lead story – generally picture and a headline – which will be followed by a series of pictures with headline choices, allowing users to click on either the picture or the headline to get to the story.

Smartphone users will see a simplified, one-column version of the website, but computer users will probably see one or two additional columns with a mixture of ads and more news stories.

Online Headlines

The online headline performs much the same function as the broadcast lead; its primary job is to capture attention in order to get someone to click on it for more information. The challenge is to grab attention without going too far. Straightforward headlines work best. In many cases, the headline may be the only thing a user sees in order to decide whether to click on it. A cute or humorous headline may just puzzle the user.

Problem headlines:

- Supreme Court: Smith Can Proceed With DTF Hearings
- Honda Leads List of Top 10 Most Stolen Cars
- Diabetes, Erectile Dysfunction, Heart Disease Share Common Link
- Witnesses Decry Horse Doping in House Testimony

Headlines need to be clear instantly, and they need to attempt to grab the user's attention. The first example, above, has two problems. First, it doesn't make clear that it was the *State* Supreme Court, and, second, it uses initials that aren't widely and instantly recognized (Drug Task Force). The second example says too much. Better to tell people that there's a new list of the 10 most-stolen cars. People will check to see if theirs is on the list. The third example is much too long and involved, despite its lack of clarity. In the last example, "decry" is a short, but almost never-used term, and "in House Testimony" can be read multiple ways and is confusing. Keep it simple.

Utilitarian headlines:

- US Judge Blocks Oil, Gas Drilling in Wisconsin
- Two Injured in SW Las Vegas Shooting
- Jeep Recalls More Than 650,000 SUVs
- Report Cites Abuses by Mexican Military

These are all simple and straightforward. Notice that most are shorter than the first group. This is especially important given that most people now access the web on a mobile device. Shorter is generally better.

Better headlines:

- Wounded Officer Battles for His Life
- Car of the Future Not So Far Away
- Iraq Handing Out Cash to People on the Street
- Rapist Gets 25 Years and a Little Mercy

Still short, all of these are more interesting, more compelling and more likely to have users click on them – which, after all, is what the headline is supposed to accomplish. Here's one I saw that I especially liked:

5 bulls found dead in Oregon; then the story gets weird.

Remember that the user is frequently scanning for information rather than reading.

Online Leads

Because web stories have headlines and maybe subheads, the lead of the web story doesn't fulfill the same role as in broadcast. Generally, the web story starts with something akin to newspaper's inverted pyramid – a sentence that generally tells what the story is about. The opening paragraph (which is frequently just one sentence) needs to tell the overall story tightly and succinctly. Remember that every sentence determines whether the next sentence will be read. Every choice provides alternative ways to go. Make sure there's a clear geographic identifier in the headline, subhead or lead.

Some sample leads from stations around the country:

The leader of the City of Spokane's efforts to establish new homeless shelters before wintertime is resigning as the city still struggles to prepare enough space to house everyone on the streets.

— KREM-TV

A fiery crash on southbound I-5 left drivers throughout the Seattle area stranded for hours Friday morning.

— KOMO-TV

A fast-moving lava flow, spewing fountains more than 200 feet into the air, is making its way through lower Puna, sparking immediate evacuations as it covers major roads and threatens more homes in the area.

— Hawaii News Now

Residents of the Bay Area were shaken awake this morning when a magnitude 3.6 earthquake struck off the San Mateo coast near Colma.

— KQED-FM

If you've spent any time waiting for the train to arrive at the Amtrak station in Alpine, you may have noticed it, too: a telephone pole, sticking clear through the pitched roof of a warehouse on the other side of the tracks — as if it just grew there, like a tree.

— Marfa Public Radio

Crews are working to tow away a private jet that veered off into the grass at Signature Airfield near Nashville International Airport.

— WSMV-TV

Some Wake County parents have hired an attorney to demand that the Wake County Public School System halt a program in which students are asked to share their feelings, emotions and thoughts with other students.

— WRAL-TV

Burlington police say a man already convicted of punching strangers is at it again.

— WCAX-TV

The United States Coast Guard said it is searching for a man and three children who went missing off the coast of Maine on Saturday.

– WCVB-TV

New York is one of roughly 20 states where people who aren't lawyers can be elected judge at the town and village level – and one of an even smaller group of states that endows its "non-lawyer" judges with authority over criminal cases.

– North Country Public Radio

A small plane from Rochester ended up short of its destination and landed in Pennsylvania's Susquehanna River on Friday.

– WHTM-TV

Notice that you can tell whether most were written by journalists with a print background and those with a broadcast background.

Online Stories

Stories posted on station websites generally vary quite a bit in length and complexity. Ideally, they all have a picture or pictures and, very preferably, video. Inevitably, the site will include local news done by the station (generally, first choice), with a mix of local, regional, national and international news from the Associated Press, CNN Newsource, other stations owned by the same company and maybe material found on the web.

Along with those daily news stories with a relatively short shelf-life, stations also need longer, more in-depth material that can stay on the website longer and engage users for a longer period of time. More and more, that includes stories done just for the web. Sometimes these stories resemble regular TV reports, but the internet is a different medium, and, more and more, these stories are done quite differently. Some might just be someone telling their own story – without reporter narration. Some just use subtitles to explain what's going on or to bridge different elements of the story. Some include databases, allowing users to look up something in their neighborhood or their school district. Some use data visualization to help users understand complex issues. The opportunities are endless. And these stories tend to be longer – three minutes or more is common. Sometimes much longer.

It's also possible to break stories up into chunks. That might include a basic story – with video. The story might link to a list of warning signs (or whatever is listable in the story). Another link could take users to a map showing where there are more or fewer of whatever you're talking about. Lists, charts, maps, tables and, especially, video all work extremely well on the web.

It's not local, but NBC News is experimenting with a series of vertical sites that reside on the website (nbcnews.com). They're topic specific, and at this writing include *Mach,* on emerging technology, *Better,* which concentrates on health, wellness and productivity, and *Think,* with analysis and essays on current hot topics. And there are newsletters available for email delivery on each of the areas.

Natural sound packages are reported to work well on the digital side – better than traditional TV packages. Natural sound packages simply use the sound of what the story is about, including the comments of people involved in the story – but without (or without much) reporter narration. The idea is to let the characters tell the story. Narration – if needed – is best handled by subtitles. YouTube reports that preferred length is three or even four+ minutes.

The following online story, from WBFF-TV (Fox) in Baltimore, is fairly typical of an online web story:

● ● ● ● ●

"It's a Huge Relief," Parents Win Fight for School Bus

After months of battling Baltimore County schools, and reaching out to Project Baltimore, the fight is finally over for a group of Essex parents.

"It's a huge relief," says Theresa Charney, a Baltimore County mother who wasn't sure she would ever see a school bus drop off her five-year-old son, Owen.

Project Baltimore was there in early January, when that finally happened. For Owen, it was memorable, as he stepped off the bus and excitedly said to his mother, "I got to ride the bus!"

Until this month, Owen was expected to walk about a mile home from Middleborough Elementary. Baltimore County would not provide a school bus, saying the families on Monacacy Road in Essex live less than a mile away, which is the cut off for bus service.

"He's been telling me since school started, 'Mommy why can't I ride the bus home like the other kids do?'" says Charney.

In October, Project Baltimore walked and measured the route. We found, it's a matter of feet. After our story, the County agreed to also measure the route. Our cameras were rolling while the parents and the school system argued over a few feet. During it all, a school bus pulled up to take the staff back to their vehicles, which were parked about a mile away at the school.

When Fox45 walked up the steps of the bus, we saw a full-sized bus apparently sent, for just two people. The parents on the street were outraged that County schools would send a bus to pick up staff, but not students.

After that story aired, the County agreed to work with parents to find a resolution. They planned to come back and re-measure. But then, last month, Charney says she got a call from the director of transportation for Baltimore County Public Schools.

Charney says the County told her they met and decided the parents were right, the route was not safe for four and five-year-old students to walk.

"I'm grateful for Project Baltimore and all the help that you guys have given us, for the help to get us our school bus back, for our kids and for their safety," Charney says.

– WBFF-TV

Could the station have done more with the online story? Sure. It could (and probably should) have highlighted the first reference to "Project Baltimore" so people could have clicked on that for more information. The story could have included a couple of maps – one showing where in Baltimore the story is talking about and another showing the route the kids were walking.

Online Writing Style

Writing for the web is like writing for anything else: quality counts. Still, there are some things to keep in mind specifically for the web:

- Write tightly and succinctly. Online users frequently scan material rather then read deeply or carefully.
- Put as much of the critical information in the first paragraph and virtually everything of note in the first four paragraphs. Most won't read beyond that point.
- As with print writing, one idea per paragraph.
- Use as many keywords as you can in the first 25 words of the story.
- Use bullet points, lists and links to split up stories and make them more visually interesting.
- Remember that your online headline is designed to capture attention and get people to read the story.
- Summaries should be short – and not use the same words as in the headline or lead of the story.
- Whenever appropriate, use multimedia components:
  - Text
  - Still pictures

- Video
- Sidebar
- Charts
- Previous related stories
- Discussion
- Tables
- Surveys

Theoretically, the web has the ability to provide the best of what both print and broadcast can offer. Obviously, it can offer words and information – and it can even exceed print in total volume if warranted. It can offer moving pictures and audio. While newspapers can run a few pictures, the web can run a gallery. While newspaper or TV can run a chart, the web can do that along with a searchable database of information that can answer questions about each user's zip code, local school district or neighborhood. It can take a newspaper's depth of coverage to new levels. It can provide the animation that television is capable of but seldom uses. And it can be as immediate as radio.

Links within a story can also allow a reporter to provide the detailed evidence to support statements written in the story, documents the story may refer to, side issues, background and older articles in the archive. Each of those areas involves depth that most readers won't want but at least some may find interesting.

The writing style for the web appears to be a cross between print and broadcast. The traditional print AP style is common, but the writing tends to be tighter and more conversational – like broadcast. There's more detail – like print. In some cases, stories appear to be print stories, written in broadcast style. In these cases, more attention is given to tight, short, declarative sentences, active, one idea per sentence, logical flow of information. At some sites, there appears to be a trend toward more use of humor or opinion. Or snark.

●●●●●
Beyond Text and Pictures

Data journalism involves the use of numbers to convey information. It could involve things like school test scores by school district or even individual school. It could involve crime statistics by neighborhood. It's not that you couldn't do data journalism within a variety of media, it's just that online can do it so much better than any other.

Data journalism online requires three skill sets: coding, design and journalism. ProPublica's Scott Klein wrote on the NICAR listserv, reprinted by Nieman Lab, a series of steps for a small to medium size newsroom to take to establish a data journalism team. Among his excellent tips: it's all right to start small; recruit people who can do at least two of the three needed skills – and teach the third; have each person be owner of a project (rather than trying to create an assembly line of people who each handle separate aspects of a project); treat members as journalists, not "data monkeys."

Data Visualization

We have a tendency, perhaps, to think of data as numbers. Certainly, they can be: the salaries of state workers; school failure rates by school district; crimes by zip code. There are databases for all of those things, and all of them can be illustrated interactively online. But it's not just numbers. You can map restaurants that fail health inspections, roads that have been flooded out in a storm, and the most dangerous intersections in your community. You could list a number of these things, but interactive maps and timelines and such can help visualize stories in a much more interesting and useful way. One of the best places to go for ideas and how-to insights on this is IRE, Investigative Reporters and Editors. Great toolkits, training, tip sheets and newsletters are available through IRE. Some of the following software suggestions come from IRE, and some come from Al Tompkins at The Poynter Institute in Florida. Al is a wealth of ideas, and you can follow him on Twitter @atompkins. Most of the software includes tutorials of some kind, and the best bet is to try these things out to see how they might be able to help you tell stories.

Charts and Graphs

- Datawrapper . . . create charts, maps and tables from data. The free version allows 10,000 charts and tables per month and 1 locator map per month.
- Google Flourish: flourish.studio . . . data visualization website that turns data into motion graphics (without coding).
- Adobe Spark . . . allows you to create custom graphics for presentations, online or social media. There's a free starter plan . . . then it costs.
- Infogram.com . . . you upload data and then build cool charts and graphs (free).
- BatchGeo.com . . . you drag and drop data files, and it'll map the data (free).
- Awesome-table.com . . . displays data from Google spreadsheets in various types of visuals: maps, tables, etc.
- Tableau Public . . . converts data into charts and tables and more.

Maps

- Vidometer . . . is an iPhone app that embeds a street map or satellite map on your video while you record. Tompkins notes that can be great for breaking news.

- MapChecking.com . . . it's a crowd estimator . . . upload a crowd shot or a picture of an area, and the site will tell you how many people can fit into the space (free).
- StoryMap JS . . . can help tell stories by highlighting a series of locations on a map – and slide for more information (free).

Pictures

- Juxtapose.knightlab.com . . . allows you to build before and after slider for still pictures (free).
- Jeffrey's Image Exif Viewer: http://exif.regex.info/ . . . you can drag an image or enter its url and the software will provide metadata on the image.
- Mojo.video . . . an iPhone app that puts text and animation on top of images and video . . . there are free templates and charges for others.

Audio

- Descript.com . . . is a website that transcribes audio and then allows you to edit the audio by editing the text . . . designed to make podcasts easier to do (free).

Other

- ThingLink.com . . . it's an editor for desktop or tablet . . . to tag photos with an interactive link and then embed them in social media (free).
- Photomath . . . is an iPhone or Android app that allows you to photograph an equation . . . and the app will show you how it solves it (free).
- TimelineJS . . . allows you to create timelines from Google spreadsheets.
- DocumentCloud . . . can create a spreadsheet from a document you upload – even a pdf . . . pulling out dates or data which can then be checked or visualized in some way.

Important Tips

- Before you post a database, make sure it's clean: run it through Open Define. It's a free Google tool that cleans databases.
- Remember the old maxim: garbage in/garbage out. Good-looking graphics won't save bad data. Make sure the data is accurate and clean.
- Never post a picture – still or video – without context. Put a headline with it or an explainer underneath, but tell the audience what they're seeing.
- The best data stories don't look like data stories . . . they're just stories that include data.
- The audience will get the most out of data visualization if it's clean and simple.
- Among the most effective visualizations: bar charts, line charts and maps.

- If you make the visualization interactive, it increases the time the audience will spend with it (and that's good) . . . things like searchable maps, public salaries, crime, health, education, home prices, etc. by zip code.
- Provide useful information.
- If you've put up a searchable database and it gets a fair amount of traffic, be sure to update it on a regular basis.
- Make sure that what you want to post will also be mobile-friendly.
- Be consistent with colors and placement. Newer data can go on the left or right, but it should always be the same. If red represents the current year in a line chart, it should always represent the current year on related charts.
- Too many colors in a graphic can be overwhelming. Moderation in all things.
- It's a good idea to sketch out in advance how you see your graphic looking when you're done. That will help and actually speed the process.
- One of the best sources for help in digital storytelling is the Journalist's Toolbox produced by SPJ, the Society of Professional Journalists. You can find it at journaliststoolbox.org.

One of the best, recent examples of a multimedia online story comes from WXIA-TV in Atlanta. Here's the url (although there's no guarantee it'll still be up when you read this):

www.11alive.com/mothersmatter

Here's the introduction to the story:

> Mothers are dying from childbirth. It's getting worse in the United States while it gets better in other countries. The statistics are alarming, especially for black women. According to the Centers for Disease Control, black moms are three to four times more at risk of dying from pregnancy-related causes. For every 13 white women who die during pregnancy or within one year of giving birth, there are 44 black women. Most of these deaths are preventable. Judge Glenda Hatchett's family shares their heartbreaking delivery room story to raise awareness about pregnancy-related deaths in hopes of finding solutions to maternal mortality.

The story has multiple parts and a variety of links to other, related stories as well as statistics and data from the Centers for Disease Control and elsewhere. The stories themselves include still pictures along with the video, and titles frequently substitute for voiceover narration. There's also the use of data visualization:

Figure 18.1

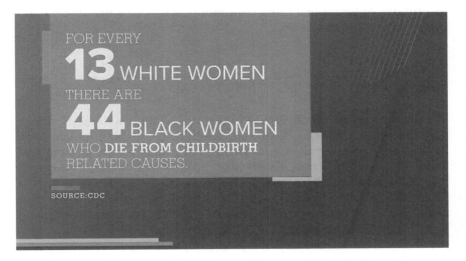

Figure 18.2 Note that the graphic in Figure 18.1 is animated, showing the mortality rates moving along the horizontal axis.

• • • • •

Multimedia

Most of what news organizations put on the web isn't multimedia – it's multiple media. Text with pictures or video or audio isn't multimedia; it's just two media put side by side. Real multimedia – the true integration of text, information graphics (with animation, rollovers and so on), video and slideshows is really reserved for special stories done by a handful of larger, mostly newspaper websites. You can find some of the best work at the NYTimes.com, washingtonpost.com, and pro-publica.org.

Few broadcast websites have moved into real multimedia. In past editions, I've suggested a variety of newspaper websites and some of the best of their multimedia stories. But most of those excellent examples are now dated and have disappeared, and they have not been replaced by the same volume or quality of new multimedia efforts. Good multimedia is time-consuming and, therefore, expensive to do.

Some of the Tegna stations have done some really interesting multimedia work. Check out WXIA-TV in Atlanta (noted earlier), KARE-TV in Minneapolis and KUSA-TV in Denver in particular. KNTV in San Jose did a terrific job on the Camp Fire. So did KOMU-TV in Columbia, Missouri (governor's resignation), WCVB-TV in Boston (gas line disaster) and Mariner East 2 by StateImpact Pennsylvania.

Undoubtedly, there are other first-rate examples.

Real multimedia presentations take time, and they're not applicable for the fleeting news of the day. But for ongoing stories, for significant institutions or issues in a given community, it can be a real demonstration of what the web can do.

● ● ● ● ●

Mobile

Mobile is a unique platform and frequently requires a different mindset from other platforms. First and foremost, it's a small screen. Even the biggest phone involves a small amount of real estate, and content and design need to accommodate that. Shorter headlines, less copy . . . but pictures and video for sure. Frequent updates, too. People using the phone for information are likely to check in often on any story that captures their attention. And the latest Pew Research Center numbers (2019) found that 57% of US adults "often" get news on a mobile device – compared to just 30% on desktop or laptop computers.

The first way to capture that attention involves push alerts. Those are typically short notices on important stories that the audience has signed up to receive. Don't abuse that sign-up with too many alerts or alerts on stories that don't justify it. A successful alert leads the receiver to click on for more. Catalog those responses to see exactly what the audience is really interested in. That applies to general news alerts. More and more stations are also offering subject-specific alerts for weather, sports, traffic, etc.

Some stations allow mobile users to post directly to the station website (although there are some risks with that), but, in any case, you want it to be easy for your audience to send you pictures (especially video) of news that they happen to encounter.

• • • • •

Video

There's substantial evidence that video is one of the biggest attractions on the web. Even for mobile users. Ideally, all stories that you post online would have video – whether it's local and generated internally or something you get from the network, other stations in your group or online. Make sure you don't violate copyright laws. Just because it's online doesn't mean you can post it, and even material from your own network may have restrictions. Second choice is a still picture.

Information on shooting video and picture composition is in Chapter 17.

• • • • •

Podcasts

A podcast is a digital audio file designed to be downloaded from the internet to a computer, tablet or smartphone for consumption whenever the person who downloads it wants to listen.

Podcasts can be a onetime thing or a regular (or irregular) series. They can be free or available at a charge. Information on podcasts is in Chapter 16.

• • • • •

Hyperlocal News

Just like it sounds, hyperlocal news is simply news about a much smaller community than we commonly see covered. Most often, hyperlocal means geography – coverage of relatively small communities within the larger market. That could be anything from a defined neighborhood to a small town. Hyperlocal could also be defined by a common or shared area of interest, like a school or water district. The web is the vehicle of choice for hyperlocal news distribution.

As this is written, a number of the hyperlocal news sites that I noted in the last edition of this book are now gone, and what remains is a shell of what had been. Patch, the largest collection of hyperlocal news sites around the country was spun off from AOL, and a much slimmed-down Patch is now separate and owned mostly by Hale Global. The company says it operates just over 900 sites in 23 states with about 125 full time staffers. That's stretched pretty thin with a fraction of the employees who once populated the company.

There are still a variety of efforts at hyperlocal news, but, so far, the business models have simply not been able to self-support what is an inherently people-intensive industry.

Hyperlocal frequently translates into backpack journalists working out of a car or home rather than an office. But the model and (business) future of hyperlocal news is very much up in the air at this point. Hyperlocal also tends to reflect a blending of traditional news and more broadly-defined information, like community bulletin boards.

Some stations are experimenting with hyperlocal news coverage – especially in markets that combine multiple municipalities.

● ● ● ● ●

Search Engine Optimization and Keywords

If you're posting stories online, you want people to be able to find them . . . preferably ahead of their finding stories from someone else. The keys to that involve SEO and keywords. The acronym SEO stands for search engine optimization and it's about making your site and stories stand out in order to increase the (unpaid) traffic that your site and story gets from people using a search engine.

Most of the major work on SEO is done by the company itself, but the key to traffic involves the selection of keywords that you use to tag your story. These are the specific words that you think someone might use if they were searching for a story like the one you're working on.

SEO responds to changing algorithms by the various search engines and is way more complicated than the few words describing it here. It's also well beyond the scope of this text, but you should at least be aware of what it is.

● ● ● ● ●

Other Issues

The nature of the web and its 24-hour news cycle also offer the opportunity to amplify the biggest problems in the media. Mistakes can live forever in the system unless media develop and follow-up on a comprehensive plan to correct stories, including those already archived.

It's clear that there's a lot more "point of view journalism" on the web than we see in traditional media. That raises questions about whether anyone does or should care about your opinion . . . and whether "point of view journalism" is really journalism at all.

The web offers a competitive world much more like TV than newspaper. In most communities, there is one paper, take it or leave it. There are almost always choices in television. Even more so on the web. That kind of intense competition can energize reporters and editors. It can also lead to bad choices resulting from inadequate thought. And because the web is potentially even more immediate than television, it can amplify TV's potential for speed ahead of facts, accuracy and context. Remember that, in the end, the audience is less likely to remember who got the story first than who got the story wrong.

●●●●●

Summary

Online news has become a critical part of virtually every traditional news outlet, although even the most successful information websites produce only a small fraction of the revenue of the station (or newspaper). Video is critical online and in social media.

Remember, it's still journalism. Do it right. Speed is helpful; mistakes are not.

Think interactively. Think about what you can present or include that can get the user involved. That could include the ability to personalize the data for each user or a variety of multimedia tools.

Try new things. There's still a lot we don't know about using the web. Experiment and learn.

●●●●●

Key Words and Phrases

information websites . . . web design . . . podcasts . . . hyperlocal news . . . data journalism . . . SEO . . . keywords

●●●●●

Exercises

A. Compare the website for your local newspaper with the website of one of the major local television stations. How are they different, and how are they similar? Compare how each handles a major local news story that both are covering. Which does a better job on local, national and international news? Support your views with concrete examples.

B. Compare the websites of the local television stations within your market. How are they different, and how are they similar? Compare how each handles a major local news story that both are covering. Which does a better job on local, national and international news? Support your views with concrete examples.

C. Using the story scenarios at the end of Chapter 11, develop a multi-media online plan for the handling of each of the stories. List all the possible elements that you could include for each of the stories – including elements that would require additional reporting.

D. Based on the discussion in the chapter, evaluate which local information websites do the best job of real multimedia reporting. Pick out the three best, local multimedia stories, and explain why you think so.

19

• • • • •

News, Weather and Sports

• • • • •

Why News, Weather and Sports?

That's the triumvirate we think of when we think about TV newscasts, and that tradition goes back right to the beginning of local TV news. Note that all newscasts do contain news and weather, but not all newscasts include sports.

Research today tells us that, on an average day, more people are interested in the weather than any other single news story. That explains why weather is always a part of TV newscasts and why, if the weather is unusual, stations will frequently lead with it. Absent unusual meteorological conditions, stations generally use weather as the main draw for the second quarter hour of the newscast (see more on this in Chapter 15).

It's not that more people are interested in the weather than in the news itself; it's that weather is more likely to be of more widespread interest than any single news story. Major breaking news changes that equation.

Sports is more complicated. Research tells us that sports is of interest to a minority of the audience, and the most serious sports fans now get their sports news from a myriad of options, including online, mobile or cable/satellite/telco.

Because of all those alternatives in sports information, some stations have dropped sports as a regular part of the news. Most of those efforts have been rescinded. As this is written, there are a few stations that have no sports anchor and simply cover sports the same way they cover any news story. But most have returned sports to the primary newscasts (early and late evening), and there is no evidence that sports is disappearing as a part of TV newscasts.

Still, because sports appeals to a smaller segment of the audience, virtually all TV stations run sports at the end of the newscast, so that if people tune elsewhere or turn off the TV, that desertion won't harm the station's ratings (see more on this in Chapter 15).

Wait a minute, you might think, weather is also readily available from other sources. That's true, but there's something about the personalized delivery of weather in a newscast that has enabled it to maintain its peculiar appeal to a large segment of the audience.

● ● ● ● ●

Reporting Weather

Few topics interest people as much as the weather. Weather and time are the two most important bits of information the morning radio audience wants, and weather shows up as the number one item in most television markets. But the audience doesn't want all of the data available.

First and foremost, people want to know the current sky condition, the temperature and whether anything is going to fall from the sky. Next, they want the short-range forecast. In the morning that means what it's going to be like that day, including sky conditions and temperature. Around noon that means what it's going to be like that afternoon and evening. In the early evening it's the forecast for that night and tomorrow. In the late evening it's the forecast for overnight and tomorrow. Commonly, in radio, we give the audience three day parts. This is what a typical morning radio weather forecast might sound like:

```
In the weather forecast, we'll have partly cloudy
skies today with a high around 55. Tonight, mostly
cloudy, with lows in the mid-30s. Tomorrow,
overcast skies and light rain expected, with highs
in the upper 40s. Right now, we have partly cloudy
skies and 41 degrees.
```

Next in interest tends to be the longer-range outlook: three to seven days. The audience knows (or should know) that it isn't terribly accurate, but they want it anyway. Weather forecasting has gotten better and better over the years, but its accuracy drops considerably as the forecast attempts to look beyond the next two to three days.

Notice all the weather conditions *not* in the previous forecast. Generally, most members of the audience don't care about barometric pressure (since most don't know what it means, anyway). Other than boaters, people don't care about the winds unless they're going to be really noticeable.

Few care about humidity unless it's going to be markedly different from usual or it's high in the summer. High humidity readings in the summer strike the same kind of endurance chord that the wind chill does in the winter. We do like to know when we've endured really bad weather. Tides are relevant for a relatively small number of people right on the coast.

A couple of points on television weather graphics. First, weather isn't a fast-paced video game. Less – and simpler – is almost always more in weather. Graphics are there to help tell a story – not to confuse the audience. Second, daytime highs are normally pretty obvious in TV graphics. That's not always the case for night-time lows. Make sure it's clear whether the night-time low is overnight from Tuesday to Wednesday, for instance, rather than for Wednesday into Thursday.

Severe Weather

Nothing sends people to radio and TV faster than the threat of severe weather. A severe weather warning (meaning that the severe weather condition definitely exists) should be broadcast as soon as it's known and repeated at regular intervals. Generally included in this are tornadoes, hurricanes, tropical storms, severe thunderstorms or other conditions and flooding. Severe weather watches (meaning that the conditions are right for the development of the severe weather) should also be broadcast. **It's important that you make clear what the condition is, the geographic area involved, the duration of the watch or warning, what the watch or warning means and what action, if any, people should take.**

Delivering severe weather information on radio tends to be fairly easy. It can be trickier in television when cutting into longer form programming – especially live sporting events – can enrage the audience. Most TV stations will not cut into programming for a weather watch. That information will normally be conveyed by a crawl (a super that usually runs across the lower part of the screen). Depending on the weather event and the station, the next level of interruption is the split screen . . . with the audio and picture of the station weathercaster on one side of the screen and the regular programming on the other side of the screen. This works fairly well for sports since the audience can still see what's happening in the game, but that won't work as well for entertainment programming where missing the audio means losing track of what's going on. Obviously, the most intrusive weather warning is cutting into regular programming with full screen weather reports. But if the safety of a meaningful part of your audience is at stake, it's far better to apologize for the interruption than to try to explain why you missed a crucial warning.

Careers in Weather

There are plenty of people doing weather on television who do not have degrees in meteorology. But it's increasingly difficult to get a job as a main weathercaster in major, large and even medium markets without that degree and "seal" in meteorology. There are schools that have specialty programs for those seeking meteorology careers, but it's also possible to put together an acceptable program of study at some other schools as well. The most common certification (CBM – certified broadcast meteorologist) is the AMS seal that comes from the American Meteorological Society. The National Weather Association (NWA) also has a certification program.

• • • • •

Defining Weather Terms

blizzard: A winter storm with winds of 35 mph or more, lots of snow falling or blowing and visibility near zero.

Celsius (centigrade): The temperature scale of the metric system, based on 0 degrees as freezing and 100 degrees as boiling (at sea level). To convert temperatures to Celsius, subtract 32 from the Fahrenheit reading, multiply by 5, then divide by 9. Unless your station insists on using Celsius readings along with Fahrenheit, don't use Celsius. Americans have clearly shown that they neither understand nor care about Celsius readings. See also *Fahrenheit*.

chinook wind: A warm, dry wind occurring along the Rocky Mountains, sometimes reaching speeds of 100 mph.

climate: The average of weather conditions *over time*. Just because it's really hot doesn't mean that it's climate change – although climate change could be making it worse. And just because it's cold doesn't disprove climate change. Don't confuse *weather* with *climate change*. And climate change is real so don't be an idiot denier.

coastal waters: Waters within about 69 miles of the coast.

cold front: The leading edge of a cold air mass advancing on a warm air mass. In the summer, thunderstorms can form a squall line in front of the edge. In the winter the result is often a cold wave.

cyclone: A storm with strong winds rotating about a moving center of low atmospheric pressure. Not the same as *tornado*. See *hurricane*.

degree-day: An index that is used to determine the amount of heating or cooling required to maintain constant temperature. The calculation assumes no demand for heat or cooling when the mean daily temperature is 65 degrees. To determine heating degree days, subtract the mean (average) temperature for the day from 65. If the high for a day is 56 degrees and the low 32 degrees, the mean is 44, resulting in 21 heat degree days. Cooling degree days also lead to a calculation of the energy required to maintain a comfortable indoor temperature – using the same formula except subtracting 65 from the mean temperature instead of the other way around.

dew point: The temperature at which the air is saturated with moisture and dew starts to form. When the dew point is below freezing, it's called the frost point – and that's what you'll get.

drought: An abnormal dry period lasting long enough to have a serious impact on agriculture and water supply.

dust storm: Blowing dust of 30 mph or more with visibility one-half mile or less.

earthquake: Involves a shaking of the earth's crust – the release of built-up stress caused by portions of the earth's crust grinding against each other. Commonly measured on the Richter scale. Minor earthquakes occur frequently; a reading of about 2.0 on the Richter scale can be felt by people. Each full point increase represents a doubling of strength. There is no upper limit to the Richter scale, although the highest ever recorded is 9.5 (Chile in 1960). Anything above about 4.5 can cause considerable damage. The Richter scale measures an earthquake's strength. The less commonly used Mercalli scale measures the earthquake's intensity in a given area. On a 1 to 12 scale, 1 means hardly felt, and 12 means total damage.

El Niño: A warming of the tropical Pacific Ocean – starting along the coasts of Peru and Ecuador – that can cause disruption in the world's weather systems. Major El Niño events occur every 5 to 10 years.

equinox: When the sun is directly over the equator. The autumnal equinox is usually September 23 (sometimes the 22nd); the vernal equinox is usually on March 21 (sometimes the 20th). The astronomic starts of fall and spring.

Fahrenheit: The temperature scale that is in common use in the United States. Freezing is 32 degrees; boiling is 212 degrees. In the unlikely event that you need to convert Fahrenheit to Celsius, subtract 32 from the Fahrenheit reading, then multiply by 5, then divide by 9. See also *Celsius*.

flash flood: A sudden, violent flood, usually after heavy rains or considerable, rapid melting of snow.

flood: Streamflow in excess of a channel's capacity. Remember that reporting how high a river or *the water* will crest is meaningless without some comparison – particularly height above flood stage.

fog: A stratus cloud with its base at ground level, reducing visibility to less than 0.62 mile (1 kilometer). *Heavy fog* means visibility is down to one-quarter mile (0.4 km) or less.

freeze: When the temperature remains below 32 degrees long enough to damage crops. *Hard freeze* and *severe freeze* are synonymous and mean that the freezing conditions are expected to last at least two days.

freezing drizzle, freezing rain: Both terms mean that the precipitation will freeze on contact with a cold object or the ground, resulting in a coat of ice called glaze. See *ice storm.*

frost: Normally, *scattered light frost* is the term used. It is the freezing of dew on the ground.

funnel cloud: A violent, rotating current of air that does not touch the ground. If and when it touches the ground, it becomes a tornado.

gale: Usually, gale force winds, meaning sustained wind speeds between 39 and 54 mph.

heat index: A calculation by the National Weather Service of what the combination of heat and humidity feels like. Given as a "temperature," it's based on the idea that when the humidity is high, the temperature feels even hotter than it is. Sometimes called the *misery index.*

Table 19.1 National Weather Service heat index

Relative Humidity	Air Temperature (Degrees F)						
	80	*85*	*90*	*95*	*100*	*105*	*110*
40%	79	84	90	98	109	121	135
50%	80	86	94	105	118	133	
60%	81	90	99	113	129	148	
70%	82	92	105	122	142		
80%	84	96	113	133			
90%	85	101	121				

Table 19.2 National Weather Service – effects of heat index

When The Heat Index Is:	The Possible Reaction:
80–90 degrees	Fatigue – with prolonged exposure and physical activity
90–105 degrees	Sunstroke, heat cramps and heat exhaustion
105–130 degrees	Sunstroke and heat cramps likely . . . Heat stroke possible
130+ degrees	Heat stroke highly likely with continued exposure

heavy snow: Generally, 4 or more inches of snow within 12 hours or 6 or more inches of snow within 24 hours.

high winds: Generally, winds of 40 mph or more for at least an hour.

humidity: The amount of moisture in the air. *Relative humidity* (the term more commonly used in weather forecasts) is the amount of moisture in the air as a percentage of the amount of moisture that air of that temperature can hold.

hurricane, typhoon, cyclone: A tropical storm with a warm core and wind speeds of at least 74 mph. Hurricanes that drop below that wind speed are downgraded to tropical storms. Hurricanes start east of the international dateline; typhoons start on the west; cyclones occur in the Indian Ocean. Otherwise, all three are identical.

hurricane season: When hurricanes are most likely to take place. In the Atlantic, Caribbean and Gulf of Mexico, that's June through November; in the eastern Pacific, it's June through November 15; in the central Pacific, it's June through October.

ice storm: When rain falls through a thin layer of below-freezing air at the earth's surface, causing the rain to freeze on contact; glaze.

Indian summer: An unseasonably warm spell in October or November. Purists insist that you can't have Indian summer until after a cold spell or frost.

jet stream: A narrow band of strong wind, normally 6 to 9 miles up, that influences the development and path of weather conditions.

knot: Used for offshore wind speed and the speed of boats and ships. Because *knot* means one nautical mile (6,076.1 feet) per hour, it's redundant to say *knots per hour*. To convert knots to approximate miles per hour, multiply knots by 1.15.

Northeaster: Strong, steady winds from the northeast – along with rain or snow – associated with a strong low pressure system moving northeast along the east coast of North America. Commonly called a *Nor'easter*.

offshore waters: Generally, from 69 to 288 miles off the coast.

relative humidity: See *humidity*.

sandstorm: Same as dust storm, but for sand: blowing sand of 30 mph or more with visibility one-half mile or less.

Santa Ana wind: A warm, dry wind blowing west into southern California from the high desert plateau to the east, associated with very high temperatures, dust storms and fires.

seasons: Meteorologically, spring is March, April and May; summer is June, July and August; fall is September, October and November; and winter is December, January and February.

severe blizzard: Same as *blizzard* but with higher winds (45 mph or more) and temperatures of 10 degrees or colder.

severe thunderstorm: Intense thunderstorms with high winds (58 mph or more), heavy rainfall, hail, flash floods and/or tornadoes.

sleet: Formed from the freezing of raindrops or refreezing of melted snowflakes into ice pellets 5 mm or less in diameter.

smog: Commonly used to describe polluted air that reduces visibility, especially common over large cities.

snow avalanche bulletin: Issued by the US Forest Service for appropriate areas of the western United States.

snow flurry: A light, on-and-off snow shower.

snow squall: A heavy but short snow shower.

solstice: The summer solstice usually occurs on June 21 (sometimes the 22nd) when the sun is right over the Tropic of Cancer – the longest day of the year in the Northern Hemisphere and the astronomical start of summer. The winter solstice is usually on December 22 (sometimes the 21st), when the sun is over the Tropic of Capricorn – the shortest day in the Northern Hemisphere and the astronomical start of winter.

squall: A sudden increase of wind speed by at least 16 knots and lasting at least one minute.

stockman's advisory: Public alert that livestock may require protection because of a combination of cold, wet and windy weather.

tidal wave: Popularly used to describe an unusually large and destructive wave that reaches land.

tornado: The most destructive of all atmospheric phenomena – a violent rotating column of air that forms a funnel and touches the ground. Not the same as *cyclone.*

travelers' advisory: Alert that difficult road or driving conditions exist over a specified area.

tropical depression: A tropical cyclone with surface wind speed of 38 mph or less.

tropical storm: A warm-core cyclone with sustained wind speeds from 39 to 73 mph. See *hurricane.*

tsunami: A seismic sea wave, generally caused by an underwater earthquake.

typhoon: See *hurricane.*

urban heat island: The higher temperatures in urban areas caused by the burning of fossil fuels and the absorption of heat by pavement and buildings.

UV (ultraviolet) index: A World Meteorological Organization index that measures the exposure to ultraviolet rays on a scale of 0 (least exposure) to 15 (extremely high exposure).

Table 19.3 UV (ultraviolet) index

Index Value	Exposure Level
0 to 2	Low
3 to 5	Moderate
6 to 7	High
8 to 10	Very High
11+	Extreme

warm front: A front created by warm air moving into an area with colder air.

warning: Generally means the existence or suspected existence of whatever the condition is that's being warned about.

watch: Generally means the possibility of or correct conditions for whatever is to be watched.

wind chill: A National Weather Service calculation of what the combination of temperature and wind feels like on exposed skin. The lower the temperature and/or the higher the wind, the larger the wind chill factor or index – and the more miserable and cold we feel.

Table 19.4 Wind chill factor

Wind Speed	Air Temperature (MPH) (Degrees F)													
CALM	40	35	30	25	20	15	10	5	0	−5	−10	−15	−20	−25
5	36	31	25	19	13	7	1	−5	−11	−16	−22	−28	−34	−40
10	34	27	21	15	9	3	−4	−10	−16	−22	−28	−35	−41	−47
15	32	25	19	13	6	0	−7	−13	−19	−26	−32	−39	−45	−51
20	30	24	17	11	4	−2	−9	−15	−22	−29	−35	−42	−48	−55
25	29	23	16	9	3	−4	−11	−17	−24	−31	−37	−44	−51	−58
30	28	22	15	8	1	−5	−12	−19	−26	−33	−39	−46	−53	−60
35	28	21	14	7	0	−7	−14	−21	−27	−34	−41	−48	−55	−62
40	27	20	13	6	−1	−8	−15	−22	−29	−36	−43	−50	−57	−64
45	26	19	12	5	−2	−9	−16	−23	−30	−37	−44	−51	−58	−65
50	26	19	12	4	−3	−10	−17	−24	−31	−38	−45	−52	−60	−67

At minus 18 degrees (wind chill), frostbite can occur in 30 minutes. At minus 32 degrees (wind chill), frostbite can occur in 10 minutes. At minus 48 degrees (wind chill), frostbite can occur in 5 minutes.

● ● ● ● ●

Reporting Sports

For the most part, sports stories are just like news stories – except they're about sports. Maybe it's the local high school star who breaks into the majors. It could be the success of a soccer program in keeping kids off the street and out of trouble.

But sports is more complicated than that. Broadly speaking, sports involves three very different activities.

Reporting Sports Stories

There's sports reporting. If you're reporting a local news story, you would never (or should never) root for one side over another. But if your local major league, college team or even high school team is playing a team from elsewhere, you're not going to last long if you really take a news-like neutral approach. In those cases, sports reporting is a blend of good reporting and local boosterism. Finding that middle ground can be difficult. Local sportscasters or sports reporters perceived as indifferent to the home team can wind up in the (job) loss column themselves. Going too far in rooting for the home team results in boorishness and whining that eventually irritate the audience.

Another common problem – especially at the college level – is that access to the players may be restricted if the team, school or coach is unhappy with the reporting on the team. Charges relating to drugs, violence or questionable behavior of athletes – on any level – can create issues between sports reporters and coaches and teams.

Some sports reporters, concerned about the potential difficulties in covering people who are unhappy with the reporter, tend to shy away from controversy or criticism. Some stations wind up sending news reporters to cover controversial local sports stories because the sports reporters either aren't capable of covering the "news" side of sports or are unwilling to ask tough questions and risk alienating the people they cover.

A sports reporter worried about asking tough questions should probably work in sports public relations rather than sports reporting. Ask the tough questions.

Reporting Scores

A second part of sports reporting involves reporting the game results. The seemingly straightforward delivery of sports scores poses one of the biggest challenges. There is no magic formula. The first thing you need to determine is *which* sports are *how* popular. Radio sports tends to concentrate on play-by-play and scores. Generally, don't give just the winners. The audience may not want a lot of detail, but they want to know who won, who lost and the score. It's also easier to follow sports scores when the announcer consistently gives the winning team first:

```
Boston beat Baltimore 5-to-2 ... Cleveland
over Toronto 7-to-4 ... New York edged Oakland
2-to-1 ... and Detroit shut out Minnesota
3-to-nothing.
```

The repetition of winner-first, loser-second makes it easier to follow, especially when scores are just heard. But notice the variety of expression used to say the same thing. In each case the first team won and the second lost, but vary the way you say it. If possible, no two scores (especially in a row) should use exactly the same words to describe the score. Among the possibilities are *beat, defeated, pummeled, walloped, nailed, drubbed, edged, shut out, blanked, got by, won by, humiliated, squeaked by, trounced, got past* and so on. But make sure you use the right term for the score. Hardly anything sounds as silly as an announcer saying something like

```
Dallas trounced Green Bay 13-to-10.
```

Varying the way you refer to teams is fine, but keep in mind that while everyone understands cities, considerably fewer people know the names of teams. Watch out for *New York, Los Angeles, Chicago* and *Sox*. All have two or more teams.

Television has the advantage of graphics. If you're also going to show the audience the score, you have a lot more leeway on how you say it. On particularly heavy sports days – or for certain sports – it may be best just to run the scores in a crawl, either full screen or at the bottom of the screen.

Play by Play

The third aspect of sports reporting involves play by play and color. Both of those skill sets are well outside of the purview of this text.

Local Sports

If you're in a city with a major league team (in any sport), coverage of that team is clearly a priority. But what if you're in the 80% of the US TV markets that have no major league team? How about big-time college sports? In Columbus, Ohio, Tuscaloosa, Alabama and Eugene, Oregon (among many other places), no professional team has the following of the local university. And high school sports tend to be big almost anywhere – especially for certain sports in certain areas. Minor league teams, especially in baseball, can develop sizeable local following.

The point here is that while there are a staggering number of alternative places where fans can get information on professional teams, there's considerably less competition as you move into other areas. More and more stations are (and have been) focusing on these other areas – along with less organized sports activity that people are involved with in every community.

Common Mistakes

Some general sports reporting cautions. First, the audience assumes that scores are final unless otherwise noted. Make clear if you're dealing with games in progress. Second, don't confuse men's and women's sports. It's incredibly irritating when an announcer gives a series of scores and then notes that those scores were for the women rather than the men (or vice versa). Make clear up front exactly what scores you're giving. Third, college sports involve men's and women's teams; high school sports involve boys' and girls' teams.

● ● ● ● ●

Sports and Teams

Auto Racing

Internationally, the leading types:

FIA (Federation Internationale de l'Automobile)

Formula 1

In the United States, the leading types:

AMA (American Motorcyclist Association – motorcycle racing)

IMSA (International Motor Sports Association – racing prototypes)

IndyCar (Indy Racing League – "Indy" car racing)

NASCAR (National Association for Stock Car Auto Racing – stock car racing)

NHRA (National Hot Rod Association – drag racing)

SCCA (Sports Car Club of America – Trans-Am racing and rallying)

SCORE International (High Desert Racing Association – off-road racing)

WeatherTech SportsCar Championship

Baseball – Major Leagues

Table 19.5 Major league baseball

American League

East	Central	West
Baltimore Orioles	Chicago White Sox	Houston Astros
Boston Red Sox	Cleveland Indians	Los Angeles Angels
New York Yankees	Detroit Tigers	Oakland Athletics (A's)
Tampa Bay Rays	Kansas City Royals	Seattle Mariners
Toronto Blue Jays	Minnesota Twins	Texas Rangers

National League

East	Central	West
Atlanta Braves	Chicago Cubs	Arizona Diamondbacks
Miami Marlins	Cincinnati Reds	Colorado Rockies
New York Mets	Milwaukee Brewers	Los Angeles Dodgers
Philadelphia Phillies	Pittsburgh Pirates	San Diego Padres
Washington Nationals	St. Louis Cardinals	San Francisco Giants

Basketball – National Basketball Association

Table 19.6 National Basketball Association

Eastern Conference

Atlantic Division	Central Division	Southeast Division	Division
Boston Celtics	Chicago Bulls	Atlanta Hawks	
Brooklyn Nets	Cleveland Cavaliers	Charlotte Hornets	
New York Knicks	Detroit Pistons	Miami Heat	
Philadelphia 76ers	Indiana Pacers	Orlando Magic	
Toronto Raptors	Milwaukee Bucks	Washington (DC) Wizards	

Western Conference

Northwest Division	Pacific Division	Southwest Division	
Denver Nuggets	Golden State	Dallas Mavericks	Warriors
Minnesota Timberwolves	Los Angeles	Houston Rockets	Clippers
Oklahoma City Thunder	Los Angeles Lakers	Memphis Grizzlies	
Portland Trail Blazers	Phoenix Suns	New Orleans Pelicans	
Utah Jazz	Sacramento Kings	San Antonio Spurs	

Basketball – Women's National Basketball Association

Table 19.7 Women's National Basketball Association

Eastern Conference	Western Conference
Atlanta Dream	Dallas Wings
Chicago Sky	Las Vegas Aces
Connecticut Sun	Los Angeles Sparks
Indiana Fever	Minnesota Lynx
New York Liberty	Phoenix Mercury
Washington Mystics	Seattle Storm

Boxing

Major sanctioning groups are the World Boxing Association (WBA), World Boxing Council (WBC), World Boxing Organization (WBO) and International Boxing Federation (IBF)

Football – National Football League

Table 19.8 National Football League

American Football Conference

East	North	South	West
Buffalo Bills	Baltimore Ravens	Houston Texans	Denver Broncos
Miami Dolphins	Cincinnati Bengals	Indianapolis Colts	Kansas City Chiefs
New England Patriots	Cleveland Browns	Jacksonville Jaguars	Las Vegas Raiders
New York Jets	Pittsburgh Steelers	Tennessee Titans	Los Angeles Chargers

National Football Conference

East	North	South	West
Dallas Cowboys	Chicago Bears	Atlanta Falcons	Arizona Cardinals
New York Giants	Detroit Lions	Carolina Panthers	Los Angeles Rams
Philadelphia Eagles	Green Bay Packers	New Orleans Saints	San Francisco 49ers
Washington Redskins	Minnesota Vikings	Tampa Bay Buccaneers	Seattle Seahawks

Football – Canadian Football League

East Division	West Division
Hamilton Tiger-Cats	British Columbia (BC) Lions
Montreal Alouettes	Calgary Stampeders
Ottawa Redblacks	Edmonton Eskimos
Toronto Argonauts	Saskatchewan Roughriders
	Winnipeg Blue Bombers

Golf

Major events sanctioned by the Professional Golfers Association (PGA), the Senior Professional Golfers Association (Senior PGA) and the Ladies Professional Golfers Association (LPGA).

Hockey – National Hockey League

Table 19.9 National Hockey League

Eastern Conference

Metropolitan	Atlantic
Carolina Hurricanes	Boston Bruins
Columbus Blue Jackets	Buffalo Sabres
New Jersey Devils	Detroit Red Wings
New York Islanders	Florida Panthers
New York Rangers	Montreal Canadiens
Philadelphia Flyers	Ottawa Senators
Pittsburgh Penguins	Tampa Bay Lightning
Washington (DC) Capitals	Toronto Maple Leafs

Western Conference

Central	Pacific
Chicago Blackhawks	Anaheim Ducks
Colorado Avalanche	Arizona Coyotes
Dallas Stars	Calgary Flames
Minnesota Wild	Edmonton Oilers
Nashville Predators	Los Angeles Kings
St. Louis Blues	San Jose Sharks
Winnipeg Jets	Vancouver Canucks
	Vegas Golden Knights

Soccer – Major League Soccer

Eastern Conference	Western Conference
Atlanta United FC	Colorado Rapids
Chicago Fire	FC Dallas
FC Cincinnati	Houston Dynamo
Columbus Crew SC	LA Galaxy
DC United	Los Angeles FC
Inter Miami CF	Minnesota United FC
Montreal Impact	Portland Timbers
Nashville SC	Real Salt Lake
New England Revolution	San Jose Earthquakes

(Continued)

Eastern Conference	Western Conference
New York City FC	Seattle Sounders
New York Red Bulls	Sporting Kansas City
Orlando City SC	Vancouver Whitecaps FC
Philadelphia Union	
Toronto FC	

Ultimate Fighting Championship – UFC

Mixed Martial Arts (MMA) fighting in various weight classes.

20

•••••

Reporting: Seasonal Coverage and the Calendar

•••••

Seasonal Reporting

There is a cyclical nature to our lives, and much of that cycle is based on the calendar. Some of it's based on religion, some based on historical events and some on the seasonal nature of weather. People who live in cold climates spend more time outside in the summer; our major shopping of the year comes in late November and December because of Christmas and Chanukah.

Our non-breaking news coverage tends to mirror those cycles. Every year, we do stories on New Year's resolutions, major holidays, Groundhog Day, Daylight Saving Time, the busiest travel and shopping days, and so on.

The listings in this chapter will help remind you to plan for seasonal, holiday and religious coverage.

•••••

Solar and Lunar and the World's Major Religions

The calendar in this section lists the major holidays celebrated in the United States, Canada and Mexico. In addition to the important Christian holidays, the major Jewish, Muslim, Buddhist and Hindu holidays are included.

Unlike the Roman, solar-based calendar, Jewish, Muslim, Buddhist and Hindu calendars are all lunar-based, and all have 354 days in a year (rather than 365). However, the Jewish, Buddhist and Hindu calendars add a month periodically (about every three years) which keeps the calendar generally in line with the seasons. That's why Jewish, Buddhist and Hindu holidays will always occur at the same general time of the (solar) year – but on varying days. The Muslim calendar, however, stays at 354 days. That means that, over time, Muslim holidays will cycle through the entire solar calendar. That's why they're listed separately at the end.

● ● ● ● ●

Calendar Holidays

JANUARY

1 New Year's Day: LEGAL HOLIDAY. If it falls on a Saturday, it's observed on Friday. If it falls on a Sunday, it's observed on Monday.

6 Epiphany: Observed by many Christians worldwide, although not necessarily on the same date as in the United States.

Dr. Martin Luther King Jr. Day: LEGAL HOLIDAY. Observed on the third Monday in January.

Chinese New Year: January 21–February 19 depending on the moon.

Sarasvati Puja: (sehr AH swah tee POO jah). Hindu festival honoring Goddess Sarasvati, who represents wisdom, intellect and knowledge, as well as inspiration, arts and music.

FEBRUARY

2 Groundhog Day

5 Constitution Day: Observed in Mexico.

12 Lincoln's Birthday

14 Valentine's Day

Presidents Day: LEGAL HOLIDAY. Observed on the third Monday in February.

22 Washington's Birthday

Ash Wednesday: Seventh Wednesday before Easter.

Lent: Forty days from Ash Wednesday to Holy Saturday (the day before Easter). Lent starts 42 days before Easter in Orthodox Eastern Church.

29 Leap Day: Almost every four years (2004, 2008, etc.). Technically: every 4 years – as long as the year can be divided evenly by 4 . . . unless it can be divided evenly by 100 . . . in which case it's not a leap year . . . unless the year can be divided evenly by 400. So 1900 wasn't, 2000 was, 2100 won't be.

Maha Shiv Ratri: (MAH hah shihv rah TREE). Hindu fast, night vigil and feast for God-Goddess Shiva-Shakti (union of will and power), who dances to create, destroy and re-create the universe. Observed in February or March, depending on the lunar year.

MARCH

Daylight saving time starts: In the United States, except Arizona and Hawaii, clocks are set forward one hour at 2 a.m. on the second Sunday in March. (DST used to start on the first Sunday in April, but the law was changed in 2005 – effective in 2007.) Worldwide observance is variable. Note *saving* is singular.

17 St. Patrick's Day

21 usually the first day of spring: (Some years the first day of spring will be March 20). The vernal equinox.

21 Benito Juarez's Birthday: Observed in Mexico.

Palm Sunday: The Sunday before Easter.

Good Friday: The Friday before Easter.

Easter Sunday: The first Sunday after the first full moon occurring on or after March 21 (March 22-April 25).

Passover: One week occurring in March or April after the first full moon occurring on or after March 21 (14–21 in the Hebrew month of Nisan).

Magha Puja Day: (mahg POO jah). Fourfold Assembly or "Sangha Day." Observed to commemorate a special honor in the life of Buddha. On the full moon day of the third lunar month.

Hindu New Year: This doesn't actually mark the beginning of a new calendar year, but usually marks the beginning of spring, although it is different in different parts of the country.

Holi: (HOE lee). Hindu festival celebrating the courting of God Shiva by Goddess Parvati, and the efforts on her behalf by Kama (God of Love) and Fati (Goddess of Passion).

APRIL

1 April Fools' Day

8 Buddha's Birthday: Observed in Korea and Japan.

14 Pan American Day

15 Income Tax Due: Because of Emancipation Day in Washington, DC, if April 15 falls on a Friday, then taxes are due the following Monday, April 18. If April 15 falls on a Saturday or Sunday, taxes are due the following Tuesday – either April 17 or 18.

Ram Navmi: (rahm NOE mee). Birthday of Hindu God Rama (avatar of Vishnu).

MAY

1 May Day/Labor Day: Observed in Latin America, most of Europe, Russia and the countries of western Asia.

Mother's Day: The second Sunday in May.

Victoria Day: The first Monday before May 25. Observed in Canada.

Memorial Day: LEGAL HOLIDAY. The last Monday in May. (May 30 was the original Memorial Day.)

Vesak or Visakah Puja: (WEH sock POO jah; note that Vesak and Visakah are pronounced the same). Buddha Day. This major Buddhist festival of the year celebrates Buddha's birth, enlightenment, and death on one day. Observed on the day of the first full moon in May.

JUNE

14 Flag Day

Father's Day: The third Sunday in June.

21 usually the first day of summer: (Some years the first day of summer is June 22). The longest day of the year with the most sunlight. Summer solstice.

JULY

1 Canada Day: Canadian national holiday.

4 Independence Day: LEGAL HOLIDAY. If it falls on a Saturday, it's observed on Friday. If it falls on a Sunday, it's observed on Monday.

Asalha Puja Day: (AHS lah POO jah). "Dharma Day." Commemorates Buddha's first teaching. Observed on the full moon day of the eighth lunar month.

AUGUST

15 Assumption Day: Observed in Catholic countries.

Janmastami: (juhn muhst MEE). In Hinduism, this holiday celebrates the birth of Krishna, believed to be an incarnation of Vishnu and the author of the Bhagavad Gita, the most important book of the Mahabarata. Observed in August or September, depending on the lunar calendar.

Ganesh Chaturthi: (guhn EHSH cha toor THEE). Hindu festival honoring God Ganesha (son of Goddess Parvati and God Shiva) as the challenger/creator and remover of obstacles. Observed in August or September, depending on the lunar calendar.

Saradhas: (shrahd). Hindu festival in which offerings are made for departed ancestors. Observed in August or September, depending on the lunar calendar.

SEPTEMBER

Labor Day: LEGAL HOLIDAY. The first Monday in September.

Grandparents Day: The first Sunday in September.

23 usually the first day of fall: (Some years the first day of fall is September 22). Autumnal equinox.

Rosh Hashanah: (rah shih SHAH nah). Jewish New Year. In September or October (1, 2 in Hebrew month of Tishri).

Yom Kippur: (YOHM kih PUUR). Jewish Day of Atonement. In September or October (10 in Hebrew month of Tishri).

NavRatri/Durga Puja: (NAHV rah tree/DUHR gah POO jah). Hindu festival of Great Goddess Maha Devi as Durga, protector of the powerless, celebrating her destruction of evil and the restoration of cosmic order. Observed in September or October, depending on the lunar calendar.

Dashera: (dahsh heh RAH). Recounts the rescue of Hindu Goddess Sita (avatar of Lakshmi) by God Rama (avatar of Vishnu) from an evil demon. Observed in September or October, depending on the lunar calendar.

OCTOBER

Columbus Day: LEGAL HOLIDAY. The second Monday in October. (October 12 was the original Columbus Day.)

Canadian Thanksgiving: The second Monday in October.

31 Halloween

Pavarana Day: (pah WEHR nah). In Buddhism, it marks the conclusion of the rains retreat (Vassa) during the rainy season, which corresponds to the monsoon season in Asia – usually the end of October.

NOVEMBER

1 All Saints' Day: Observed primarily by Catholics in most countries.

2 All Souls' Day: Observed primarily by Catholics in most countries. Observed as the Day of the Dead in Mexico.

Daylight saving time ends: In the United States, except Arizona and Hawaii, clocks are set back one hour at 2 a.m. on the first Sunday in November. (Until 2007, DST used to end on the last Sunday in October.) Worldwide observance is variable. Note *saving* is singular.

Election Day: The first Tuesday after the first Monday in November.

11 Veterans Day

20 Anniversary of the Revolution: Observed in Mexico.

Thanksgiving Day: LEGAL HOLIDAY. The fourth Thursday in November.

Advent: The Sunday nearest November 30 marks the start of the Christmas season.

Chanukah: (KHAH nu kah). Jewish Feast of Dedication. Eight days in November or December (starting on 25 in the Hebrew month of Kislev). Various spellings.

Kathina Ceremony: (kah THEE nah). Robe offering ceremony. In Buddhism, the laity gather to make formal offerings of robe cloth. Observed on a convenient date within one month of the conclusion of the Vassa Retreat.

Anapanasati Day: (UHN puhn uhs TEE). At the end of one rains retreat (Vassa), the Buddha presents his instructions on mindfulness of breathing (Anapanasati). This marks the end of the fourth month of retreat.

DECEMBER

8 Feast of the Immaculate Conception: Observed in most Catholic countries.

Nine Days of Posada: Observed in Mexico during the third week in December.

22 usually the first day of winter: (Some years the first day of winter is December 21). Day of the year with the least daylight. Winter solstice.

25 Christmas: LEGAL HOLIDAY. If it falls on a Saturday, it's observed on Friday. If it falls on a Sunday, it's observed on Monday.

26 Boxing Day: Observed in Canada.

26 Kwanzaa: Observed through January 1.

Buddhist Holidays

Some Buddhist holidays are celebrated at differing times of the year depending on the country. Take the **Buddhist New Year,** for example. In Thailand, Burma, Sri Lanka, Cambodia and Laos, the new year is celebrated for three days starting with the first full moon day in April. In China, Korea, Vietnam, Mongolia, Nepal, Indonesia, and parts of rural Japan, the new year starts on the first full moon day in January, but the celebration can be in late January or even later, depending on the country. Most of Japan celebrates the new year for at least three days, most often starting on January 1.

Uposatha: (uu poh SAH thah). Observance Day. Four monthly holy days, every month: the new moon, full moon and quarter moon days.

Hindu Holidays

Hindus celebrate many religious holidays, but the diversity of the religion leads different parts of the country and different sects to celebrate different holidays. The dates in the calendar represent the major Hindu holidays and approximate month in which they occur.

Muslim Holidays

Muharram 1: (moo hah RAHM). Muslim New Year.

Mawlid an-Nabi: (MOU lid). Celebrates the birth of Mohammed (the 12th day of the 4th month).

Ramadan: (RAH mah dahn). Holy month of fasting for Muslims (9th month of the Islamic year).

'Id al-Fitr: (EED ahl Fah tr). Shawwal 1. The Muslim celebration at the end of Ramadan (the 1st day of the 10th month).

'Id al-Adha: (EED ahl AHD hah). Dhul-Hijjah 10. Biggest day of celebration in Islam. Pilgrimage day for Muslims (the 12th and last month of the Muslim calendar).

●●●●●

State Holidays

Along with the national holidays of New Year's Day, Martin Luther King Day, Presidents Day/Washington's Birthday, Memorial Day, Independence Day, Labor Day, Columbus Day, Veterans Day, Thanksgiving and Christmas, listed next are any additional holidays when state offices close.

In most states, a holiday that falls on Saturday is observed the previous Friday, and a holiday that falls on Sunday is observed the following Monday. There are also discretionary holidays for state workers – frequently including the day after Thanksgiving and the day before or after Christmas. Note that Arizona, Colorado, Florida, Idaho, Kansas, Minnesota, Ohio and Wyoming just have the holidays listed above and are not included in the list below.

ALABAMA

Robert E. Lee Day is observed with Martin Luther King Day in January.

Confederate Memorial Day: Fourth Monday in April.

Jefferson Davis's Birthday: Observed on the first Monday in June.

ALASKA
Seward's Day: Observed on the last Monday in March.
Alaska Day: Observed October 18.

ARKANSAS
Robert E. Lee Day: Observed on the third Monday in January with Martin Luther King Day.

CALIFORNIA
Cesar Chavez Day: Observed on March 31.

CONNECTICUT
Good Friday: Observed on the Friday before Easter.

DELAWARE
Good Friday: Observed on the Friday before Easter.
Election Day.

GEORGIA
Robert E. Lee Day: Observed on the day after Thanksgiving.
State Holiday . . . a more neutral term replacing what used to be **Confederate Memorial Day**: April 26 but observed on a Friday or Monday.
Washington's Birthday is observed the day before or after Christmas.

HAWAII
Good Friday: Observed on the Friday before Easter.
Kuhio Day: Regatta Day. Observed March 26.
Kamehameha Day: Hawaii hero who unified the islands under a monarchy. Observed on June 11.
Statehood Day: Observed on the third Friday in August.
General Election Day.

ILLINOIS
Lincoln's Birthday: Observed February 12.
Casimir Pulaski Day: War of Independence hero. Observed on the first Monday in March.
General Election Day.

INDIANA
Good Friday: Observed on the Friday before Easter.
Election Day.
Lincoln's Birthday: Observed the day before or after Thanksgiving.
Washington's Birthday: Observed the day before or after Christmas.

IOWA
Thanksgiving Friday: The day after Thanksgiving.

KENTUCKY
Spring Holiday: Observed on the Friday before Easter (half day)
General Election Day.

LOUISIANA
Mardi Gras Day: Tuesday before Ash Wednesday.
Good Friday: Observed on the Friday before Easter.

MAINE
Patriots Day: Observed on the third Monday in April.
Thanksgiving Friday: The day after Thanksgiving.

MARYLAND
Election Day.
American Indian Heritage Day: The day after Thanksgiving.

MASSACHUSETTS
Patriots Day: Observed on the third Monday in April.

MICHIGAN
Election Day.
Thanksgiving Friday: The day after Thanksgiving.

MISSISSIPPI
Robert E. Lee Day: Observed on the third Monday in January with Martin
    Luther King Day.
Confederate Memorial Day: April 26 but observed on the last Monday
    in April.
Jefferson Davis' Birthday: Observed the last Monday in May with Memo-
    rial Day.

MISSOURI
Lincoln's Birthday: Observed on February 12.
Truman Day: Observed on May 8 (or nearest weekday)

MONTANA
Election Day.

NEBRASKA
Arbor Day: Observed on the last Friday in April.
Thanksgiving Friday: The day after Thanksgiving.

NEVADA
Nevada Day: Observed on the last Friday in October.
Family Day: Observed on the Friday after Thanksgiving in November.

NEW HAMPSHIRE
Thanksgiving Friday: The day after Thanksgiving.

NEW JERSEY
Lincoln's Birthday: Observed on February 12.
Good Friday: Observed on the Friday before Easter.
Election Day.

NEW MEXICO
President's Day: Observed the day after Thanksgiving.

NEW YORK
Lincoln's Birthday: Observed on February 12.
Election Day.

NORTH CAROLINA
Good Friday: Observed on the Friday before Easter.
Confederate Memorial Day: May 10 but observed on Friday or Monday.

NORTH DAKOTA
Good Friday: Observed on the Friday before Easter.

OKLAHOMA
Thanksgiving Friday: The day after Thanksgiving.

OREGON
Thanksgiving Friday: The day after Thanksgiving.

PENNSYLVANIA
Thanksgiving Friday: The day after Thanksgiving.

RHODE ISLAND
Victory Day: Observed on the second Monday in August.
Election Day.

SOUTH CAROLINA
Confederate Memorial Day: May 10 but observed on a Friday or Monday.
Thanksgiving Friday: The day after Thanksgiving.

SOUTH DAKOTA
Native American Day: Observed on the second Monday in October.

TENNESSEE
Good Friday: Observed on the Friday before Easter.

TEXAS
Confederate Heroes Day: Observed January 19.
Texas Independence Day: March 2.
San Jacinto Day: Observed April 21.
Emancipation Day in Texas: June 19.
Lyndon Baines Johnson Day: August 27.
Thanksgiving Friday: The day after Thanksgiving.

UTAH
Pioneer Day: Observed on July 24 (or nearest weekday)

VERMONT
Town Meeting Day: The first Tuesday in March.
Bennington Battle Day: Revolutionary War battle: August 15 (or nearest weekday).

VIRGINIA
Lee-Jackson Day: Confederate Generals Robert E. Lee and "Stonewall" Jackson: January 16 but observed on Friday or Monday.
Thanksgiving Friday: The day after Thanksgiving.

WASHINGTON
Thanksgiving Friday: The day after Thanksgiving.

WEST VIRGINIA
West Virginia Day: June 20.
Thanksgiving Friday: The day after Thanksgiving.

WISCONSIN
Good Friday: Observed on the Friday before Easter.
Election Day.

DISTRICT OF COLUMBIA
Emancipation Day: April 16.

21

●●●●●

Reporting: The GA and Specialized Coverage

●●●●●

The General Assignment Reporter

Most reporters in radio and television are general assignment (GA) reporters. That just means that there's no telling what a reporter might be covering from one day to the next. Today, it's a house fire and traffic tie-ups; tomorrow, it's a city council meeting and pollution control.

Some larger stations still have at least some specialized reporters. The most likely by subject area are investigative units, education, politics, crime and consumer. Some stations that cover a large territory might also have reporters who specialize in a specific geographic area of the market. They're still general assignment reporters; they just do that reporting in a defined geographic area.

This chapter is designed to help the general assignment reporter cope with the wide variety of topics that he or she might face on any random day.

●●●●●

Business, Economy and Taxes

So many of the stories we deal with on a day-to-day basis – and should deal with more in investigative, enterprise and process reporting – concern money. Some estimates say that as many as a quarter of all the stories we do concern money. Yet business and economic subjects remain perhaps the most underreported and misunderstood of any that we cover.

Part of the problem may be that so many of the people who are involved in reporting and producing the news are young enough that they have too little experience with the financial side of day-to-day survival. Frequently, *young* translates to unmarried, no children, renter and transient, with few ties to the community. Audience members, in contrast, are older, have lived in the community for years, are married, have children, frequently own their own homes and so on. Studies tell us that there's a direct correlation between how long people have lived in a community and how likely they are to watch broadcast news . . . and how often they do so. In other words, the audience is frequently not "just like us." Among other things, they're a lot more involved in the economic life of the community and care a lot more about it. You need to recognize that and respond.

This section will make no one an expert in the field. It's designed as a quick reference guide to demystify some of the most important business and economic terms we encounter every day – keeping in mind the concept that our audience cannot understand what we do not.

Top Money Terms

assessed valuation: Most commonly used in reference to real estate taxes. A house and lot might be *worth* $100,000, but the local government where the house is located may not tax at full value. It may tax at *assessed valuation* – a government-set figure that is a government-determined percentage of the total value. For instance, a community may levy property taxes on an assessed valuation that's set at half the real value of the property. That means you cannot compare the tax *rate* in one community with the tax *rate* in another unless they either tax at the same assessed value (50% in this example above) or you adjust for the difference. A mill rate (see *mill rate*) is then set as a tax on assessed valuation. Without knowing local assessed valuation, you cannot calculate the actual effect of a property tax hike. Generally, the best way to deal with property tax stories is to calculate how much the property taxes are on a home of typical value in the community, then talk about how much the taxes on that property will go up or down.

bankruptcy: BE CAREFUL. The term has more than one meaning because there are varying stages of bankruptcy proceedings. Without any other modifiers, this is a legal term meaning that a company's or individual's assets must be sold with the proceeds going to creditors. *Do not use this term incorrectly. You must differentiate between companies or individuals involved in bankruptcy proceedings and those actually bankrupt.* Most often, companies and individuals file for protection under the federal bankruptcy laws, temporarily halting lawsuits and actions by creditors while an attempt is made to reorganize. The three individual bankruptcy proceedings involve filings under Chapters 7, 11 and 13 of the federal bankruptcy laws. Chapter 7 is final liquidation. In Chapter 11 (reorganization bankruptcy) an individual or company seeks protection from creditors but remains technically out of bankruptcy as a payment schedule is worked out to avoid bankruptcy. In Chapter 13 an individual's wages are garnished. You need to find out under which chapter or section of the law a person or business is filing. Commonly, you should say that an individual or company is filing for *bankruptcy protection* rather than saying that they're filing for *bankruptcy*.

bonds: Interest-bearing obligations issued (sold) by businesses and governments to raise money. *General obligation bonds* are issued (money is borrowed) by governmental units (with voter or governmental approval) and are secured or guaranteed by the governmental unit's ability to tax. *Municipal bonds* are general obligation bonds issued by a city, county, possession, state, territory, town or village. *Industrial revenue bonds* (IRBs) are actually private bonds that are issued through a governmental unit on behalf of private business. Note that the security (what backs the bonds) may be the government, an agency of the government, the project itself or the private business(es) involved. *Revenue bonds* are bonds backed only by the revenue of the project built with the money raised by the bond issue. What backs the payback of the bonds determines how secure the bonds are.

company, corporation, firm, partnership, professional association, sole proprietorship: The terms *business, firm* and *company* are all synonymous in that they all mean an entity that conducts business. Those terms convey no legal status to the firm or business. Anything that does business may be called a company, business, or firm. Corporations, partnerships, sole proprietorships and professional associations (PA) are all viewed as legal entities; most are legally created with documents filed with one or more states and one or more federal agencies – the IRS at the very least. A *sole proprietorship* is owned by one person. *Partnerships* involve two or more people. Although usually small, many enormous real estate companies are really partnerships because of some tax advantages. *Corporations* are formed, among other reasons, to limit liability. The corporate "shell" provides an ability to raise substantial funds while shielding the owners of the stock from personal liability (in most cases except fraud). Most corporations and all large ones are regular corporations. Many smaller ones and new ones are Subchapter S corporations. Sub S corporations operate the same as regular corporations except that the profits or losses of a Sub S corporation are passed directly to the limited number of shareholders. *Professional associations* are the same as corporations. The name is used mostly by groups of professionals (e.g., doctors, lawyers, accountants, etc.) because they believe the name sounds better and less impersonal than "corporation" and because state law does not allow individuals to be shielded from malpractice.

cost of living: The total money needed to pay for goods and services based on varying standards of living normally released with the figures. The difference between cost of living and CPI (consumer price index) is that cost of living includes how people spend their money rather than the fixed market basket comparison of the CPI and includes the effect of income taxes and Social Security.

Dow Jones Industrial Average: This is the total cumulative value of one share of stock in each of 30 specific major industrial companies, most of which are listed on the New York Stock Exchange. This is used as a general guide for what's taking place in the stock market because the 30 companies represent a cross-section of US industry and because they're so big. If the Dow Jones Industrial Average is up 11.02, that means the total dollar value of the industrial shares of stock in the companies followed (weighted for stock splits and changes in the stocks sampled) rose 11 dollars and 2 cents from the closing prices the day before. Stock market reports should state whether the Dow was up or down, by how much and the closing (or latest) figure. The next most important information is the volume of trading, with an indication of whether the trading volume was light, moderate or heavy.

Exchange traded funds (ETF): Similar to mutual funds (see mutual funds), refers to companies that invest money in businesses, the money market, bonds or other defined investments. ETFs get their money from the shareholders or investors. ETFs differ from mutual funds in that they are bought and sold throughout the trading day the same as stocks, while mutual funds are bought and sold at the end of each trading day.

Index of Leading Economic Indicators: A Commerce Department measure (index, not dollars) of where the economy is heading based on 12 economic guideposts. The items measured are (1) average work week, (2) average weekly initial unemployment claims, (3) new orders for plant and equipment, (4) vendor performance (companies receiving slower delivery from vendors), (5) net business formation, (6) contracts and orders for plant and equipment, (7) building permits, (8) change in inventories on hand and on order, (9) change in sensitive materials' prices, (10) stock prices (500 common stocks), (11) money supply (M-2), and (12) change in credit – business and consumer borrowing. Note that the eighth item (change in inventories on hand and on order) is late every month, which leads to preliminary figures being released and then adjusted later.

mill rate: A unit of measure by which real estate or property taxes are levied. A mill is a tenth of a cent (one-thousandth of a dollar). The mill rate is the amount of taxes due per thousand dollars of assessed valuation. See *assessed valuation.*

mutual funds: Refers to companies that invest money in businesses, the money market, bonds or other defined investments. Mutual funds get their money from the shareholders or investors in the mutual fund. In addition to being divided by types of investments, mutual funds are also divided into load and no-load. A load fund means that a commission (percentage) is taken with each purchase of shares (typically 2 to 8% of the investment) by the fund itself for operation, profit and so forth. No-load means that all invested money goes to the purchase of shares with no commission. See exchange traded funds.

prime rate: A critically important term of dubious meaning. Theoretically, it's the interest rate at which banks lend money to their best, most secure customers. It's important because so many other rates are pegged to it. Most business loans float (go up and down) above prime – commonly 1 to 3% higher – adjusted monthly. More and more consumer loans and even some home mortgages and credit card rates are pegged to the prime rate. What makes the figure dubious is that the best, most secure companies frequently borrow money below the prime rate, making the figure arbitrary. The federal discount rate, set by the Federal Reserve Board, is one of the major determinants of the prime rate.

real estate taxes: Always a plural unless used as an adjective. This is actually a combination of taxes levied on all taxable real estate. Normally collected by a local jurisdiction, commonly counties, it's a combination of county tax, school or education tax, plus a variety of taxes for other services. Real estate taxes are assessed in mills based on assessed valuation and mill rate (see both).

unemployment: Figures are released monthly by the Labor Department. The figures include people the government says are actively seeking employment but who are still unemployed, with seasonal adjustments figured in. Unemployed figures do not include those the government says are no longer looking for work, which is why critics charge that the figures understate actual unemployment and completely ignore under-employment. Members of the military are not included in the figures since there's no such thing as unemployed military.

● ● ● ● ●

Crime and Legal

Great care must be taken when writing about crime to avoid violating the spirit of our system: People are innocent until proven guilty. That same care also avoids potentially costly libel actions.

Journalistically, we'd probably be better off if we applied the same standards to crime stories that we apply to just about everything else. There's no question that the audience is interested in and concerned about crime, but there's no evidence that the audience cares about meaningless, petty crime that has no implications beyond the one or two people involved. Yet that's exactly what so many stations seem to spend so much time covering night after night.

Years before her death from cancer, Carole Kneeland, then news director of KVUE-TV in Austin, Texas, determined that the notion, "if it bleeds, it leads," really shouldn't be the credo of local TV news. With help from others, she developed five criteria that crime stories had to meet to go on the air:

1. Is there an immediate threat to public safety?
2. Is there a threat to children?
3. Do people in the audience need to take some action?
4. Is there a meaningful impact the story has on the community?
5. Is the story about crime prevention?

A crime story that didn't meet at least one of those criteria didn't go on the air. The effect was to decrease the amount of crime coverage the station did, but Kneeland and others at the station argued that all they really did was apply the same standards for crime coverage that they already applied to other things.

Attribution

Always use qualifiers and attribution when dealing with someone accused of a crime until and unless that person is found guilty in a court of law. Sometimes that attribution can seem cumbersome, but there's no shortcut. Every time you link an identifiable person as a possible perpetrator in an illegal, immoral or questionable activity, you must have some form of attribution. And remember that a person may be identified not only by name, but also by picture or even a description that sufficiently allows that person to be singled out.

Alleged

Alleged is a legal term that generally means *charged.* Alleged will serve as a form of attribution but should not be first choice because it's not a word commonly used in conversational English, and the way it's commonly used will frequently *not* protect a station in a legal action.

LEGALLY
OKAY: Police allege that John Smith committed the
robbery....

Although the attribution in the sentence above is fine, the writing isn't. No one speaks like that.

POOR
USAGE: John Smith allegedly robbed....

This is not the way people speak, nor does this sentence make clear who's alleging that John Smith robbed anyone.

BETTER: Police arrested John Smith for the robbery....

ALSO
BETTER: POLICE SAY JOHN SMITH ROBBED....

ALSO
BETTER: Police have charged John Smith with robbing....

Note in the first example, "Police arrested John Smith for the robbery..." requires no further attribution for that part of the sentence. Someone was either arrested or not – that's a fact, not a defamatory statement. In our system people are innocent until proven guilty, so there's no problem with *correctly* stating that someone was arrested.

A story that includes details of a crime along with an identifiable suspect is usually best handled by citing police:

PROPER
ATTRIBUTION: Police say Smith entered the office holding a
shotgun and left with a bag stuffed with 20-dollar
bills.

That last example contains proper attribution that's both conversational and makes clear the source of the charges.

Misplaced Attribution

Watch out for misplaced attribution:

PROBLEM: `Police arrested John Smith for the alleged robbery....`

The attribution for *John Smith* is fine, but the *alleged* before *robbery* means you're questioning whether the robbery itself took place. If that's really what you mean to do, make that issue clear. Hardly anyone is *allegedly murdered*. Usually, we know whether the person was killed; at issue is who did it. *Alleged* or any other qualifier is normally both unnecessary and inappropriate in front of the crime. Qualifiers are needed only in reference to the accused.

Cautions

Using a phrase like *the alleged murderer* provides a writing shortcut that may be technically correct but potentially unfair because of the ease with which the audience may either miss *alleged* or not fully understand the critical qualifier. Note also that only someone actually charged with a crime can be considered *alleged* to have done it. Again, if a prosecutor or police say that someone is a murderer, make that clear – and skip *alleged*.

Suspected technically applies to the process of investigation before any charge is made.

ACCEPTABLE: `Police say James Smith is a suspect in the case....`

The bigger question is whether you should be identifying people who are merely suspects but have not been charged with a crime. Generally, don't identify suspects unless there's a compelling reason to do so. And remember that *suspected* applies only when authorities suspect someone of a crime – not when you do.

Increasingly, law enforcement agencies are identifying "people of interest." That's just another way of saying that someone is a *suspect*. Be careful. Remember that if police had enough evidence, they'd have charged the person with a crime. Identifying suspects or *people of interest* appears to be a way to have the news media help police gather evidence. Quite a few high profile *people of interest* have never been charged with crimes but have had their reputations damaged by overzealous law enforcement and complicit news media.

Get the Terms Right

Burglary, holdup, larceny, robbery, stealing, theft. *These terms are not interchangeable. Theft* is the general term meaning the unlawful appropriation of someone else's property. *Stealing* and *theft* may be used as alternative descriptions for *larceny* and *burglary*. *Larceny* is the legal term for *theft*, broken down between petty larceny and grand larceny. Each state determines where the line is drawn, but it's usually pretty low (e.g., $25 to $150). *Burglary* and *robbery* are the terms to describe *how* an unlawful appropriation took place. *Burglary* is frequently regarded as a crime against property – involving the unlawful entry into a house or building for the purpose of theft; *robbery* is a crime against people – involving the forcible taking of valuables or possessions from a person through the use of weapons or intimidation. *Holdup* may be used for a robbery committed with a weapon – officially called *armed robbery*.

Homicide, manslaughter, murder. These terms are similar in meaning *but cannot be used interchangeably. Homicide* is the unlawful death or killing of someone, as opposed to lawful state or military action. *Manslaughter* is also killing someone but normally without malice, sometimes unintentionally. This is a formal legal charge and generally carries a considerably lighter potential penalty than murder. *Murder* is the premeditated killing of someone or, frequently, killing someone during the commission of another crime (such as robbery).

Top Crime and Legal Terms

acquitted, innocent, not guilty: All these terms mean the same thing, although neither judges nor juries actually declare someone accused of a crime *innocent*. However, because of potential confusion either because the audience missed the word *not* or the announcer dropped it, some consider it better to use *acquitted* or *innocent* rather than *not guilty*.

arraignment: A court proceeding in which a person charged with a crime is informed of the charges against him or her. At this proceeding, bail may be set, a defense attorney may be appointed, and a plea may be entered.

civil, criminal: *Civil* actions concern violations of private (individual, business or governmental agency) rights. Civil suits seek monetary damages and/or relief by a court order. *Criminal* actions are brought by a governmental unit charging the commission of a crime. Criminal charges may result in a fine or imprisonment or both.

concurrent sentence: Sentences for more than one crime in which the guilty party serves the sentences at one time (concurrently) rather than successively. See also *cumulative sentence*.

cumulative sentence: Sentences for more than one crime in which the guilty party serves the sentences one after the other. The same as accumulative – although *cumulative* is a better word – and the opposite of concurrent. See also *concurrent sentence*.

deposition: Sworn testimony of a witness that is taken outside of court.

felony, misdemeanor: Both terms relate to the commission of a crime but differ in the severity of the charges and potential punishment. A *felony* is normally a serious charge carrying a potential punishment of a lengthy (one year or more) prison term or death. A *misdemeanor* is a less serious charge usually carrying a potential punishment of a fine and/or a shorter term in jail or a workhouse.

grand jury: Typically, a group of 12 to 23 individuals who are empaneled to hear evidence about potential wrongdoing and empowered to decide whether formal charges (an indictment) should be issued against someone.

indict, indictment: Use these words only in the legal context of bringing charges. *Indictment* involves the formal charges placed by a grand jury against one or more people, organizations or businesses alleging the commission of a crime. Charges brought without a grand jury are called an *information*.

jail, prison: Both *prisons* and *jails* do the same things: confine people convicted of crimes and some people awaiting trial. Normally, a *jail* serves to confine people convicted of lesser charges and serving shorter sentences. All penitentiaries are *prisons*.

pardon, parole, probation: *Pardon* means forgiveness. It is the release from sentence for someone accused – and convicted – of wrongdoing. Note that the person pardoned is not absolved from the wrongdoing but is simply released from confinement or the prospect of confinement. *Parole* is the release from confinement (usually for good behavior) before a full sentence is served. *Probation* is the release from the *prospect* of confinement (suspension of sentence) for someone who has been found guilty of a crime. Normally, the person must remain on good behavior and is under supervision.

plea bargain: Negotiation between the prosecution and defense in a criminal proceeding that results in a reduced charge and reduced sentence or other arrangement in exchange for a guilty plea.

●●●●●

Education

When stations look over a list of what their audience is most concerned about – either a list they've constructed by surveying their audience or a list supplied by a consultant – education is always near the top.

Despite all the national and political discussion, education is fundamentally a local issue. There are some national mandates, but most of what happens in education is determined by a local board and administration within the guidelines established by a state board of education or the equivalent.

For the K (kindergarten) through 12 grades, states commonly have a commissioner or superintendent of education. That person is most often appointed by the governor, but it's an elected position in some cases. States frequently determine educational minimums like the number of school days per year and the number of credits required for graduation and so on. A state office or a board may also prescribe minimum statewide testing results.

From a public school standpoint, most states offer half- or full-day kindergarten, and kids continue in elementary school through fifth grade. Middle school commonly includes grades 6, 7 and 8, with high school 9 through 12. For a variety of reasons – most often economic – an increasing number of communities are trying alternative combinations.

On a local basis, it's common to have an elected school board. It's frequently a non-partisan election, which means candidates are not identified by party affiliation. The school board is responsible for hiring and overseeing a superintendent for the school district. The superintendent then oversees a central administration staff and is typically responsible for hiring and managing principals for the various schools in the district. There are a number of variations on this theme, so check on how your local system operates.

Private schools typically are required to follow certain key state guidelines, but since they normally do not receive local or state tax dollars, they are largely free to administer themselves as they see fit. There is also an increasing trend toward home schooling, where one or both parents take on the responsibilities for schooling kids at home. Sometimes those students can also get involved with public school after-school activities. Sometimes a student may be home schooled because the parents want nothing to do with the public school system.

While private schools do not normally receive public tax dollars, there are a variety of plans with school vouchers taking place. Under that system, parents may be eligible for a voucher (a predetermined amount of tax dollars) that can go to either the local public school or another public school or even a private school – wherever the child goes. In a 5–4 decision, the US Supreme Court upheld the constitutionality of school vouchers, but some state courts have held that a given state constitution does not permit vouchers.

In most places in this country, the biggest source of school funding comes from local property taxes. But because courts found that poorer school districts offered fewer educational opportunities, a varying amount of state money commonly supplements local tax dollars to help toward evening out the per pupil support system. At the same time, there appears to be a growing trend in having state government pick up more of the tab for public education. Again, check on how things work in your state.

Higher education commonly operates differently. Some states have a board or commission that oversees public higher education; some do not. As higher education expenses have risen and states have cut budgets, more and more state schools argue that they have moved from "state-supported" to "state-assisted." Some not too jokingly worry that they're moving rapidly toward simply being "state-located."

As expenses have increased and relative state support has dropped, student tuition and fees have picked up more and more of the operating costs. Depending on the size of the state, there are commonly different tiers of state institutions. The top rung includes the large research institutions; the second rung might include smaller or more specialized research institutions or even non-research institutions; a third rung might be two-year (freshman and sophomore) or community colleges. As state money has become tighter, there has been a tendency to limit duplication among state schools, and more schools now have subject areas of defined strength where extra resources are put. Other than requirements needed for accreditation, private universities are largely free to operate as they choose.

Top Education Terms

accreditation: A process by which an outside organization certifies the minimum qualifications of the staff, facilities and operation of an educational organization. For instance, the National Council for the Accreditation of Teacher Education sanctions most teacher-education programs, and there are six regional accreditation associations for colleges and universities.

alternative schools: Generally, public schools set up by states or school districts for students not succeeding in traditional public schools.

at risk: Describes students with socioeconomic challenges, such as poverty or teen pregnancy, which may place them at a disadvantage in achieving academic, social or career goals.

Brown v. Board of Education (of Topeka, Kansas): The 1954 Supreme Court decision that banned racially segregated schools.

busing: Usually refers to the racial integration of schools by busing students to achieve racial balance. Note that most students are bused simply for transportation and not to achieve any form of integration.

charter schools: Schools that receive public funding but are independent of traditional public schools.

Common Core: Developed by a group of government and business leaders, it's a set of grade-by-grade standards for what should be learned in English and math related areas. Most states have adopted some or all of the standards – which was a requirement to receive special federal school funding dollars.

corporal punishment: Generally refers to spanking or paddling students for disciplinary reasons. At this writing, 19 US states permit corporal punishment. Most are in the South, Southwest and Midwest.

Individuals with Disabilities Education Act (IDEA): A 1975 federal law, originally known as the Education for All Handicapped Children Act, where federal money goes to schools that must then guarantee that all children with disabilities receive a free public education.

magnet school: A school that specializes in a particular field such as science or the arts, to attract students from elsewhere in a school district.

No Child Left Behind Act of 2001: Signed into law in 2002, the bill was structured on four principles: accountability, choices for parents, more local control and using research to determine what works. At this writing, the law has become less popular because, many have charged, that it emphasizes testing more than actual learning.

tenure: Most commonly refers to the controversial practice of near-guaranteed employment for teachers and professors who have successfully taught at one place for a certain period of time and met other job requirements.

Title I, VII and IX: Title I is the nation's largest federal education program. Created in 1965 during the War on Poverty, Title I of the Elementary and Secondary Education Act addresses remedial education programs for poor and disadvantaged children. Title VII refers to a federal program to make non-native students proficient in English. Title IX is commonly noted in regard to sports programs; it bars gender discrimination in schools that receive federal funds.

●●●●●

The Environment

Historically, the environment has shown up as a major local issue only when there's been a major local environmental problem: a particularly polluted river, a toxic waste site or spill, controversial battles over land use and endangered animals. When the local problem has been addressed, the environment has tended to fade as a pressing issue.

Global warming/climate change has changed that. While individuals and groups may disagree over how severe or immediate the threat of global warming, few now disclaim its existence. To be clear: climate change is not an unproven theory; it is fact. That's raised the consciousness on the issue and led to increased news coverage, including new coverage on how the people and businesses in each area contribute to making the environment better – or worse.

Top Environment Terms

altered weather patterns: The theory that global warming will, among other consequences, lead to unnatural changes in the weather. Note that natural occurrences, like El Niño, can also alter weather patterns.

carbon footprint: The measure, in units of carbon dioxide, of greenhouse gases added to the environment by individuals, groups or organizations. Calculations can be made of the direct or primary contribution based on fossil fuels consumed and the indirect or secondary contribution made by others (individuals or organizations) whose services we use.

Clean Air Act: Air quality regulation started in 1955, with The Clean Air Act coming in 1963, with significant changes in 1967, 1970, 1977 and 1990. The act defined air pollution and provided for federal authority to regulate it.

Clean Water Act: First passed in 1972 with significant amendments in 1977 and 1987, the CWA defined water pollution and provided for federal authority to regulate it.

endangered species: A species that is in danger of extinction through either natural (e.g. overpopulation of predators) or unnatural (e.g. use of pesticides) conditions.

fossil fuels: Non-regenerative sources of fuel found within the Earth's crust as a result of millions of years of pressure on the remains of animals and plants, where energy is given off as a result of burning. Examples include coal, oil and gas. Non-fossil fuels include nuclear, hydroelectric, geothermal, solar and wind power as well as wood and some other materials.

global warming: The increase in the average temperature of the Earth's air and water. Generally attributed primarily to the burning of fossil fuels, which has resulted in the accumulation of greenhouse gases, which traps the heat produced on Earth and prevents that heat from escaping into space. There is concern that as heat builds up, there will be more and more significant changes in the climate and melting of glaciers which will increase the water level of the oceans, resulting in increased coastal flooding.

greenhouse gases: Gases in the Earth's atmosphere that prevent heat from escaping into space, thus forming a "greenhouse" effect, trapping the heat in the Earth's atmosphere and raising the temperature of the Earth's air and water.

nuclear power: The generation of energy through nuclear technology – most often nuclear fission, the splitting of the nucleus of an atom. The only nuclear reactor to go online in the US since 1996 is the Tennessee Watts Bar Unit 2 in 2016. Even so, nuclear power supplies almost 20% of US electricity and about 14% of the world's electricity. At this writing, there are two new US reactors under construction.

ozone: At the Earth's surface, ozone is a pollutant. In the atmosphere, a part of the stratosphere called the ozone layer, ozone helps to filter harmful ultraviolet rays from the sun.

renewable energy: The generation of energy by using natural resources that regenerate themselves naturally. Most commonly, hydroelectric (water), windmills (wind), solar (sun), geothermal and some others.

risk assessment: The term frequently applies to public health or the environment and involves the determination of the amount of risk involved in any enterprise or activity along with the potential size of the loss.

● ● ● ● ●

Geography

As with many things in life, the geographic lines identifying where we are and where we're near are not as clear-cut as we might like. Even terms like *here* and *there* can get us in trouble, depending on where we are and where the audience is. *Local* usually works well, although from one end to the other within a market may not seem very local. It gets worse beyond that.

We frequently refer to stories as being *regional*, and the government and private business frequently release data by regions, but there is no universal agreement about where one region starts and the next one begins. To an Easterner, Texas may be in the Southwest, but to a Texan or a New Mexican it all depends. And some terms we think of as *geographic* are really more *political*.

Major US Geographic Terms

Appalachia: Geographically, the term applies to all of the area through which the Appalachian Mountains pass. However, we commonly mean the poorer areas of eastern Tennessee, eastern Kentucky, southeastern Ohio and western West Virginia.

Bible Belt: A subjective phrase that is variously applied to parts of the South, Midwest and Southwest. Limit the use of this phrase to quotes.

Corn Belt: North central Midwest (where corn is a major product), including parts of Ohio, Indiana, Illinois, Iowa, Nebraska and Kansas.

Cotton Belt: Parts of the South and Southeast where cotton is (or was) grown.

Deep South: Generally viewed as Alabama, Georgia, Louisiana, South Carolina and Mississippi.

Down East: The southeastern part of Maine.

Eastern Shore: Parts of Maryland and Virginia east of the Chesapeake Bay.

Great Lakes: Forming part of the border between the United States and Canada. From west to east, they are Lake Superior (bordering Minnesota, Wisconsin and Michigan), Lake Michigan (bordering Wisconsin, Illinois, Indiana and Michigan), Lake Huron (bordering Michigan), Lake Erie (bordering Michigan, Ohio, Pennsylvania and New York) and Lake Ontario (bordering New York).

Great Plains: The grasslands of the United States, running from North Dakota, South Dakota, Nebraska, Kansas and Oklahoma to Texas and including portions of Colorado, Wyoming and Montana.

Gulf Coast: Running along the Gulf of Mexico, it includes the western shore of Florida and the shores of Alabama, Mississippi, Louisiana and Texas.

Nevada: Pronounced neh VA dah (as in Canada) . . . not neh VAH dah (as in ah ha).

New England: Connecticut, Maine, Massachusetts, New Hampshire, Rhode Island and Vermont.

New York City: Includes the five boroughs of Manhattan, Queens, Brooklyn, the Bronx and Staten Island.

North Slope: The area of Alaska north of the Continental Divide and draining into the Arctic Ocean, running across northern Alaska.

Outer Banks: The islands along the coast of North Carolina.

Sea Islands: The islands along the coasts of South Carolina, Georgia and Florida.

Sun Belt: Generally viewed as those states in the South and Southwest from Florida all the way west into California.

Voice of America Pronunciation Guide

One of the best places to locate pronunciations of names in the news – both geographic and people – is the Voice of America Pronunciation Guide (pronounce.voanews.com). You can look up pronunciations from a long list of names (mostly international) in the news or type in exact or approximate names in order to find the pronunciation. Along with a phonetic spelling, VOA also provides an audio file to hear how the name should be pronounced.

Major World Geographic Terms

Asian Subcontinent: Bangladesh, Bhutan, India, Nepal, Pakistan and Sri Lanka.

Baltic states: Formerly part of the Soviet Union, the independent states of Latvia, Lithuania and Estonia.

British Isles: The group of islands including Great Britain, Ireland and the adjacent islands.

Caribbean: The Bahamas, Cuba, Hispaniola (Dominican Republic, Haiti), Jamaica, Puerto Rico and the West Indies.

Central America: The southernmost part of North America: Belize, Costa Rica, El Salvador, Guatemala, Honduras, Nicaragua and Panama.

China: Use for mainland China (People's Republic of China). Note that the Chinese capital is Beijing (bay JING), formerly known in the West as Peking. Use Taiwan (tye-WAHN) – formerly known as Formosa – for the island country off China. Note that China considers Taiwan to be a renegade province.

down under: Marginal reference for Australia, New Zealand and some of the other countries in the area, which are better referred to as being in the South Pacific.

Far East: The easternmost part of Asia: China, Hong King, Japan, North and South Korea, and Taiwan. Technically also refers to Siberia, but don't use the term that way.

Germany: East (German Democratic Republic) and West (Federal Republic of Germany) Germany reunified in October 1990. The capital is Berlin.

Great Britain: Includes England, Scotland and Wales. The United Kingdom includes Great Britain and Northern Ireland. Ireland itself is separate.

Indochina: Part of Southeast Asia including Cambodia, Laos and Vietnam.

Latin America: Countries south of the United States where Romance languages (Spanish, Portuguese, French) predominate.

Maritime Provinces: Nova Scotia, New Brunswick and Prince Edward Island in Canada.

Middle East: Afghanistan, Cyprus, Egypt, Iran, Iraq, Israel, Kuwait, Jordan, Lebanon, Oman, Qatar, Saudi Arabia, South Yemen, Sudan, Syria, Turkey, the United Arab Emirates and Yemen. Note that *Middle East* refers to a general region that crosses continents.

Nordic countries: A general reference to the Scandinavian countries: including Denmark, Finland, Iceland, Norway and Sweden.

Persian Gulf: The major oil shipping waterway to the Gulf of Oman and the Arabian Sea, bordered by Bahrain, Iran, Iraq, Kuwait, Qatar, Saudi Arabia, and the United Arab Emirates.

Scandinavia: Denmark, Iceland, Norway, Sweden and, arguably, Finland.

West Indies, the: Anguilla, Antigua, Aruba, Barbados, Caribbean Netherlands (Bonaire, Sint Eustatius and Saba), Curaçao, Dominica, Grenada, Guadeloupe, Martinique, St. Kitts and Nevis, St. Lucia, St. Vincent, Trinidad, Tobago, and all Virgin Islands (British and US islands of St. Croix, St. John and St. Thomas). Common usage places the West Indies as part of the Caribbean, and that description is acceptable.

●●●●●

Government

The federal government is divided into three branches: executive (White House, federal agencies); legislative (Congress) and judicial (the federal court system, including the US Supreme Court). All must operate within the current interpretations of the Constitution by the federal courts and, ultimately, the US Supreme Court.

The give and take of those three branches shape the contours of the system. The executive branch proposes policies, makes appointments and administers the law. The legislative branch passes laws (which the president signs or vetoes). Financial matters generally originate in the House of Representatives, commonly in response to presidential initiatives. High-level presidential appointments and international treaties must be approved by the Senate. Exceptions are those who work for the president in a personal, staff capacity, such as the national security adviser and press secretary.

Although Congress enacts legislation, the laws themselves are administered by the various federal agencies under the control of the executive branch. Those agencies – and the courts – promulgate rules and regulations based on their interpretation of congressional law and the legislation itself. Any rule or regulation may be changed by the implementing agency or by congressional law, assuming presidential approval or congressional ability to override a presidential veto. Legislation passed by Congress may be vetoed by the president but can only be changed by Congress. The process is commonly called a system of checks and balances or the separation of powers.

State governments frequently operate in a similar manner to the federal system. States have either a legislature or a general assembly. Massachusetts and New Hampshire call it a General Court, and North Dakota and Oregon call it a Legislative Assembly. All states have a senate; Nebraska has a unicameral legislature, so the senate is the only game in town. All other states also have a house of representatives except California, Nevada, New Jersey, New Mexico, New York and Wisconsin, which have assembly members, and Maryland, Virginia, and West Virginia, which have delegates.

All states have counties except Alaska, which has boroughs, and Louisiana, which has parishes.

Top Government Terms

adopt, approve, enact, pass: Amendments, ordinances, resolutions, and rules are *adopted* or *approved*. Legislative bills are *passed*. Laws are *enacted*. Committees *approve* legislation or plans of action.

bill, legislation: A *bill* is proposed legislation. *Legislation* is what a bill becomes after enactment.

conservative, left, liberal, moderate, right: We use these terms all the time; unfortunately, their meaning is, at best, subjective and may say more about the political views of the writer than about the person being labeled. Generally, it is best to avoid the terms unless someone so described agrees with the label or the term is used in a bite.

departments: Federal departments: Department of Agriculture, Department of Commerce, Department of Defense, Department of Education, Department of Energy, Department of Health and Human Services, Department of Homeland Security, Department of Housing and Urban Development, Department of the Interior, Department of Justice, Department of Labor, Department of State, Department of Transportation, Department of the Treasury, Department of Veterans Affairs. All are headed by secretaries (except Justice, which is overseen by the attorney general); all are appointed by the president and confirmed by the Senate.

European Union: The idea behind the EU is the promotion of economic and social progress of the member nations – along with enabling the combined strength of the countries to form a strong economic world unit. Predecessor organizations include the European Economic Community and the Common Market. The 27 current members include Austria, Belgium, Bulgaria, Croatia, Cyprus, Czech Republic, Denmark, Estonia, Finland, France, Germany, Greece, Hungary, Ireland, Italy, Latvia, Lithuania, Luxembourg, Malta, Netherlands, Poland, Portugal, Romania, Slovakia, Slovenia, Spain, and Sweden. Candidates for admission at this writing: Albania, Macedonia, Montenegro, Serbia and Turkey. Use European Union on first reference, E-U second reference. At this writing, the existence of the EU is uncertain, with Great Britain pulling out in a movement called Brexit.

filibuster: The process of using legislative rules to make (or threaten to make) long speeches to prevent proposed legislation from coming to a vote.

legislative bodies and titles: Some local governing units have city councilors, some have aldermen; some state legislative bodies are legislatures, some are assemblies; Louisiana has no counties; they're parishes. In Alaska, they're boroughs. Make sure you know the correct local terms before writing.

Medicaid: A joint federal-state program for the poor, disabled and elderly that helps to pay for health care.

Medicare: A federal insurance program for people 65 and older or disabled that helps to pay for health care.

NATO (North Atlantic Treaty Organization): Western defense and mutual interest organization. The 29 members are Albania, Belgium, Bulgaria, Canada, Croatia, Czech Republic, Denmark, Estonia, France, Germany, Greece, Hungary, Iceland, Italy, Latvia, Lithuania, Luxembourg, Montenegro, Netherlands, Norway, Poland, Portugal, Romania, Slovakia, Slovenia, Spain, Turkey, United Kingdom and the United States. Headquarters is in Brussels, Belgium. Use NATO first reference.

OPEC: Organization of the Petroleum Exporting Countries. The 14 members are Algeria, Angola, Congo, Ecuador, Equatorial Guinea, Gabon, Iran, Iraq, Kuwait, Libya, Nigeria, Saudi Arabia, the United Arab Emirates and Venezuela. Use OPEC first reference.

Supreme Court: The nine justices appointed by the president and confirmed by the Senate make ultimate decisions in court cases in the United States through final interpretations of the Constitution. The Chief Justice is *of the United States* (not *of the Supreme Court*). Others are Associate Justices of the Supreme Court.

●●●●●●

Health and Medicine

Reporting health and medical stories can be especially tricky. First, they can be technical, and few reporters are trained in the technical aspects or the jargon involved. Second, those most likely to pay the closest attention are those most in need of new developments and discoveries. If anything, stories about possible breakthroughs should be underplayed to avoid arousing misplaced hope.

The Patient Protection and Affordable Care Act and the Health Care and Education Reconciliation Act of 2010

Both bills were signed into law by President Barack Obama in March of 2010 . . . and they have resulted in significant changes in health care in the United States. Among the earliest provisions to go into effect: ending lifetime limits on health care coverage, the elimination of non-coverage for pre-existing conditions, more access to preventive care and allowing young people to stay on parents' insurance policies until age 26. Mandatory health care coverage went into effect in 2014. "Obamacare," as the law has become known, was upheld in major rulings by the US Supreme Court in 2012 and again in 2015. The Trump administration and a Republican Congress from 2017 to 2019 made a number of changes designed to weaken the law. At this writing, the bill remains under attack in the courts.

Health Insurance Portability and Accountability Act

Reporting on health matters became more difficult because of a provision of HIPAA, the Health Insurance Portability and Accountability Act of 1996. The Department of Health and Human Services regulations implementing HIPAA went into effect in April 2003. Basically, the regulations make it a crime to release any health-related information about anyone unless the person has specifically authorized disclosure. The privacy provisions of the federal law apply to health information created or maintained by health care providers who engage in certain electronic transactions, health plans and health care clearinghouses. That includes hospitals, physicians, emergency medical personnel, health plans and people who work with these groups. Police, firefighters and law enforcement agencies are not covered, but a combined ambulance and fire department may make it impossible to get information from both of those areas. Family members aren't covered, nor are journalists, although journalists could be liable for invasion of privacy depending on how they got the information. There are serious civil and criminal penalties for violations of HIPAA – enforced by the HHS Office of Civil Rights.

Hospital Conditions

Most often, the medical conditions of hospital patients are issued after medical care has been administered. Someone is injured or becomes sick; the person is taken to a hospital. Keep in mind that the extent of injuries at a traffic accident, for instance, bears no relationship to the condition given out by the hospital. Someone police describe as "seriously" injured at the scene could easily be in "fair" or even "good" condition according to the hospital. Police may well describe what the injuries look like at first glance; the hospital will give out a condition after doctors have worked on the patient.

When information is released at all, hospitals provide condition information within a broad framework of how the patient is doing. While there's no absolute uniformity here, these are the conditions and what they generally mean:

undetermined: Means just what it says. Patient is in E-R (emergency room) and not yet diagnosed.

treated and released: Patient received treatment but was not admitted to the hospital.

good: Patient is usually conscious, comfortable and alert. Vital signs are within normal range and stable. Prognosis is good.

fair or satisfactory: These mean the same thing. The patient is usually conscious but may be uncomfortable and may not be fully alert. Vital signs are within normal range and stable. Prognosis is fair.

poor: This term is seldom used today but means somewhere between fair and serious.

serious: The patient is seriously ill or injured. Vital signs are not within normal range and are not stable. Prognosis is uncertain.

critical: The patient is in life-threatening condition. Vital signs are not within normal range and not stable. Prognosis is unfavorable.

stable: Used in conjunction with some of the terms above (e.g., the patient is in serious but stable condition). This means the patient's condition is not changing and is not expected to change in the immediate future. If someone tells you the patient is in *critical but stable condition*, get more information. Since critical means unstable, that really doesn't make much sense.

Make sure you use whatever condition the hospital has given you. Never invent your own – not even based on what someone at the scene may have said.

●●●●●

Top Health and Medical Terms

abortion: The deliberate termination of pregnancy. Given the controversial nature of the subject, make sure stories are done evenhandedly, including the references to the two sides. It's probably best to use *pro-life* and *pro-choice*, rather than *pro-life* and *pro-abortion* or *pro-choice* and *anti-abortion*. Known by opponents as partial birth abortion or PBA, the medical community refers to the procedure as dilation and extraction, commonly called D & X, intact D & X, D & E or intrauterine cranial decompression. There are probably about 3,000–4,000 cases a year, nationwide, but there are no reliable numbers. The procedure involves dilating the cervix and partially removing the fetus, feet first. A cut is then made in the back of the fetus' head and a vacuum tube extracts the fetus' brain. That contracts the head and allows the rest of the fetus to be removed more easily. The procedure is usually performed in the fifth month or later. Opponents argue that the procedure is never required; proponents argue that there are cases when it's the safest medical procedure to save the life of the mother.

AIDS (acquired immune deficiency syndrome): A virus that destroys the body's immune system, leaving it subject to a variety of other ailments. AIDS is transmitted by body fluids, usually sexually. Use AIDS at first reference. Note that there's a big difference between someone testing positive for the HIV virus and someone with AIDS. Someone who has tested positive for HIV has been exposed to the virus. That person may or may not contract AIDS at some unknown time in the future. Write stories carefully.

Alzheimer's disease: A degenerative disease, characterized by a loss of mental function, most commonly in elderly people.

cancer: A series of different and only marginally related diseases characterized by a rapid and destructive growth of cells.

Centers for Disease Control (CDC): Located in Atlanta, the CDC monitors illnesses across the country and especially the spread of illnesses. Use C-D-C second reference, and note that *Centers* is plural.

COVID-19: The CO is from corona, the VI from virus, D from disease and 19 for the year discovered. It's a disease caused by a new (novel) coronavirus first identified in Wuhan, a city in Hubei Province in China at the end of 2019. Symptoms include cough, fever, muscle aches, shortness of breath and more. While most recover, COVID-19 is highly contagious and has resulted (at this writing) in over 370,000 deaths worldwide and more than 106,000 in the United States. At this writing, there is no proven treatment or vaccine for the disease.

Down syndrome: A congenital disease, characterized by some level of mental retardation and facial characteristics. Used to be known as *Down's syndrome* but the *'s* has disappeared over the years.

drugs: The term *drugs* has come to mean illegal drugs. Generally, use the word only in that context. If you mean medicine, use that term to refer to legal drugs used for treatment of illness or injury. Avoid *medication;* it's just a longer way of saying medicine.

epidemic: A widespread outbreak of a disease. May be declared only by a medical authority. See pandemic.

Food and Drug Administration (FDA): Oversees most food, drugs and cosmetics. Use full name first reference.

flu: Short for *influenza*. Don't confuse the flu with a cold; the flu can be serious stuff. Primarily involves the lungs and not the intestines. *Flu* okay first reference.

Medicaid/Medicare: Medicaid is a joint federal-state program for the poor, disabled and elderly that helps to pay for health care. Medicare is a federal insurance program for people 65 and older and disabled that helps to pay for health care.

National Institutes of Health (NIH): The center of federal, government-run health and medical research, located near Washington, DC. Use N-I-H second reference, and note that *Institutes* is plural, and it's *of* health.

pandemic: An epidemic of wider proportions . . . generally across multiple countries and/or continents. See epidemic.

22

• • • • •

TV Script Form, Supers and Glossary

There is no universal script marking system for television. Every station seems to do things a bit differently. Newsroom computer systems dictate some designations, but most systems allow stations to customize the look and approach to suit themselves. Most newsroom computer systems are integrated with control room equipment to make the appropriate supers virtually automatic – assuming they've been entered into the system correctly. This chapter lays out a reasonably typical system which can be used as a base suitable for alteration.

• • • • •

Abbreviations

CG: Character generator. Designate what it's to look like by using separate lines and uppercase and lowercase to correspond to use on air. Sometimes abbreviated CH, CI or CY (after Chyron, the company that once dominated the field).

CU: Close-up, standard bust shot for a single anchor.

GFX: Graphics. Note what it is.

IN: In cue of SOT in VO/SOT.

MATTE: To indicate more than one live video source on the screen at the same time.

OUT: Out cue of SOT in VO/SOT.

PKG: Reporter package that ends with standard signature (sig) close unless otherwise noted (e.g., *Jane Smith, XXXX-TV, Cityville*). Sometimes abbreviated PK.

SOT: Full screen sound on tape.

SS: Still store (electronic). Sometimes designated as *BSS* (box still store) or *FSS* (full [screen] still store). Make clear what it's to be.

3-shot: Three-shot on camera. Since most stations have more than three anchors, designate which three. Also note the order – for example, Jean/Jan/George where Jean and Jan are the usual co-anchors and George either is normally on the right doing, for example, sports, or is a reporter who is to be sitting on the right.

2-shot: Two-shot on camera. Because most stations have more than two anchors, designate which two (although it may be understood that it means the two news anchors unless otherwise noted).

VO: Voiceover; presumes natural sound under unless designated as silent (VO/sil).

● ● ● ● ●

Script Form

Standard Anchor Read

To indicate standard medium/close-up shot of the anchor who's reading the copy:

VIDEO	AUDIO
CU: Jean	((Jean))
	Three more arrests in the latest drug roundup on the west side today.

Standard 2-Shot

To indicate a standard two-shot:

VIDEO	AUDIO
2-shot: Jean & Jan	((Jean))
	Three more arrests in the latest drug roundup on the west side today.
	((Jan))
	It's a follow-up to the two dozen arrested....

Standard Anchor Read With GFX

To indicate a medium/close-up shot of anchor with box graphics:

VIDEO	AUDIO
CU: Jean BSS: drugs	((Jean)) Three more arrests in the latest drug roundup on the west side today.

Anchor With Voiceover

To indicate anchor read to voiceover copy with super:

VIDEO	AUDIO
CU: Jean BSS: drugs	((Jean)) Three more arrests in the latest drug roundup on the west side today.
VO———— CG: West Cityville IN: **:02** OUT: **:06**	It's a follow-up to the two dozen arrested yesterday at the Village Apartment Complex.

Note the *IN:* and *OUT:* after the super, giving the time during which a super can be run.

Anchor With VO/SOT

To indicate a VO/SOT:

VIDEO	AUDIO
CU: Jean BSS: drugs	((Jean)) Three more arrests in the latest drug roundup on the west side today.
VO———— CG: West Cityville IN: **:01** OUT: **:05**	It's a follow-up to the two dozen arrested yesterday at the Village Apartment Complex. Police Chief George Smith says it's all part of a new "get-tough" approach.
SOT————	((————SOT————))

CG: Chief George Smith Cityville Police	"We're going to go in there and clean things up. The people of the city have a right to live
IN: **:08**	in peace, and we're going to keep up the pressure until
OUT: **:13**	we've gotten rid of every one of them."
	((Jean))
VO————	Officers confiscated cocaine, marijuana, and L-S-D.

Remember after SOT to note who is reading and whether it's VO or on camera.

Anchor VO/SOT With Package Intro

To go into a reporter package:

VIDEO	AUDIO
CU: Jean BSS: drugs	((Jean)) Three more arrests in the latest drug roundup on the west side today.
VO − − − − CG: West Cityville IN: **:02** OUT: **:06**	It's a follow-up to the two dozen arrested yesterday at the Village Apartment Complex. Police Chief George Smith says it's all part of a new "get-tough" approach.
SOT———— CG: Chief George Smith Cityville Police	((————SOT————)) "We're going to go in there and clean things up. The people of the city have a right to live
IN: **:08**	in peace, and we're going to keep up the pressure until
OUT: **:13**	we've gotten rid of every one of them."
VO————	((Jean)) Officers confiscated cocaine, marijuana, and L-S-D. Reporter Sam Jones says the county prosecutor plans to file hundreds of charges.
SOT/PKG————	((————SOT/PKG————))

• • • • •

SUPERS

Names

STANDARD NAME SUPER. Notice that in the previous examples, name supers took up two lines while place supers occupied one. With a few exceptions that's the way supers should appear on the air. For most people supers, the first line gives the name, the second line the reason why that person is on the air:

CG: Molly McPherson
      Airline Spokesperson
CG: Ann Bishop
      Witness

Note that even if you use all caps for the script, you'll have to use uppercase and lowercase for supers. Otherwise, whoever types in the supers won't know how to spell a name like *McPherson*. Make sure to use gender neutral terminology. People who fight fires are called firefighters; those who fight criminals are police officers.

NAMES WITH COMPANY IDENTIFIERS. Generally, specific company names are not used in supers unless the story is about that company or about several specific companies. In the latter case the super might be like this:

CG: John Smith
      State Savings Bank Manager

But if John Smith has been sought out simply because he's in banking, use this:

CG: John Smith
      Bank Manager

PEOPLE IN AUTHORITY. People who are in some position of authority require some different handling of supers. There should be no need to super the president or vice president of the United States. The governor of your own state may be supered on one line:

CG: Gov. Pat Smith

Everyone else runs two lines. In most cases the name goes on the first line and the title on the second:

CG: Dana Greene
Cityville Police Chief
CG: Dana Greene
Village County Sheriff
CG: Dana Greene
Ohio Lt. Governor
CG: Dana Greene
Alaska Governor

TITLE AND RANK. Titles or ranks are used in the first line with the names in the case of clergy, the military, and police and fire officers who are *not* the people in charge:

CG: Rev. Ralph Taylor
United Methodist Church
CG: Sgt. Ralph Taylor
US Army
CG: Capt. Ralph Taylor
Cityville Police Dept.

POLITICIANS. Politicians – US and state – should be supered with federal/state and House/Senate designation along with name on line one and party affiliation and place represented (excluding district number) on line two:

CG: US Sen. Jane Doe
(R) Kansas
CG: US Rep. John Doe
(D) Detroit
CG: Indiana Rep. Betty Smith
(R) Indianapolis

Remember that *congressman/congresswoman* has no real meaning (all senators and representatives are members of Congress); don't use the term.

CANDIDATES FOR OFFICE. Super all candidates for public office – even those who currently occupy elective or appointive office – by party affiliation and the office they're seeking. You can make clear in the story itself if any of the candidates now hold some office:

CG: Betty Smith
(R) Governor Candidate
CG: John Smith
(I) Legislature Candidate

DOCTORS. There are too many doctors of too many different things to use *Dr.* in a super preceding a name anymore. Medical practitioners should have the appropriate letters follow a comma after the name:

CG: Jane White, M.D.
　　　Family Medicine
CG: Stephen Glenn, D.D.S.
　　　General Dentistry
CG: Elizabeth Flint, D.O.
　　　General Osteopathy

Do not use either *Dr.* or *Ph.D.* in a super:

CG: Henry Appleman
　　　Cityville School Supt.
CG: Louise Appleman
　　　OSU Economist

INITIALS AND ACRONYMS. Minimize both initials and acronyms in supers. The same guidelines apply for supers that apply to copy. If the organization is well enough known to use initials or an acronym first reference, then it's okay for a super. Acceptable initials: AFL/CIO, CIA, FBI, NAACP, NFL and a few others. Otherwise, write it out:

CG: Ken Jones
　　　United Auto Workers

CELEBRITIES. Celebrities are best identified with either their last major work or, if that's not appropriate, a general identifier:

CG: Mark Harmon
　　　"NCIS"
CG: Jim Gaffigan
　　　Comedian

NAME ALIAS. If someone is on the air who does not wish to be identified, have the person pick an alias, and put it in quotes:

CG: "Patrice"
　　　Rape Victim

SOMEONE NOT ON CAMERA. An exception to the two-line super is the use of a voice of someone who will not be seen – either for more than five seconds of a first bite or not at all. In that case, identify as follows:

CG: Voice of:
Sam Jones
Gay Homeowner

MULTIPLE NAMES. If more than one person is on the screen, it may be necessary to call for a super screen right or screen left. But be careful about the timing on this:

CG: John Smith (screen rt.)
Auto Mechanic

UNUSUAL SPELLING. And if the spelling is unusual, make clear that the way you've spelled it is correct:

CG: John Smythe (sp ok)
Charged with murder

In the last two examples those directions on screen location and spelling apply only to stations that manually enter the supers into the system. Newsrooms that are completely computerized simply need to enter the correct codes to make it happen properly.

MOS. *MOS* is short for *man-on-the-street* (although including both men and women). There's normally no reason to super MOSs. That's assuming that you've just gone out on the street to collect *short* comments from people about some issue in the news that you're using in a montage of bites.

CREDITING OUTSIDE HELP. When crediting outside help, like a courtroom sketch artist or a freelance photographer, use the same form as a *voice of* super:

CG: Artist:
Sam Smith
CG: Photojournalist:
Janet Jones

Location, Date and Miscellaneous

LOCATORS. The first rule is to think about whether you need a locator at all. If the story is about disposable diapers and you *happened* to shoot it in North Cityville, don't bother with a super. If it could have been anywhere, let it be.

If the story is outside the core city of coverage, super the name of the town, county, area – however the place is known:

CG: Marysville
CG: Delaware County

If the story is within the core city of coverage, use whatever broad terminology local residents use:

CG: Downtown Cityville
CG: East Cityville

If a specific address is necessary (especially on a crime story), use it all (including street, road, city, etc.):

CG: 2201 Velvet Place
Cityville

The second rule for using locator supers is to make sure that they're going to run over location video – not a tight shot of some document or a medium shot of a person who's been interviewed. Locators are inevitably a balancing act between being as broad as possible and as meaningful as possible.

DAY AND DATE. The viewer understands that video on the news was shot that day for that story. If that's not the case or there might be any question, then make sure the video is properly identified. A story on farm produce prices using last week's general farm video probably doesn't need a super. It probably really doesn't matter when that video was shot. But a story about John Smith being charged with a crime shouldn't run over any unidentified video of John Smith unless it's from that day. Crime video must always be specifically dated.

Be as general in dating as you can, given accuracy and context. If you're doing month-by-month comparisons, exact dates are not relevant:

CG: February
CG: Last Month

If you're using video from last Tuesday:

CG: Last Tuesday

That's almost always preferable to the exact date. If the event you're showing happened during the current calendar year, leave off the year; if it happened in a previous year, use the whole date:

CG: January 15
CG: January 15, 2020
CG: January 2020

If all else fails and you absolutely must use a particular piece of previously shot video, and it can't go on unidentified, but an exact date isn't known or doesn't make sense, use:

CG: File Tape
CG: File Video

This is an absolute last resort.

The only time a super saying *this morning* would be used on the air would be on a morning or noon show to indicate how timely the video is (or to show a comparison with later video, which would be so marked). The same concept would apply for *tonight*.

LOCATOR AND DATE. Locators may be used with dates:

CG: January 15
        Nassau County
CG: Tonight
        North Cityville

IDENTIFYING OUTSIDE VIDEO. Video must also be identified if the station (or the station's network) didn't shoot it. That includes movie video, video from other networks, public service announcements and commercials, with clarifying "courtesy" in parenthesis:

CG: (courtesy) Columbia Pictures
CG: (courtesy) Public Service Announcement
CG: (courtesy) Commercial

On movies or music videos, just courtesy the distributor or producer, not the title. Spell out *public service announcement*. Most people don't know what *PSAs* are.

● ● ● ● ●

Glossary of Broadcast and Online Terms

actuality: The "actual" sound of someone in the news on audio tape. This applies only to a newsmaker, not a reporter. *Bite* is the television equivalent.

ATSC 3.0: Advanced Television Systems Committee has established what TV groups hope will be a new digital broadcast standard – the first to be based on Internet Protocol (IP). Commonly called Next Gen

TV, it allows for higher quality picture and sound and addressable content – which will allow better targeting of advertising. The system is not backwards compatible so consumers will have to get new TV sets to receive ATSC 3.0.

affiliates: Stations with an agreement with one of the networks in which the stations have first call on programs carried by the network. Today, most TV affiliates pay the networks for the programs (and the commercials within them). It's called reverse compensation because it used to be the networks paying the stations. In radio, larger stations are paid, but smaller stations are not – depending on the size of the audience the station delivers. NPR affiliates pay NPR based on market size and size of audience.

anchor: The *talent* on the set who delivers the news. Also used to refer to on-the-set talent who present sports and weather.

app: Short for application, it's software designed for a particular purpose, most commonly, software downloaded for mobile use.

assignment desk, editor: Common in TV, rare in radio except the largest stations, this is the nerve center of the newsroom. Assignment editors, working at the assignment desk, schedule stories for reporters to cover and photographers to shoot. The desk may also perform research for reporters and other news people.

ax: Common abbreviation for accident.

B-roll: An old film term: Pictures shot to accompany reporter or anchor script. See the second definition of *cover shot*.

background/bg: Usually in TV, the natural sound on video that is run at lower volume, under the voice of a reporter or anchor. Same as *wild sound under* or *natural sound under*.

backtiming: Timing a story or, more commonly, a newscast from the back forward to help ensure that the newscast ends on time.

beat: An area of coverage that a reporter deals with on an ongoing basis, e.g., health, consumer, police.

bg: See *background/bg*.

billboard: Used variously, but most commonly as an announcement on the air – sometimes by a commercial announcer, sometimes by a newscaster – that a particular advertiser is sponsoring a news program or segment.

bite: The selected section of sound on tape (SOT) of a news maker or news event on TV to be run at full volume as SOT (see *SOT*). The TV equivalent of a radio *actuality*.

blog: Short for web log. Individual or group commentary or observations online.

bonded cellular: Bonded cellular is now the most widely-used system for TV stations to broadcast live material from practically anywhere. The system combines two or more internet signals in order to send large video files quickly enough for live transmission.

bridge: Used variously but usually refers to an internal stand-up (see *stand-up*) within a reporter package (see *package*).

BSS: Box still store. See *SS*.

character generator: Electronic equipment that produces supers (titles . . . also called lower thirds) used to identify people, places and things on TV. Abbreviated *CG:* (sometimes *CH:* or *CI:* or *CY:* – short for common brand name of Chyron) on script paper.

chromakey: The electronic merging of two video sources. Often the generation of pictures behind news, sports and weather anchors.

close-up/CU: A picture in which the subject is framed fairly tightly on the screen, generally no wider than head and shoulders.

cold open: Starting a TV newscast with video or a bite from the lead story rather than starting with the anchor or a standard show open.

copy: Scripts written for a newscast.

cover shot: (1) A scene of video used to cover or bridge what would otherwise be a jump cut (see *jump cut*) or simply to bridge scenes for time transitions; (2) in some shops, *cover shots* or *cover video* refers to video that accompanies narration. Also called *B-chain* or *B-roll*.

crawl: Text running across (usually) the bottom of the screen.

crowdsourcing: In media, generally asking people in the audience (online or mobile devices) to determine or verify information.

CU: See *close-up*.

cut: A direct, abrupt change from one video scene to another. The most common form of editing in TV news.

cutaway: Same as first definition of *cover shot*.

dayside: Refers to the newsroom staff who work generally between 8 a.m. and 7 p.m., culminating in the early evening news. See *night-side*.

digital first: The idea that news stories (information) should go out to the audience on the first available channel – which will almost always be online rather than on-air.

DVR: A Digital Video Recorder allows the digital recording of TV content for later playback. About half of US homes have a DVR.

dissolve: A video cross-fade in which one image is slowly (typically one-half to three seconds) replaced with another image. This softer form of editing (than cuts) is used most often in features to denote scene changes or passing of time.

domain: The end of the basic web address – after the period but before any slashes.

drive times: The time periods when radio station audiences are generally highest – because so many people are in cars. Morning drive usually runs from 6 a.m. to 10 a.m. weekdays (peak radio listening overall). Afternoon drive usually runs from 3 p.m. to 7 p.m. weekdays.

dub: As a noun, a copy of audio or video material. As a verb, the act of copying audio or video material.

ENG: Electronic news gathering. The term applies to videotape or digital video (rather than film) material from the field.

ESS: Electronic still store. See *SS*.

engagement: Engagement is the common measure of success in social media, tabulating likes, comments and responses in general to material posted and running online.

establishing shot: Typically, the first shot in a video story, which shows the general context of the location rather than a tighter shot of some of the details.

evergreen: A story, typically a feature, that can be held for later airing because it's not timely.

feed: Video or audio from an outside source, e.g. a network or from a station's live truck.

5G: 5G is the next generation of mobile transmission. Operating at up to 100 times the speed of 4G, it allows for near-instantaneous downloads of huge amount of data (including video). It could well revolutionize streaming, but since the signals don't travel as far, it will require a huge build-out before it can operate.

Flash: Animation program for web pages from Adobe.

font: Set of typeface styles in a character generator. See *character generator*.

FSS: Full (screen) still store. See *SS*.

future file: Filing system (physical file or on computer) to keep track of events coming up in the future, usually involving days of the month and months of the year. Sometimes called *futures file*.

GFX: Common abbreviation for graphics.

gif: Graphics Interchange Format . . . mostly used for illustrations and graphics on the web.

green screen: In TV, most commonly used in weather, it's a green screen or board which allows the chromakey or superimposition of video or maps behind a weathercaster or other talent. Technically, any color could be used, but green is chosen because whoever is in front of the green screen can't wear that color (and not wearing bright green is easy to do).

handout: A press release given or sent to the news media.

heavy: In a newscast, means that the show is running long and something will have to be cut back or eliminated. See *light*.

html: Hypertext markup language for coding instructions on the web.

hyperlocal: News about a much smaller community than we commonly see covered, most often a geographic area.

ifb: Interrupt feed or fold back. Usually refers to both the anchor's and reporter's earpieces and the audio that goes through it on live shots. Designed for the reporter to hear the station audio without his or her own voice and enables the producer or director to talk directly to the anchor or reporter to provide cues or information.

impression: In advertising, an impression is how web advertising is sold – based on a count of people who see or could see an ad by virtue of clicking on something that includes an ad. TV companies are moving to use the same system because they think their content – which includes online – is being undervalued.

IN: Script notation to mark in cue of SOT in VO/SOT. See also *OUT*.

interactivity: Generally, the ability of the audience to respond and participate in an activity, either online or through television.

jpeg: Joint Photographic Experts Group . . . compression for good quality photos at relatively fast download speeds on the web.

jump cut: An unnatural movement between edits caused by the internal editing of material such that two similar but not identical or flowing video shots are placed next to each other. The result is a discernable *jump* in the picture.

kicker: An unusual, light or humorous story – usually short – run at the end of a newscast.

lav: Short for lavaliere – a small mic that clips on to clothing.

light: In a newscast, means that the show is running short and something will have to be expanded or added. See *heavy*.

livechat: In media, generally software that allows a live connection between an audience and a live person.

localizing: Finding a local news aspect to a story that is not otherwise directly related to your community.

long shot/LS: Similar to an establishing shot, this is a picture showing a wide view of the story the camera is capturing. Same as *wide shot/WS*.

MATTE: Split screen. Term indicating more than one live video source on the screen at the same time.

medium shot/MS: Between a close-up and a long shot, the medium shot shows some detail of the picture without getting too close.

message board: A web page where comments can be posted.

mix minus: An engineering term referring to the elimination of the reporter's or anchor's audio through an ifb – thus preventing feedback or disconcerting delayed audio.

MP3: Motion Picture Experts Group, Audio Layer 3 . . . an audio compression format used for downloading.

MPEG: Motion Picture Experts Group . . . a system for digitizing and compressing video for downloading. Pronounced m-peg.

multimedia: Online, generally refers to the mixed use of text, audio, video, graphics, animation, and so on.

natural sound: The actual sound of whatever is being recorded (audio or video), generally intended to be run under a reporter's or anchor's voice. Same as *wild, ambient, nat* or *background sound*.

nightside: Refers to the newsroom staff who work generally between 2 p.m. and 11:30 p.m., culminating in the late evening news. See *dayside*.

O & O: Abbreviation for *owned and operated* – in reference to stations that are actually owned and run by the networks or group owners rather than just affiliated with the networks.

OTT: Stands for over the top and refers to the transmission and reception of video via the internet – rather than traditional broadcasting signals that most people receive via cable, satellite or telco.

OUT: Script notation to mark out cue of SOT in VO/SOT. See also *IN*.

outtakes: Audio or video material recorded for a story but not used on the air.

package: A report, usually put together by a reporter, usually including the reporter, reporter voiceover, natural sound, and one or more interview segments (bites). Usually abbreviated *PKG*, sometimes called *pack*. Normally ends with standard signature (sig) close (or out) unless otherwise noted.

paywall: Requiring payment in order to access an online site.

pixels: Short for picture elements . . . the tiny circles of color that make up a video screen. The more pixels, the more detail and sharper the image.

podcast: Online, material available for download to be played on a computer or portable electronic device.

pool: Generally refers to the use of shared (or pooled) resources, most commonly a single photographer or group of photographers at an event where all media can receive and use the material.

pre-pro: Short for pre-production, the advance production of material done prior to the newscast.

producer: A *field producer* works with a reporter to determine the audio and video aspects of a story. A *segment producer* typically oversees the writing and production of various segments within a newscast (e.g., health, consumer). A *show producer* or *line producer* typically oversees the writing, graphics, sequence and, to varying degrees, content of a newscast. An *executive producer* typically oversees one or more newscasts and the producer or producers who handle those newscasts. Depending on the station, the *executive producer* is likely to be the number 2 or number 3 management person in the newsroom (after the news director and assistant news director, if the station has one).

PSA: Most commonly used as an abbreviation for public service announcement – spots run for free by radio and TV stations for non-profit events or organizations. Also refers to pre-sunrise authority, by which certain AM radio stations operate at reduced power between 6 a.m. and average monthly sunrise.

QuickTime: Video format developed by Apple.

rating: The percentage of people or households listening (radio) or watching (TV) of all the people or households who could listen or watch (in the defined area and have a radio or TV). See *share*.

reader: In TV, a story to be read by an anchor on camera.

SEO: Search engine optimization . . . the process of choosing words, especially in headlines or key words, to maximize the ability of search engines to locate material.

share: The percentage of people or households listening (radio) or watching (TV) of all the people or households who are listening or watching at that time. See *rating*.

sig out, sig close: The standard line used by reporters to end all packages. Typically something like *Sue Smith, WXXX-TV, Cityville.*

sil: Abbreviation for *silent* – to indicate that there is no usable audio on a piece of video. See also *VO*.

slug: Refers to the word or phrase identifying a given story on assignment listings and show rundowns. Also refers to the slug line plus the initials or last name of the writer, the date and the newscast the story is being written for – all of which generally appear in the upper left or across the top of the page.

SNG: Satellite news gathering, as opposed to in the studio or via microwave.

SOT: Stands for *sound on tape*. Usually used to indicate that a segment of video should be run at regular, full audio level (with accompanying picture).

spots: Radio and TV term for commercial announcements.

SS: Still store (electronic) frequently designated as *BSS*, box still store (the box accompanying an anchor shot), or *FSS*, full (screen) still store (where the video fills the screen).

stand-up: A story or segment of a story during which a reporter at the scene talks on camera.

stick mic: Handheld microphone. See *lav*.

streaming: For computers and mobile devices, a system of sending and receiving a continuous flow of audio and/or video. That flow could be live streaming (as it's being sent) or material available for streaming (transmission) on demand.

super: The superimposition of lettering over video – most commonly names and titles. Sometimes called lower-thirds because many (but not all) supers are placed there.

sx: Common abbreviation for sports. Also sometimes Spx.

tag: Scripted close to a radio or TV package, story or commercial – usually at least one full sentence.

talent: People who perform on the air, including newscasters, weather and sports, but not usually reporters.

tease, teaser: Usually a short bit of information on an upcoming story that is used to *tease* the audience so they will continue to listen or watch the newscast, especially used just before commercials.

toss: The introduction of another person or video by an anchor or reporter.

URL: Uniform resource locator . . . the address of a website.

visuals: Pictures or graphics accompanying a story. See *B-roll*.

VO: Short for voiceover, used to indicate anchor or reporter reading during a video segment. Presumes voiceover natural sound unless indicated otherwise (VO/sil).

voiceover: See *VO*.

voicer: In radio, a story read by a reporter, with the reporter's voice (and perhaps natural sound under) the only audio on the tape (no actualities).

VTR: Videotape recording.

webcast: Audio or video feed on the web . . . usually streamed live.

wide shot, WS: See *long shot/LS*.

wild sound: See *background/bg* and *natural sound*.

wrap: In radio, a voicer that includes one or more actualities. Also a time cue directing talent or reporter to conclude presentation or interview.

wx: Common abbreviation for weather.

Index ●●●●●

Note: *Italicized* entries reference words that appear in defining terms sections of Chapters 7, 19, 20, 21 and 22.